MASSIVE RETALIATION

THE POLICY AND ITS CRITICS

by
PAUL PEETERS

Published in cooperation with
FOUNDATION FOR FOREIGN AFFAIRS, INC.

FOUNDATION FOR FOREIGN AFFAIRS SERIES

NUMBER 2

The Foundation for Foreign Affairs, 64 East Jackson Boule-
vard, Chicago 4, Illinois, is a non-profit corporation devoted
to the promotion of a wider understanding of international
relations—political, economic, and cultural. Books in the
Foundation for Foreign Affairs Series are published in the
interest of public information and debate. They represent the
free expression of their authors and do not necessarily indicate
the judgment and opinions of the Foundation.

To M. S. and to L.

CONTENTS

PREFACE

COMMUNIST IMPERIALISM and the new balance of power resulting from the unleashing of nuclear energy have radically altered the United States' role in world affairs. Americans have fully accepted the changed situation, but do they really comprehend the tasks and processes of this new role of leadership? This question must be answered in the framework of American political tradition, which demands popular support of government policies, and we have therefore chosen to seek its answer in the necessary and continuous intercourse between public debates and national policy.

Foreign policy—the present administration's supporters and critics alike will agree—can be quite flexible. It is capable of adjusting itself, day by day, to the demands of the diplomatic situation. Unfortunately, however, public debates seem to be far less flexible, incapable of adjustment, as if bound to conform to some prescribed pattern; regardless of varying circumstances, the same debating techniques are used again and again. Deliberation on national policy has been made uniformly rigid by complexes of socially accepted values and by dynamisms, or built-in forces that exert a prevailing influence on public opinion. These values and dynamisms operate as a set of rules that must be obeyed in American politics, even though they are not always consistent with the requirements of U.S. policy. Our broad purpose in this work is to formulate and illustrate the patterns or laws that govern public opinion and to determine the nature and the extent of their interference with the conduct and success of U.S. foreign policy.

If our work is to carry conviction, it must proceed as a case study, and our conclusions, if they are to be genuine, must be drawn in positive terms. We must show how the techniques of debate, the dynamisms that determine public behavior, and the

ix

values that society professes to cherish have, in fact, affected the conduct of our foreign policy in an instance of major importance. We must be sure that it is our own conduct that is under scrutiny. How did we act in a past which is distant enough to permit a sober examination of ourselves and yet close enough to allow a genuine self-evaluation? We must make our examination now—judging the past on the basis of what we knew at the time—not merely for the sake of establishing what is true, but in order that we may profit in the future from the experience of the past.

The doctrine of massive retaliation, which Secretary of State Dulles formulated on January 12, 1954, was chosen as the subject in our case study of public opinion and government policy for several reasons, the first and foremost of which is that the Eisenhower administration introduced massive retaliation as a major element of U.S. foreign policy. The proponents of massive retaliation have argued that there was no other course of action, that the doctrine had to be upheld or the United States would have no global strategy. Yet, as we shall see, in the acid test of public discussion, this cast-iron doctrine has corroded considerably. The administration, after defining, in piecemeal fashion, every aspect of the policy, has not been willing to present a compact, consistent summation of its plan of action.

It is remarkable that massive retaliation has become officially taboo because of criticism. Still more remarkable—and of special importance for our purpose—is the fact that although no real alternative to massive retaliation has been offered, the opinion has come to be generally held that massive retaliation may have been nothing more than a slip of the tongue by Secretary Dulles—what we Americans call a "catchy" slogan or "political poppycock."

When the doctrine of massive retaliation was first formulated, its American critics professed not to understand it. "The American people . . . do not understand parts of it," said Senator Stuart Symington on March 30, 1954. "Neither do I. Neither do many of my colleagues."[1] The public was apathetic. Since Dulles' pronouncement was considered to represent a far-reaching shift in American policy, the lack of public interest was openly regretted. But the debate eventually got under way, and massive retaliation was declared to be an empty phrase. "This was the period," Senator Symington said on June 20, 1955, "in which we first created, and then abandoned, such word weapons as massive retaliation."[2] The policy had frightened our allies without sobering our enemies. It had been discarded almost immediately. In all its wisdom, public opinion had declared that there was nothing new in it. Massive retaliation had caused a controversy and had therefore become controversial.

Whatever the merits of the case might have been, the massive retaliation debate has been inept. No one really attempted to offer workable alternatives; no one made distinctions of the various situations to which the doctrine was to apply. The debate on the issue drew its life from grossly erroneous assumptions and finally floundered into inconsistency, pretending, apparently with some reason, to carry the national policy down with it.

It is not easy to follow the development of a debate of such importance. Political attitudes are complex, arguments rarely terminated. A patient labor is required from those who want to separate the grain from the chaff, for public opinion readily chooses to remain in a state of paralyzing confusion—as if it possessed no valid evidence that could guide its conduct, as if nothing were certain or trustworthy. Public opinion is also satisfied to act on the basis of false evidence. Alleged facts which are no facts at all are taken as truths, while the validity of the most intelligible principles is overlooked and denied.

In order to overcome the difficulties posed by the dialectics of public debate as it is generally conducted in the United States, we have divided our work into three parts. First, we have presented the doctrine of massive retaliation as stated by the administration, much of it in the administration's own words. In the second part, we have analyzed, one by one, the various arguments against massive retaliation. On the basis of this double evaluation, we have shaped the third part into a study of the patterns of public discussion in America as they revealed themselves in the massive retaliation debate.

Our discussion of the doctrine of massive retaliation has been limited to the rational contents of every argument; we have not written a history of recent American diplomacy. Our analysis is based upon sources of information available to the general public: campaign speeches, the administration's policy statements, and newspaper editorials. This material, with the exception of certain background information which does not require identification because it is generally known, is our primary source. Furthermore, we have considered only those arguments which have reached maturity; by "maturity," we mean the simple, naked form in which concepts are conveyed in political speeches and other media of mass communication. An argument that has reached such a state is always devoid of intellectual alibis; it must mean what it says, which is not always the case in many scholarly studies of massive retaliation.

American public opinion accepts, without bitterness, the most unfair criticisms from abroad. Will it also accept a study which attempts to do justice to the great realist tradition of American foreign policy and which denounces, with equal frankness, some of America's faults? Like individuals, nations are inclined to endure, with noble patience, sweeping and unfounded accusations, but they can hardly bear the realization of one true weakness. The same contradictory attitude is found in those nations which indulge in anti-Americanism. A global indictment of America comes easier to them than a justified charge which is limited in scope. They well know how unreasonable is the frequent and unqualified censure of everything America really is, yet they will not attempt to clarify their charges lest more precise accusations force them to recognize the fundamental good faith of their appointed victim. In this manner, human relations are perpetually carried on waves of changing opinion and changing events by an irrational force that only a free will can control.

PAUL PEETERS

New York
March 25, 1959

xii

The Doctrine of Massive Retaliation

The Decline of the Republic

CHAPTER I

Strategic Postulates

THE FOREIGN POLICY of the United States is ruled by strategic considerations. It logically starts with a definition of the problem with which it intends to cope. This can best be done in the form of postulates that deductively describe the various aspects of the global situation with which the United States is confronted. As President Eisenhower said in his press conference of June 10, 1954, the problem that the democracies have to look in the face is not only "broad in scope" but also "great in depth." It possesses several dimensions which will now be analyzed.

At the very start of the Eisenhower administration, Secretary of Defense Charles E. Wilson canceled substantial Air Force contracts—a decision which raised the question of whether a change in basic defense policies by the new administration was under way. Shortly thereafter, in April, 1953, the Council of the North Atlantic Treaty Organization met in Paris, and there were reports in the United States that the build-up of forces, instead of proceeding as originally planned, was to be spread, or "stretched out," over a period of many years. This double development forced the new administration to elaborate publicly on the "long-haul" concept—which thus became the first feature of the new policy of massive retaliation to appear in articulate form.

As Admiral A. W. Radford later said on December 14, 1953, "the motif and tempo" for the new strategy stemmed from the directive given by the President in his speech of April 16, 1953. Mr. Eisenhower said that the policy of his administration would not be tied to "any magic critical year which then had to be stretched out because of economic and production problems." Policy was to be based on the "sounder theory that a very real danger not only exists this year, but may continue to exist for years to come." American strength, which was already very real when he assumed office, was to be made stronger by steady improvements that would replace what the President called "inefficient and expensive starts and stops."

This is the substance of the long-haul concept: any attempt to establish some date of maximum danger is futile. The strategic position of America is essentially defensive; and, as the President said on April 23, 1953, "for anybody on the defensive position . . . to base his defense on his ability to predict the exact date of attack was crazy." He insisted that he had never looked at this problem in any other way and that he had "raised his voice in inner circles time and time again" before becoming President of the United States.

Acceptance of the long-haul concept meant that defense planning had first to provide what the Budget Message of January 21, 1954, called a "strong military posture which can be maintained over the extended period of uneasy peace."[1] But never before had the United States even attempted to keep over a long period of time, forces of the size it now had to maintain. Was such a program economically feasible? How did the administration define the economics of national defense?

As Secretary of State Dulles explained on April 29, 1953, President Eisenhower believed that it was "safest to adopt a pace which can be maintained with growing strength, rather than to run the risk of dropping exhausted by the wayside before the haven is reached." Recalling at this point that Nikolai Lenin had taught that "the United States of America, like all capitalist countries, will eventually spend herself into bankruptcy," the President told his press conference of April 23, 1954, that "the first thing for any nation . . . in order to defend themselves would be to be able to make a living." Otherwise, he said, "in the long run your peoples were ground down."

How much the United States could safely invest in defense without running the risk of dropping exhausted by the wayside or spending itself into bankruptcy, the administration has made no great effort to say. The President was certainly on more solid ground when he warned on March 10, 1954, that the free world had picked up a burden that "it might have to carry on indefinitely." It was not possible to look forward to a solution "as of next year or even in the next decade, possibly not in our life-time." Consequently, he added, the United States must "be able to carry this forward and in such a way that it would not wreck the very concepts on which all free government was constituted." In other words, a defense effort which was not an emergency measure had to be carried out in the social and the political framework of a free country. This new concept had been clearly defined by the President on May 14, 1953. "We didn't want to become a garrison state," he said, "we wanted to remain free. Our plans and programs had to conform to the practices of a free people, which meant essentially a free economy."

This obviously points to the acceptance of a calculated risk. The defense needs of today must be met; to build less would expose the country to aggression; to build excessively under the influence of fear would be self-defeating. Since Soviet power will constantly increase, America must become stronger and stronger, yet normalcy and peaceful pursuits must be allowed to continue. It is clear, then, that our economy is pitted against our military needs.

Nor is that all. Military strength and economic expansion are wedded. In the face of a growing Soviet economy, it might become dangerous for the United States to let its military effort interfere unduly with economic expansion. As the President wrote in his public letter to Secretary Wilson on January 5, 1955, "true security for our country must be bonded on a strong and expanding economy, readily convertible to the tasks of war." If war were forced upon the United States, gigantic amounts of equipment and supplies would be needed. It might be wasteful to produce these now, but the means to produce them must exist.

A defense effort that the country can support indefinitely with-

3

out ruining the fabric of its own institutions is a program that can progress from year to year. The Budget Message of January 17, 1955, reiterated the doctrine that security must be achieved on a long-term basis without the "letdown" that would result from "peaks and valleys"[2] in defense spending and procurement. The strain upon the economy must be endurable; otherwise defense spending would have no stability.[3] American capabilities are finite, but the nature and duration of the Soviet threat are not. It must be assumed that this threat will continue without abating, perhaps for an entire historical era. We now turn to a qualitative analysis of this threat.

The two great dimensions of the Soviet threat are Communism as an ideology and the might of the Soviet Union as a state. To use here the words of the State of the Union Message of January 5, 1956, the United States must face "the continuing reliance of the Soviet Communists on military force . . . their continuing effort to dominate or intimidate free nations on their periphery." The United States must also consider the assets the Soviets possess, the power of their weapons, and their increasing strength. "This power," the Message continued, "combined with the proclaimed intentions of Communist leaders to communize the world, is the threat confronting us today."[4]

Basic to the administration's evaluation of the Soviet threat is the axiom that Communism is totally unacceptable as a way of life. The issue of Communism is not "a struggle merely of economic theories, or of forms of government, or of military power," declared the State of the Union Message of January 6, 1955. "The issue is the true nature of man."[5] Consequently, it goes to "the roots of the human spirit and its shadow falls across the long sweep of man's destiny." However much the Soviet rulers are moved by a primitive lust for power, the most significant aspect of their imperialism is the doctrinal garb that cloaks their ambitions. As Mr. Dulles said on May 15, 1954, aggressive imperialism "has never before attained the status of the well-thought-out intellectual creed taught throughout the world and pursued fanatically by many men of many nations." In other words, the threat does

4

not represent the personal ambitions of an individual dictator or group of men. The threat is the Communist ideology, an ideology that is now identified with a powerful state, and from this identification flow a number of consequences which must be taken into account in the formulation of policy.

The first of these consequences is that the U.S.S.R. can never really live in peace alongside the free nations. Political processes generally tend to corrupt the morality of political action, but in the case of the Soviet Union, the opposite holds true: the legitimate pursuits of the Soviet Union as a state tend to give moral sanction to its corrupt ideology. The U.S.S.R. as a state is indeed entitled to receive assurances against aggression. Its sovereignty must be respected. Its economy must be allowed to grow. The free nations naturally fear that their antagonism toward the Communist ideology might be interpreted as an act of hostility toward the Soviet state. They are inclined, for that reason, to compromise with the state at the risk of appeasing the ideology.

For the Soviet Union, the situation is reversed. Its necessary identification with Communism makes impossible any true compromise with the free nations. As a force system attempting to suppress man's most sacred aspirations, Communism is fundamentally opposed to everything human. For Communism, freedom is subversion, and because the Soviet state and Communism are identified with each other, freedom threatens the existence of the U.S.S.R. Even the existence of freedom abroad is subversive. And since the call to freedom tends to reach the Soviet people only through the voices of other states, these states must be described as enemies of the Soviet Union. In this way, the Soviet Union is forced, by its own system, to remain "frozen" in a condition of basic hostility toward the democratic world. It cannot, without subverting itself, promote genuine peace and collaboration among nations.

A second consequence, which follows from the first, is that international security will remain threatened by Communism as long as the Communist ideology remains unchanged. One must therefore take seriously Lenin's statement that "war is inevitable" and

5

his threat that "as soon as we are strong enough to defeat capital-ism as a whole, we shall immediately take it by the scruff of the neck" and destroy it. However, it is highly dangerous for the Soviet state to hold, in the age of atomic bombs and intercontinental mis-siles, the doctrine that the existence of the Soviet Union side by side with capitalist states for a long time is unthinkable.

This feature of Communism is, as far as the free world is con-cerned, a definite asset, but one to be used with care. The Com-munist ideology is firmly settled on the rock of Soviet power, yet by reason of its being a state, it is open to considerations of political realism. Rational responses can be elicited from the Soviet state, which can never endanger its continued existence for the sake of its ideology. It should be kept in mind, however, that the realism of the Soviet state, which calls for a flexibility of approach, is quite consistent with Communism as ideology. Since Communist ide-ology holds that morality is what serves the state, we can never trust the Soviet Union. We can have no faith in Soviet promises, Mr. Dulles explained on November 29, 1955, "unless they are given under circumstances so that the self-interest of the Soviet Union becomes an obvious reason for them to make their promises good."

Without the backing of Soviet arms, Communist conquests would be perpetually endangered. Without military power, we cannot obtain from the Soviet state the realist response that can check its ideology. Whether it resorts to open military aggression or not, Communism should be viewed primarily as a military threat. The picture of Communist advances achieved "without war" is sobering. Not very long ago, the U.S.S.R. spoke of capitalist encirclement; it now boasts of the nine hundred million people who have "firmly entered upon the road of socialism and democ-racy."[6]

The military aspect of Soviet imperialism is not the only aspect that deserves our attention. Communism will succeed again and again in creating situations that confuse the free nations, for the Communist dictatorship knows quite well that something can be gained from every division and every hatred it creates in the non-Communist world. It professes that truth can be concealed and

6

retreats accepted as long as Soviet imperialism benefits in the end. Communism demands no consistency other than its own advancement. For these reasons, it would be folly to treat subversion and indirect aggression as a "new" threat which excludes the threat of direct military aggression. Both threats are ever present, and their effects are cumulative.

The co-existence of the Communist state and the Communist ideology creates a new and final dilemma. Any change in Soviet culture (like the one vaguely initiated with the downgrading of Stalin) could conceivably create irreversible forces. If fully released, these forces could, said Mr. Dulles on July 11, 1956, "take charge of the situation." Relaxation of the Communist grip on the U.S.S.R. would require Soviet policy to become more responsive to the will of the people and for that reason might become irreversible. Communism is driven to change by a law of nature, yet its own nature cannot tolerate change, for the basic tenets of the Communist ideology are so crude, so compact, and so few that to repudiate any of them is to repudiate Communism. The day Communism truly changes, it will cease to exist. "Its basic doctrine precludes its changing of its own accord," wrote Mr. Dulles in 1957. Consequently, "self-advertised changes must be considered as mere stratagems." And yet "international Communism is subject to change even against its will. It is not impervious to the erosion of time and circumstances. . . . The yeast of change is at work."[7]

However, the evidence now available yields no reason to believe that Communism has changed in any way. The Secretary of State pointed out on June 21, 1956, that the Soviet rulers "retain capabilities which enable them quickly to revert to their old policies." The Soviet Union might occasionally wage what the Budget Message of January 16, 1956, called "a campaign of smiles without deeds," but there has been no noticeable basic change in the purposes of Communism. Upon returning from Geneva on July 25, 1955, President Eisenhower told the American people that we are still separated from the Communist camp by what he called "a gulf as wide and deep as the gulf that lies between the concept of man made in the image of his God and the concept of man as a mere

7

instrument of the State." And Nikita Khrushchev himself warned that the U.S.S.R. would never abandon Marx and Lenin. He said on September 17, 1955, that those waiting for that kind of change might just as well wait "until a shrimp learns to whistle." This, then, is the Soviet ideological threat. Let us now turn to a short description of the ominous Soviet military power that backs it up.

The Soviet Union is the leader of a formidable empire that exercises tyrannical sovereignty over the enormous land mass of Eurasia. Together with Red China, the U.S.S.R. possesses unlimited manpower, and its system of government enables it to strike a surprise blow anywhere on earth. As Mr. Dulles said to the Senate Foreign Affairs Committee on March 29, 1954, the U.S.S.R., "within an orbit of 20,000 miles . . . could strike by land twenty states of Europe, the Middle East and Asia, and by air it could strike the North American Continent," while it enjoys the protection of distance, terrain, sea, and arctic climate.

In addition to these geopolitical assets, the Soviet Union maintains a considerable number of Red Army divisions. Its mobilization system permits a rapid expansion of manpower because of exceptionally well-trained reserves. The Soviet army is the only army in the world which is maintained in a state of readiness for land operations in both limited and all-out war. Its equipment is entirely modern.

The Soviet air force is generally credited as having more than 20,000 active aircraft and approximately the same number in reserve. Its effectiveness has been dramatically improved in recent years by the replacement of the older models with up-to-date jet aircraft. The bulk of Soviet air power is believed to be devoted to tactical support of ground operations and air defense, but the Soviets also possess a transoceanic and offensive air force comparable to our Strategic Air Command in range and striking power. The Soviet Union is training scientists and technicians at a fast rate, and on August 26, 1957, it announced the success of the first intercontinental ballistic missile, a claim later supported by the launching of earth satellites, leading to the conclusion that it may be ahead of the United States in some areas of missile development.

As a naval power, the U.S.S.R. is second only to the United States, and it is outbuilding us at a considerable rate. Although the Soviet Union is actively engaged in the production of destroyers and other vessels, the Russian fleet of more than 450 submarines has received great attention. Nazi Germany started World War II with only fifty-seven submarines, and it is not difficult to imagine the havoc that the Soviet navy could wreak in European and Asian waters in time of war. In addition, the U.S.S.R. will equip its submarines with ballistic missiles, which means that American cities on the Atlantic and the Pacific coasts could be destroyed without warning.

Is it necessary to point out that this enormous war machine has not been substantially weakened by the various cuts announced by the Soviets since 1955? Those cuts were described by Mr. Dulles as dealing primarily with manpower rather than armaments, and President Eisenhower said on May 23, 1956, that the mere fact that the Soviet Union reduced manpower by 1,200,000 "when you still have 115 divisions" or reduced their air force by two or three hundred planes "when you have a total of 20,000" or reduced their navy by "a few vessels that we don't even know what they are" is certainly no reason for the United States to change its estimate of Soviet power and still less reason for the free world to change its own dispositions.

On September 24, 1949, President Truman announced the first atomic explosion in the Soviet Union. The first thermonuclear explosion in the U.S.S.R. occurred on August 12, 1953, and was announced to the American people on August 20. The Atomic Energy Commission also announced shortly afterwards that the Soviets were testing smaller atomic weapons of a tactical type that could be used against troops on the battlefield. Thus the day when the Soviet Union acquired well-rounded nuclear strength had come, and along with it had come the possibility of Russia's making a crippling attack on the continental United States. This new factor is, by itself, responsible for a complete revolution in our strategic thinking. "For the first time," said Mr. Dulles on January 11, 1955, "Western civilization can be seriously challenged by an atheistic

9

system." On the following day, the President repeated this warning and said that "for the first time in our history, we have reason for alarm as to our own safety."

However strong it may be militarily, the United States cannot prevent a break-through of enemy planes carrying hydrogen bombs. Defense has thus ceased to be a reality. It has been estimated that a reasonably well-conceived Russian attack would cause the destruction of eighty million Americans, and there is no reason to assume that the Kremlin would never resort to such an attack. The great concentration of American industry and population in urban centers makes the United States particularly vulnerable to surprise attack. There would be little warning, if any, no time for preparations, no possibility of large-scale evacuation. Finally, the logic of air-atomic warfare renders surprise attack a strategic necessity. Mr. Dulles recognized this when he said at Geneva on November 10, 1955, that "major aggression is unlikely unless the aggressor has the advantage of surprise and can hope to strike a blow that will be devastating because it is unexpected." President Eisenhower also said on March 17, 1954, that "the element of surprise, always important in war, had been multiplied by the possibility of creating such widespread destruction quickly." This picture of the Soviet threat leads to the conclusion we find expressed in the State of the Union Message of January 5, 1956: "Nuclear war would be an intolerable disaster which must not be permitted to occur."[8]

The American defense program was defined by the State of the Union Message of January 5, 1956, as a program that emphasizes "an effective flexible type of power calculated to deter or repulse aggression and to preserve the peace." The administration thus expressed a third and last strategic postulate: the concept of flexibility.

Flexible defenses must first be understood in relation to the economics of security. The resources that can safely be used for defense are finite, and the most economic use of resources absorbed by national defense must therefore be made. The ratio of combat personnel to total military manpower must be increased, and the total manpower required must be reduced by a more efficient use of weapons and techniques. "America's most precious possession is the lives of its citizens," wrote President Eisenhower to Mr. Wilson in January, 1955, which means that the number of men used in warfare must be constantly reduced. "To accomplish these ends," declared Admiral Radford on December 14, 1953, "we are improving greatly our . . . effectiveness by the application of new weapons and new techniques, and hope ultimately to achieve far greater flexibility than heretofore attainable." Flexibility thus refers to the rigid economic and political framework imposed upon military strategy by the democratic way of life. Within the inflexibility of this framework, our defense is constantly being improved—as the President said on August 1, 1956—by "substituting power, speed, mobility, flexibility for just men."

So understood, flexibility makes security generally attributable to scientific and technological development, although the progress of science and technology is continuous and unpredictable. Guided missiles, atomic-powered vessels and aircraft, new applications of electronics—every new scientific advance affects the evolution of a military planning that must be flexible enough to utilize every new weapon and technique.[9] This kind of flexibility is relative to the inflexibility of military procurement; almost as soon as new weapons are procured, they are obsolescent. We must therefore choose between what Secretary of the Navy R. B. Anderson called on March 9, 1954, "too-little-and-too-late and too-much-and-too-soon." We must, he said, "buy our security in installments with the most promising weapons of the day." Or, as the Budget Message of January 16, 1957, expressed it, "during the transition, we must continue to purchase enough of the current types to preserve our readiness until the effectiveness of the advanced weapons is demonstrated." It is no easy task, the Message states, "to maintain a proper balance between expenditures for future military strength and expenditures for current readiness."[10]

The weapons of tomorrow are not always improvements of today's weapons. New technological break-throughs have a profound impact on our global procurement of weapons. As the State of the Union Message of January 9, 1958, warned, the new weapons do not always "fit into any existing service pattern. They cut across all services, involve all services, and transcend all services, at every stage from development to operation." In some instances, they even defy classification. Since the jurisdictional disputes accompanying such situations tend to confuse the public and create wastes of money and scientific manpower, defense planning must be flexible in a different sense, one in which flexibility is relative to both the rigidity of any strategic plan already agreed upon and the services' traditional jurisdiction over tasks and weapons.

In addition, our defenses must be characterized by a stability which is not materially disturbed by the shifting methods of world Communism. The State of the Union Message of January 5, 1956, declared that "our policy must be dynamic as well as flexible, designed primarily to forward the achievement of our own objectives rather than to meet each shift and change on the Communist front."[11] This new meaning of flexibility is synonymous with that of diplomatic and strategic initiative. In his pronouncement of January 12, 1954, Mr. Dulles said:

> If the enemy could pick his time and his place and his method of warfare—and if our policy was to remain the traditional one of meeting aggression by direct and local opposition—then we had to be ready to fight in the Arctic and in the tropics, in Asia, in the Near East and in Europe; by sea, by land and by air; by old weapons and by new weapons.

A strategy of this kind would be the prototype of inflexibility; conversely, a flexible policy would mean that the United States could choose its time, place, and means of warfare. It also means a balanced security. It is a point which demands further elucidation.

The United States cannot stake its preparedness on one type of weapon, nor can it anticipate one type of situation only. Defense

12

"had to be rounded," said President Eisenhower on January 12, 1955, "because you couldn't tell where it was going to be, the place you had to use your forces, the conditions under which you would have to use them." The State of the Union Message of January 6, 1955, warned that "undue reliance on one weapon or preparation for only one kind of warfare simply invites an enemy to resort to another."[12] This type of flexibility is relative to the emphasis which will have to be placed upon air power and new weapons, an emphasis which will entail reduction of forces in certain categories and their expansion in others; it is relative, in other words, to the problem posed by the possible recurrence of local aggression.

The Eisenhower administration has said nothing that would diminish the strategic importance of such peripheral wars as those in Indochina or Korea. Admiral Radford explained on December 14, 1953, that it was not enough for the United States to be ready for "the tremendous, vast retaliatory and counter-offensive blows in event of a global war," that we had to be prepared for the "lesser military actions short of all-out war" as well. Local wars would be waged, as Mr. Eisenhower expressed it on March 17, 1954, on "the fringe or periphery of our interests." They are thus postulated as a definite strategic possibility.

It was necessary for the administration to bring the problem of localized warfare into the right perspective. Former Chief of Naval Operations Admiral R. B. Carney explained on May 27, 1954, that this problem could not be taken care of by "coming up with a succession of minor strategies to cope with brush fires." What had to be developed, he said, was a strategy which would truly counter "the centralized over-all strategy which is directing the moves in the campaigns for Communist expansion against us." In case of local attack, the free world can either rush around and try to plug the dike as well as it can, or it can adopt measures that will eventually lower the pressure against the dike. This is what the administration tried to do. A strategy for local aggression cannot pinpoint all possible threats in advance, nor can it be specific about the weapons and the forces that ought to be prepared for

13

each emergency. It can, however, postulate that any local threat is posed by Communism as a whole and go on from there in a manner that will not impair the United States' defense posture or enlarge local hostilities more than would be necessary in the national interest.

It has been said that with the hydrogen bomb, intercontinental missiles and long-range jet bombers, we have no defense except deterrence. But "wars have a way of coming about in circumstances that have not been foreseen by humans," said President Eisenhower on August 27, 1958, adding that he did not see any reason for saying that "we necessarily have to take the first blow" and that it was "silly to say that we can be defeated in a first-blow attack." The Communist rulers must be made to understand that any large-scale military venture will engulf their nations in total disaster. They can be deterred by American offensive power. The "one mission" assigned to our forces, said the Budget Message of January 16, 1957, "is to maintain ready nuclear-air-retaliatory forces so strong that they will deter a potential aggressor from initiating an attack."

Deterrence is the first priority of defense, but despite its primacy, there are other tasks that are equally necessary. The United States must maintain a system of warning and disperse its offensive power in order to minimize the effects of an all-out attack on the North American continent. Continental defense, then, is the second priority. There can be no question that to deter attack by means of adequate striking power and to blunt that attack if it comes are the two tasks which, according to the President's letter to Secretary Wilson, "logically demand priority in all planning."

The United States must be able to wage war effectively. It is true that major wars in the future will differ from past wars in that deadly blows will be delivered at the outset. There will be no long period of preparation, and this will limit the amount of force with which America can meet a surprise attack. Actual warfare is therefore a function of both deterrence and continental defense. Its priority is third. But the absence of an all-out attack on the continental United States is not synonymous with national survival, except, perhaps, in a physical sense. The ability to engage our forces, especially in local situations, is a prerequisite for effective national policy. As we shall see presently, the great merit of the doctrine of massive retaliation lies in respecting the limitations imposed on national policy by the current situation while permitting national policy to fulfill all of its necessary tasks.

CHAPTER II

The Doctrine of Massive Retaliation

In his historic address before the Council of Foreign Relations on January 12, 1954, Secretary of State Dulles declared:

> The way to deter aggression is for the free community to be willing and able to respond vigorously at places and with means of its own choosing.
>
> Now, so long as our basic concepts in these respects were unclear, our military leaders could not be selective in building our military power. . . . Before military planning could be changed, the President and his advisers, represented by the National Security Council, had to make some basic policy decisions. This has been done.
>
> And the basic decision was . . . to depend primarily upon a great capacity to retaliate instantly by means and at places of our own choosing.

Earlier in his pronouncement, Mr. Dulles had spoken about local defenses. In the framework of this particular problem, he had said that "local defense must be reinforced by the further deterrent of massive retaliatory power." This carefully drafted statement, undoubtedly the most important pronouncement made by an American statesman in many years, was summarized by American public opinion in terms of a forcible slogan. It became known as the doctrine of instant and massive retaliation. Although Mr. Dulles did not use this striking phrase, we shall make it the starting point of our inquiry and proceed immediately to define its real meaning.

The concept of massive retaliation has not one but several meanings. The Eisenhower administration has taken great pains to define each of these during the debate which followed Mr. Dulles' speech of January 12, 1954. The first and most general meaning, which applies to all types of military aggression, is, as Secretary Dulles said in Chicago on November 29, 1954, "a capacity to inflict punishing damage." The potential aggressor must be deterred, not merely punished after he has acted, as was the case in Korea. "To apply this deterrent principle, the free world must maintain and be prepared to use effective means to make aggression too costly to be tempting," for the aggressor must know in advance that he would be made "to suffer from his aggression more than he can possibly gain by it . . . that the probable hurt will outbalance the probable gain." This is the policy as Mr. Dulles defined it to the Senate Foreign Relations Committee on March 19, 1954.

Now if an aggressor is not able to calculate that aggression is a paying proposition, the retaliation to which he exposes himself is massive; it is massive in relation to his expected gains. Defined thus, massive retaliation is self-explanatory. The essence of any punitive action is to make the hurt outbalance the gain; if the aggressor knows in advance that he would lose more than what he would gain, it would be unreasonable for him to carry his aggressive plans into execution. He is deterred. This is what massive retaliation generally means. It does not mean atomic bombs being dropped all over the map, nor does it imply that the United States would fight for the complete destruction of an enemy or that local hostilities would automatically be turned into a general war. The substance of this strategy is its flexibility.[1]

Effective deterrence presupposes a capacity for instant retaliation, but as the Secretary of State explained in his press conference of March 10, 1954, "in no place" did he say that the United States would always and necessarily retaliate instantly. Noting that it took the United States four years to retaliate against Japan after Pearl Harbor, he said that the essential thing is for the United States to have the capacity to retaliate instantly under conditions that call for such action. Armaments must be kept in a state of

constant readiness and in such quantities that if it became necessary, a retaliatory action could be both instant and effective.

The applicability of massive retaliation as a strategy to all types
of aggression does not preclude its having more specific meaning.
The question now is: How could aggression be made too costly to
be tempting? It might be assumed that the aggressor acts on a
selective basis, that is, he does not engage at once all the forces that
he has available for war. He could strike on several fronts, and yet
he attacks at one point only. If retaliation would ever go beyond
the limits imposed on the conflict by the aggressor in his own interest, it would become massive in relation to the selective nature
of the aggressor's methods. It would be massive to the extent that
it would go beyond the conflict's original limitations. This, then,
is the second meaning of massive retaliation.

Reaction to an aggression must be on America's terms, not on
the enemy's. This is selectiveness. "The broad concept of our defensive policy," said Mr. Dulles on July 18, 1956, is set out "in terms
of primary reliance upon selective deterrent power." Although
selectiveness appears to be contradictory to massiveness to the
superficial observer, it is evident that massive retaliation, if and
where it is judged necessary, expresses American selectivity in the
choice of places and means of retaliation as opposed to the enemy's
selectivity. This can be illustrated by a few examples.

On January 12, 1954, Mr. Dulles said that the fighting in Korea
had stopped because the Communist aggressor was faced with the
"possibility that the fighting might, to his own great peril, soon
spread beyond the limits and the methods which he had selected."
There were areas of great importance to him in the vicinity of the
Korean borders which could eventually be deprived of what General MacArthur had called the status of "privileged sanctuary." If
this had been done, American retaliation would have become massive by going beyond the limitations imposed on the Korean War
by the aggressor in his own interest.

A warning of similar nature was issued by the Eisenhower administration with respect to Indochina. The Formosa Resolution

gave the President sweeping war powers that did not specify the area in which American forces could strike in case of a Communist attempt to seize Formosa by force.[2] Mr. Dulles said in Taipei on March 3, 1955, that the defense of Formosa would not be static and that any area from which a Communist offensive might be staged would not be immune from American retaliation. In case of Communist aggression in Southeast Asia, the Secretary warned on March 15, 1955, that "the United States could cease to exercise restraint on the Republics of China and South Korea." Or as he said in his report to the American people on March 8, 1955:

For military purposes, the Chinese Communist front should be regarded as an entirety because if the Chinese Communists engage in open aggression this would probably mean that they have decided on general war in Asia. . . . General war would confront the Chinese Communists with tasks both at the South and at the center and at the North, tasks which would strain their inadequate means of transportation.

In his message of December 26, 1953, President Eisenhower announced the recall of American forces from Korea and referred to the Korean Unified Command's Report of August 7, 1953, which warned that if hostilities were resumed in Korea, the consequences would be "so grave that, in all probability, it would not be possible to confine hostilities within the frontiers of Korea." In his address of September 2, 1953, Mr. Dulles warned the Chinese Communists not to channel to Indochina the aggressive forces that had been released by the armistice in Korea. "Such a second aggression could not occur," he said, "without grave consequences which might not be confined to Indochina." Commenting on the Khrushchev interview published in the *New York Times* of October 10, 1957, the State Department indicated that the United States would defend Turkey in case of Syrian or Russian aggression, saying that "Mr. Khrushchev is himself reported to have observed that it is dangerous in these times to assume that hostilities, once begun, will remain confined to a particular locality." These grave words

19

were made even more explicit when Mr. Dulles said that even the Soviet borders would not create a sanctuary for Russian aggressive forces if they were to strike Turkey.

These various statements do more than hint at a possible extension of a local conflict in regard to the place and methods of retaliation. They refer to an expressed willingness to alter the nature of the conflict in certain extreme cases. The aggressor might act by proxy, send "volunteers," or limit his active intervention to diplomatic and logistic support. In this case, if retaliation were ever to strike the real aggressor (assuming that he could be found), it would become massive in a new and third manner. The very nature of the aggression, as originally planned by the aggressor, would be altered.

It is true that this third meaning often overlaps the second. The "hot pursuit" concept illustrates this. If American aircraft had been permitted to pursue Communist planes into China, this particular form of retaliation would have been massive in two ways. By going beyond the borders of Korea, retaliation would also have gone beyond the limits imposed on the Korean War by the Communist aggressor. By bringing the war into China, retaliation would have altered the fundamental nature of the Korean conflict. Expansion beyond the original development of local aggression is one thing, but the fact that aggression is brought home is something else.

The fourth and final concept of massive retaliation is easy to understand. Secretary Dulles told the Senate Foreign Affairs Committee on March 19, 1954, that if the Communists attack the United States or its vital interests, "we will hit them with everything we have." Massive retaliation thus means that if the Soviet Union were to attack the United States or reveal any intention of challenging the United States militarily, it would immediately be attacked by air and sea with all sorts of nuclear weapons. Since atomic weapons can be used effectively in localized conflicts, massive retaliation, in this sense, is also relevant to limited aggression.

The ominous meaning of massive retaliation is here too clear to demand much explanation. Retaliation is massive to the extent that weapons of massive destruction are to be used. It can therefore be defined as atomic retaliation. Different as it is from the other three concepts, this type of retaliation is obviously the foundation on which they rest. In order to prove this, however, we must define what the American administration has called the requirements of a successful deterrence.

Thus far in our study of massive retaliation, we have outlined the various levels of increasing intensity through which it might have to pass. We must now consider a question of grave importance: Are we willing to carry out our policy of massive retaliation if such action becomes necessary? President Eisenhower answered this question quite clearly in his message of January 24, 1955. Our task, he said, is to "remove any doubt regarding our willingness to fight if necessary . . . and to engage in whatever operations may be required to carry out that purpose."[3] Or as the late Senator George expressed it on April 23, 1955: "No foreign policy will receive any respect unless the people who put it forth have the strength and the will to carry it to execution." In other words, our willingness to fight must be expressed in declarations so solemn that a potential aggressor will not be likely to overlook them.[4] In a democracy, such declarations serve to marshal public opinion at home. It is therefore important to analyze, in the light of the recent past, the features or conditions that statements of purpose must possess.

Logically, any declaration of policy ought to begin with a statement of the aggressor's alleged intentions. For example, in the statement he read on April 5, 1954, to the House Foreign Affairs Committee, Mr. Dulles defined Communist intentions with respect to Southeast Asia as "not only to take over Indochina, but to dominate all of Southeast Asia." When the Formosa Resolution of 1955 was being discussed, Senator George said that according to Mr. Dulles, "the Communists' intention to take Formosa [at that moment in the probing stage] . . . could become a fixed intention with considerable chances of success." On January 17, 1957, Mr. Dulles warned that the Middle East had always been coveted by the U.S.S.R. "Today," he said, "it seems to Communist rulers that events have played into their hands, and that a great victory is almost within their grasp."

When a policy is declared, the situation is described as critical. In such an event, a direct threat to American security is said to be imminent unless the United States acts and acts quickly. An entire area could conceivably be lost, and the effect of a new Communist advance would be grave.[5] To illustrate this point, if the nations of the Middle East should lose their independence, said President Eisenhower in his address of January 5, 1957, "if they were dominated by alien forces hostile to freedom, that would be both a tragedy for the area and for many other free nations whose economic life would be subject to near strangulation."[6]

The sense of urgency that is expressed in official declarations is often misunderstood by public opinion. The classic example in this respect is the Middle East Resolution of 1957. It was not clear to American public opinion that there was, as the administration seemed to suggest, imminent danger of Communist aggression in that area. However, any question about actual Communist intentions is irrelevant, for a declaration should do no more than express concern about intentions which, for one reason or another, are officially attributed to a potential aggressor. Thus it matters little whether the aggressor actually has the precise plans that are attributed to him. The only relevant factor is whether the situation that the declaration attempts to foreclose is an eventuality that would really endanger the peace and our vital interests if it were permitted to materialize. The aggressor might be bluffing; he might pursue an objective quite different from the one officially attributed to him. The intention of American policy should always be to clarify a situation in need of clarification, and it is therefore the responsibility of the potential aggressor to adjust his behavior to the terms set up by U.S. policy.

Another major stumbling block for public opinion is the diplomatic notion that our government uses in its analysis of the situation in order to make action feasible. This notion generally is that a given situation might lead to war or that it threatens the vital interests of the United States. During the Middle East crisis of

1958, the administration used the concept of indirect aggression. Mr. Eisenhower "cheerfully" admitted on August 6, 1958, that indirect aggression can be carried out "sometimes so cleverly and in such a clandestine manner" that it is difficult to prove, yet the notion was used in our declarations concerning the situation in the Middle East. "If the practices of indirect aggression as they are being developed at the present time are allowed to persist," Mr. Dulles declared on July 31, 1958, ". . . then I think the world is, indeed, in grave danger of war." In this instance, the declaration draws the line from the practice of indirect aggression to its logical consequence. If this were not done, the United States could not cope with the problem.

Public opinion wants the government to describe things "as they are"; it tends to deny the need for enlarging the problem. On September 9, 1958, the Secretary of State said, in reference to the offshore islands of Quemoy and Matsu, "You cannot isolate and say that the only problem involved here is Quemoy and Matsu. What is involved and what is under threat, is the entire position of the United States. . . . And we have to conduct ourselves in relation to that situation, not as though little bits of it could be segregated and treated as isolated problems to be dealt with entirely on their own." Mr. Dulles immediately added that there were always "some people who argue that if you fall back from an advanced position, then you are in a stronger position to hold" other areas that seem more important strategically.

The Lebanese landings were declared necessary for the protection of American lives. Nobody would quarrel with the necessity for protecting our citizens, but were their lives actually in jeopardy in Lebanon? The United States declares that the United Arab Republic tries to subvert its neighbors, and the public retorts that the United Nations has failed to detect any massive foreign intervention in Lebanon. The United States declares that Communist imperialism uses Arab nationalism, and public opinion answers that Nasser has his own Communists under lock and key. How, then, could Communism be the guiding force of his movement? In every situation, public opinion seems to forget that the analysis of a situation by the United States is authoritative and therefore correct.[7]

This is all the more so, of course, when U.S. declarations have no other purpose than to counter similar declarations by the Communist powers. The Korean aggression was declared by the Communists to be a civil war; so was the situation in the Formosa Straits. "We do not accept that view," said Mr. Dulles on September 9, 1958. "There are in this situation elements which could lead to an international war." The Chinese Communists declared that a twelve-mile limit represented their territorial waters. In a counter-declaration, the United States defined this situation as a "grab." "It cannot be effected unilaterally by any nation," the Secretary of State declared, "any more than it can grab territory." The Chinese Communists then proceeded to shell Quemoy and boasted that they would liquidate Chiang Kai-shek. But if their military operations were preliminary to an attack on Formosa, the President said on September 11, 1958, it was "clear that the Formosa Straits resolution" applied to the situation, and the United States declared that Formosa itself was threatened.

Once an aggressor's intentions have been openly declared, they are given a response. In an effort to clarify the American position in relation to Indochina, Mr. Dulles said on March 29, 1954, that the imposition of Communism to Southeast Asia, by whatever means, would not be tolerated by the United States and that it would be met "by united action." On August 17, 1954, Mr. Eisenhower reaffirmed the orders given by President Truman regarding the defense of Formosa and added that "any invasion of Formosa would have to run over the Seventh Fleet." Turkey, Pakistan, and Iran received assurances on November 29, 1956, that any threat to their independence would be viewed by the United States "with the utmost gravity."

These examples show how the form of American declarations can change and how identical their substance really is. Although all of them express deep concern and determination, they do not reveal the United States' exact intentions. This lack of exactness is deliberate, of course, for the United States must maintain flexibility of action. In his speech of March 29, 1954, Mr. Dulles called for united action in Southeast Asia, but our allies wanted no united action at the time. The Formosa Resolution clearly intimated that in case of Communist aggression, military operations would be extended to areas which the United States did not formally propose to defend. It was this flexibility that disturbed public opinion both at home and abroad. Nobody wanted to start a war for the sake of the offshore islands of Quemoy and Matsu. The Eisenhower Middle East doctrine ran into the same difficulties: What would the United States do if Egypt attacked Israel? Is Syria a Soviet satellite? What would the administration do about Communist subversion in one of the Arab states?

Obviously, this aspect of American declarations of policy is most delicate. The national interest is rarely served by spelling out for the aggressor how the United States would act in case of a still hypothetical emergency, and it is precisely that which American public opinion wants the administration to reveal. It is not easy for the United States to resist such pressures and to draw the line between what the enemy must know and what he must not know.

A declaration should certainly remove any doubt from the enemy's mind about America's intention to retaliate. Although he did not try "to attach any blame on anybody," President Eisenhower said on February 2, 1955, that he felt that "the Korean conflict started because of our failing to make clear that we would defend this small nation." Everyone knows that in his major address of January 12, 1950, Dean Acheson excluded Korea from the American defensive perimeter in the Pacific; this ill-famed statement has become the classic example of what a declaration should *not* be. In the interest of peace, it is the responsibility of the United States to remove the chance of mistaken calculations on the part of the aggressor; beyond this, the aggressor is entitled to receive no assurance of any kind. "The most effective type of policy," said Senator Knowland on January 22, 1954, is for the United States to say that in case of aggression, it would take "whatever course of action" its national interest may require. It is sound, he added, to "let those in the Kremlin worry for a while about what we might do. But why telegraph our punches, so to speak, or give a blueprint

25

of our course of action?"[8] In other words, the boldness of a policy is, to a certain extent, complementary to its vagueness. Spelling out a policy in order to appease domestic opinion serves only to hand-cuff the administration without tying the hands of the enemy. But can public opinion understand this?

Once a warning has been issued—with due publicity and seri-ousness—a rational response from the would-be aggressor can be expected. From past experience, the United States has learned a lesson, "and the lesson is this," said Mr. Dulles on September 2, 1953: "If events are likely which will in fact lead us to fight, let us make clear our intention in advance; then we shall probably not have to fight." This is a calculated risk for peace. It does not elim-inate all risk, for there is no certainty that the Communists will always heed even the most serious warning or that they will, in fact, respond rationally. "We must all admit," Mr. Eisenhower said on April 5, 1954, "that there remains a possibility that they might do this [act] in a fit of madness." However, policy can go no further.

Warnings and declarations require a proper basis for action. "Peace is not going to be obtained in any cheap way," the Presi-dent said on January 23, 1957. "We have got to look facts in the face, and we have got to realize that we do things today that a few years back in a slower, more methodical and easier-going life would not have been necessary. They are necessary now." This refers to the proper psychological and political bases for interven-tion. Otherwise, one would just "go wage a battle somewhere," he said on June 10, 1954. It is only when a proper basis for action has been achieved that intervention can take place "in such a way that you are strengthened throughout the world and not merely using up resources to win some local battle." The administration's doc-trine on this point is of paramount importance.

In his speech of June 11, 1954, Mr. Dulles said that American intervention in Indochina was considered in view of certain condi-tions. As long as Red China did not openly intervene in the con-flict, the United States would consider intervention justifiable only as part of a collective effort and on the condition that it would obtain clear assurances about the future independence of Laos, Cambodia, and Vietnam. The United Nations was to show concern about the situation then existing in the Associated States, and France was not to withdraw her troops until the battle was won. "Only if these conditions could be realized," Mr. Dulles concluded, "could the President and the Congress be justified in asking the American people to make the sacrifices incident to committing our nation with others to help restore peace to the area." It was not enough to say that the United States sought, for Southeast Asia, a peace that was true and total—and not a.fraudulent peace—or to claim, as President Eisenhower did on March 24, 1954, that Indochina had become "again one of the battlegrounds of the people that want to live their own lives against this encroachment of Communist aggression." The proper basis for action was missing. For this reason, the Indochinese War is a striking example, not because intervention by the United States was inconceivable, but mainly because the United States failed to secure a satisfactory basis for intervention.

The legal basis for American intervention in Korea was a resolution passed by the Security Council of the United Nations. In early 1955, the administration obtained from Congress the necessary stand-by powers to cope with the emergency in the Formosa Straits. The Formosa Resolution—a public law—refreshed the juridical basis of American commitments in that area, and the Senate later approved a mutual security treaty with the Chinese Nationalists. A somewhat similar procedure was used for the defense of the Middle East. The 1950 declaration by the United Kingdom, France, and the United States, in which these three countries stated their intention to maintain the *status quo* with reference to Middle Eastern boundaries, was at the time considered defunct in the United States as a result of British and French co-operation with Israel in her attack on Egypt. In contradistinction, any intervention in Hungary was clearly precluded by material circumstances. But the Indochinese crisis was remarkable in that a deterrent use of massive retaliation was conceivable but was rendered impracticable for lack of a legal basis. The treaty that established

SEATO was negotiated and signed after the Indochinese armistice. Declarations made by the administration before the treaty was signed did not meet with a full measure of success—though they well deserved it—because they lacked a legal basis.

The Eisenhower administration has well understood the need for treaty commitments and other forms of legal arrangements that do not bind the United States to automatic action and yet would justify such action if it has to be undertaken. Without such commitments under law, the United States could easily be forced into improvised and hasty actions or simply paralyzed by inaction. As a matter of fact, a commitment that has become the law of the land serves both to obligate the country and to formalize the objectives of American foreign policy. The United States thus demonstrates its unity of purpose, and Congressional sanction (which, under the Constitution, could not be otherwise attained) leaves no doubt about the seriousness of the administration's declarations.

Mr. Dulles rightly remarked on February 16, 1955, that "it would be dangerous to assume that treaties or pledges alone would relieve us of the burdensome tasks we undertake in the struggle for peace." They are not a substitute for policy. As the Senate Committee on Foreign Relations said of the Middle East Resolution, the authority granted to the executive branch of government by the joint resolution "is essential to provide an atmosphere in which other measures can be brought to bear and to provide time for those other measures to be effective," but no more.

Secretary Dulles said on June 9, 1956, that our ability to act and to prevent miscalculation is determined not by warning alone but by our forces-in-being. We cannot avoid, at this point of our inquiry, a summary description of American defenses, a description that must include a definition of the basic strategic missions assigned to each of the three services.

The Air Force comprised 48 wings just before the Korean War and 98 wings when Mr. Eisenhower took office. A goal of 137 wings by June 30, 1958, was originally planned. The program for fiscal year 1960 is based on a strength of 845,000 men and a combat structure of 102 wings, consisting of 43 strategic, 25 air defense, and 34 tactical air·wings, with an active inventory of 19,952 planes. Despite repeated cuts in the number of·wings, the over-all combat strength of the Air Force has increased constantly. As of now, it is superior to that of·the Soviet Union.

Since the United States has not reached a state of missile development in which it can afford to let its aircraft program decline, the work horse of massive retaliation is still the Strategic Air Command's manned bombers. SAC maintains a force of some fifteen hundred B-47's, medium all-jet bombers capable of intercontinental missions when refueled in flight or relying otherwise on a system of overseas bases. Except for a dwindling number of B-36's, the balance of SAC's power is composed of eleven wings of B-52's, the number of which will soon exceed five hundred.

The mission of the Strategic Air Command is quite clear. The accent is on planes that can span oceans and continents and on weapons that can destroy entire cities in one blow. SAC's mission was defined by General Curtis LeMay on February 9, 1957, as follows:

> We in SAC define the deterrent force to be "an effective intercontinental nuclear air offensive force which is secure from destruction by the enemy regardless of what offensive and defensive action he takes against it." It must be of such size and composition and be alerted to such a degree that the Soviet Union will realize that an attack on the United States will mean committing national suicide.[9]

As the General testified on April 30, 1956, all responsible airmen agree that "an airtight defense against a well-coordinated and properly executed atomic bombing attack" is not feasible. "A substantial part of the offensive force will always get through," he said. What counts is the actual atomic strike capability, or what LeMay called on February 9, 1957, SAC's "residual punch." This SAC now has and will have for several years to come. It is understandable that the Air Force has expressed concern about what General Thomas D. White called on January 27, 1959, the "growing tendency to believe that a force with less than a capability to destroy the strategic elements of Soviet military forces will be adequate to deter the enemy." At present, this doctrine does not represent national policy. Massive retaliation requires that SAC's "residual punch" be adequate to deter the enemy. And it is reasonable to assume that the enemy will be deterred by the fear of unacceptable damage to his population, industry, and strategic forces. Desirable as it is from the standpoint of continental defense, the destruction of "the strategic elements of Soviet military forces" is an objective that could never be totally achieved.

The Strategic Air Command must be capable of immediate action. LeMay wrote in the April, 1956, issue of *Air Force* magazine that SAC's "prime interest is in readiness today, this instant." In past years, bombers were kept aloft day and night, and since November 8, 1957, much of SAC's striking force has been on continuous alert. Nuclear weapons are stored at widely scattered locations, and they can be carried on routine flights. SAC's tankers are also on standard alert. In order to reduce the vulnerability and increase the response capability of its B-52's, the Air Force has decided to disperse its heavy bombers on the basis of a single squadron per base. Thirty-three home bases were needed for the dispersed B-52's and their KC-135 jet refueling tankers. According to present plans, the medium bomber force will be located on twenty bases at the end of fiscal year 1961 in order to disperse the bombers on the basis of a single wing per base. KC-97 tankers will be similarly dispersed and relocated.

The Air Force maintains more than 150 major installations overseas. In Europe, the system extends from Iceland and the United Kingdom to Spain and Greece. In many countries, such as Norway and Denmark, there are NATO bases that can be used in case of war. The European system is supplemented in the Mediterranean area by major bases in Morocco, Libya, Saudi Arabia, and Turkey. In Pakistan, the United States possesses rights that could eventually be exercised, but at present, there is a large gap in the perimeter from Dhahran to our Pacific bases, which extend from the Philippines to the Aleutians. In addition, certain U.S. bases have become involved in political wrangles, and their future has there-fore become somewhat insecure.[10]

Since the size and weight of atomic weapons have been reduced a great deal, SAC's responsibilities are now shared by the Tactical Air Command. The dividing line between strategic and tactical air power has thus been blurred, yet as long as piloted aircraft remain essential, TAC's light bombers and missiles will remain as important means to deter local aggression, support battlefield operations with versatile weapons (either atomic or conventional), and maintain wings of troop carriers.

The Budget Message of January 17, 1955, announced the crea-tion of a separate air defense command reporting directly to the Joint Chiefs of Staff and having operational control of all air de-fenses.[11] This set-up includes weapons, aircraft control and warn-ing networks, the Army anti-aircraft and guided-missile battalions, the Navy radar picket ships, and all other available means of con-tinental defense.

The policy statement issued by President Truman on December 31, 1952, announced the creation of the Distant Early Warning System (DEW). It was accepted by the Air Force on August 13, 1957, and extends, as far as its land-based portion is concerned, to the northernmost practicable part of the North American conti-nent. In a letter to Senator Russell dated April 19, 1956, Donald Quarles announced that the DEW line would be extended one thousand miles into the Pacific—as far as the Aleutian island of Attu. It is now linked to NATO's warning systems and to the two oceanic radar barriers, which stretch from the mid-Pacific to the general vicinity of the Azores in the Atlantic.

The DEW line is a combination of rotating and fixed radar equipment and is designed to flash instant warning to the joint U.S.-Canadian center (NORAD) at Colorado Springs, Colorado. It is supplemented by the Mid-Canada line, a radar "fence" ex-tending across Canada and completed since the end of May, 1957, and the Pine Tree line, which has been under joint U.S.-Canadian operation for several years. On July 10, 1958, the creation of a joint cabinet committee acting in a supervisory capacity was announced by the United States and Canada, thus making more effective the concept of air defense in depth.

Our radar warning network is also linked to radar installations within the United States, the flight centers of the Civil Aeronautics Administration, the Navy radar picket ships, to the Texas towers off the Atlantic Coast, and to the various headquarters of Ground Observer Corps. The enormous amount of information obtained from these various sources is processed by a "semi-automatic ground environment system" (SAGE), and instructions are issued accordingly. If it is ever required to proceed to the destruction phase of its activities, SAGE can order the use of weapons that range from anti-aircraft guns to guided missiles and whatever squadrons of interceptors are assigned to NORAD.

General Partridge pointed out on May 17, 1956, that "the mere existence of an air defense system in this country forces the enemy to adopt many measures which he would otherwise be able to avoid." In plainer language, NORAD's primary function is not simply to maintain a continental defense system but to make effective destruction of the U.S. retaliation potential a strategic objective that the enemy cannot hope to achieve by surprise. Since our retaliatory attack must be launched at the same time our defenses go into action, the present system constitutes a necessary aid to the navigation of our own planes and permits a close coordination between offense and defense. It will therefore remain an essential part of our defenses, although its present usefulness is, to a considerable extent, predicated on the possibility of a Russian attack with intercontinental bombers and air-breathing missiles.

Recent developments in radar technology will soon permit the early detection of ballistic missiles and the faster aircraft of the future. The construction of two installations for this new type of radar is already far advanced. As regards other developments, we should remember that the primary purpose of our air defense is to deter aggression. If we succeed in that, we will have achieved a 100 per cent effective air defense.

At the start of the Korean War, the U.S. Navy had 646 ships in the active fleet. The budget for fiscal year 1960 provides for the operation of an active fleet of 864 ships, including 386 warships, and a reserve fleet of more than 1,500 vessels. In fiscal year 1959, the Navy will receive 27 new ships. Forty vessels are included in its construction program for both 1959 and 1960. The number of submarines in the active fleet will be 113 by June 30, 1960. Up to 1959, Congress has appropriated funds for the construction of 35 nuclear-powered submarines, including nine ballistic-missile submarines. For fiscal year 1960, the administration requested funds for long "lead-time" items for three additional Polaris submarines. The Navy plans to maintain 14 attack aircraft carriers. It has long aimed at a total of 15 carriers of the *Forrestal* type, but up to now, only seven of these have been built or authorized, including one that is nuclear powered. In fiscal year 1959, the Navy will operate 95 air combat groups and squadrons in the fleet and will maintain an active aircraft inventory of more than 9,000 planes. This number will drop to 7,200 in fiscal year 1960.

The Navy is the most complex of the various elements of American power. It is passing from steam to nuclear power, from subsonic to supersonic aircraft, from guns to missiles, from conventional armaments to nuclear weapons. In the course of a few years, the battleship has lost the position it long occupied, replaced in that position by the carrier, now considered by many to be obsolescent. In a document released unofficially on May 19, 1956, the Air Force reportedly condemned the attack carrier as being ineffectual for long-range strategic bombing—mainly because of the small number of aircraft that can be based on a carrier—and as being too vulnerable to enemy attack.[12]

The Navy rightly considers the attack aircraft carrier to be essential to our military posture. International Communism occupies a central land position and thus has the possibility to radiate in every direction, but for the same reason, it can be hit by a flexible striking force using a peripheral strategy. This means that the United States must have control of the sea, and since the strength of a navy is primarily measured by the striking power of its aircraft (a power that would be ineffective if its carriers could not launch

33

their aircraft), we must have an adequate carrier force in order to dominate global waters. If we keep these simple facts in mind, the answer to the question of whether the United States ought to be a naval power is obvious. It is equally clear that as long as control of the sea remains essential, so does the aircraft carrier.

The carrier task force, an elusive target, is relatively immune to attack. With its air arm, its guided-missile ships, its submarines, and its anti-submarine force, it can concentrate enormous firepower and yet can normally spread it over an area about the size of the state of Maine. Any successful attack on a carrier task force would be a remarkable feat requiring considerable means and time, an important factor in case of all-out war. The Navy considers a ballistic missile fired at a moving target, such as a carrier, to be wasted. Since the object of modern sea warfare is the identification and destruction of aircraft carriers, only submarines and piloted aircraft have enough selectivity to identify a carrier; but they cannot do so without exposing themselves to electronic jamming and other defenses of the task force.

Equally valid is the Navy's increased emphasis on the ballistic-missile submarine. As a missile launcher, the submarine combines the versatility of the atomic-powered submarine with the deadliness of solid-fuel ballistic missiles, a sizable number of which can be carried in a single vessel without appreciably increasing her size. Like the aircraft carrier, the Polaris ballistic-missile submarine is unobtrusive and politically inoffensive, and since it is virtually free from fuel limitations, it can be kept at sea continuously and can be so well concealed that the United States can move the weight of its firepower from one area to another both quickly and secretly.[13]

The deterrent value of the Polaris submarine is limited by its strategic function. Primarily designed for attacking fixed land targets, it will be a one-purpose weapons system and will never suffice to keep control of the sea. The carrier task force has the further advantage of being ready for local situations which require both a stabilizing reminder of our global power and the means for a limited intervention. The recent events in the Middle East and in

the Formosa Straits illustrate this point conclusively. In this respect, the Navy's power is complemented by the Marine Corps'
three air wings and three divisions, which are poised for immediate action in the Pacific and Mediterranean areas. The Marine
Corps is our most compact and flexible striking force, ready for
deployment on the ground on the shortest possible notice.

The budget for fiscal year 1959 provides for 14 modern Army
divisions and other battle groups, one armored combat command,
four atomic combat commands, 28 additional surface-to-surface
missile battalions, 74 surface-to-air missile battalions, and 30 aviation companies, with a total manpower strength below 900,000
men. As these figures indicate, the Army contributes to our continental defense against air attack. In addition, nearly one-half of
its personnel strength is deployed overseas for deterring and, if
necessary, resisting aggression. A third and highly important
function is the maintenance of a mobile, combat-ready strategic
force here at home for rapid reinforcement of forward-deployed
forces or prompt suppression of small-war situations. The Strategic Army Corps (STRAC) was formed for this purpose. According
to the original plan, STRAC was to consist of two airborne and
two infantry divisions, along with their supporting units. Thus far,
only two of these divisions have reached the combat-ready stage,
and the Army announced in early 1959 that STRAC would have
three divisions instead of four.

The Budget Message of January 17, 1955, announced that the
U.S. Army had been reorganized "into smaller, but more mobile
and self-contained units with greater firepower."[14] After a study of
the effects of atomic weapons upon the tactics of warfare, the
Army decided in favor of the "pentomic" concept. In contrast to
the old "triangular" divisions, Army forces have been given a pen-
tagonal structure by increasing the number of basic combat units
within the division from three to five.

The new organization is based upon several considerations. The
division commander is given atomic weapons within the organic
structure of the division, and the division itself is so organized
that it can disperse quickly over wide areas. Dispersion, however,

is combined with perimeter defense: forcing the enemy to concentrate in order to attack and thus setting him up as a profitable target for an atomic strike.

The traditional use of masses of troops is gone forever. Since any atomic battlefield will be vast in size and since dispersed units must be able to reconcentrate rapidly in order to exploit the effects of atomic bombing, problems of command are bound to arise. Much progress has been made in signal communications, however, and a division commander can now control more subordinate units than he formerly could.

Although it has fewer men, the new division is almost equal to the old division in terms of non-atomic firepower. Unlike the old division, however, the pentomic division possesses atomic firepower, and its long-range weapons can deliver both atomic and non-atomic warheads much farther behind enemy lines than was heretofore possible.

"We used to think of troops supported by weapons," General Gruenther once said. "Now it is the case of weapons supported by troops." This aphorism expresses the difference between atomic strategy per se and the use of atomic weapons in land warfare. The Army's present strategy is decidedly atomic, but this does not mean that the Army could never wage conventional warfare. Although there exists a certain incompatibility between atomic strategy and conventional weapons, it is evident that an atomic strategy cannot operate without a considerable infrastructure of conventional power. Since the division still possesses conventional weapons, the Army's new structure does not force it to use only atomic weapons. Its strategy is atomic, but its capabilities are both atomic and conventional.

Critics who worry about the reduced personnel strength of the Army have denied that its strategy is flexible and have warned that a nuclear war would require more men and logistics than a conventional war. The administration has met this objection by pointing out that the traditional policy of concentrating on the mobilization of a large and fully equipped expeditionary force has lost all relevance in the atomic age. The size of the force to be kept in a state of constant readiness should therefore be reduced in view of the practical limitations that oppose its transfer to a battlefield at the outbreak of all-out aggression. The administration has also pointed out that the U.S. Army is today regarded, in part, as a complement to the local defenses maintained by friendly nations. The principle of collective security presupposes that each partner contributes what he best can with the least strain to himself and the greatest advantage to his allies. In this context, the American contribution mainly consists in providing the means of massive retaliation for integration into the free world's system of local defenses.

The United States has developed an atomic stockpile of growing diversity and size. Our nuclear armaments include offensive and defensive weapons and superweapons, as well as tactical weapons of very small yield. In our missile stockpile, we have what Mr. Eisenhower called on November 7, 1957, "weapons adapted to every kind of distance, launching and use." Although it recognized a temporary lag in intercontinental ballistic missile development, the administration said flatly that the transition to missiles had to be made in an orderly manner and that this would not be done at the expense of our forces-in-being. Many of the functions now performed by conventional armaments will eventually be taken over by missiles, creating new problems of defense, but all of this will be worked out gradually and to the best possible advantage.

The United States has no intention of matching the Soviet Union in the production of intercontinental missiles. The administration's policy is to rely on a diversified delivery system, which is better suited to our requirements. As President Eisenhower said on February 3, 1959, we are not going "to assume that our entire forces were going to be wiped out instantly . . . in one volley all over this world." There is "such a thing," he said, as "a logical limit to capability, and we just know that there is not that kind of capability existing in the world today."

The new weapons developed by the three services can be used for strategic and tactical bombing, for launching from land bases, in the air, or at sea, as anti-aircraft defenses, or as diversionary targets. Interim weapons, though operational, must be replaced by more sophisticated missiles with longer range, better guidance, and new propellants. Research in this revolutionary field is, says the administration, progressing satisfactorily according to a program that is well balanced in spite of definite weaknesses in some sectors.

There can be no doubt that the United States still possesses what George Washington called "a respectable military posture." General Twining rightly warned in January, 1958, that "it would be an unnecessary tragedy if our national policy, or the will of our allies—to say nothing of the confidence of our people in their civilian and military leaders—were weakened because of the mistaken impression that the Soviets have achieved military ascendancy over the free world." He added that "such mistaken conclusions could actually increase the probability of total war because they might result in bolder courses of Soviet action and greater opportunity for fatal miscalculations."[15]

CHAPTER III

Applications of the Doctrine

THE VALIDITY OF massive retaliation as a strategy for all-out war is hardly open to question. Although the Eisenhower administration has been exceedingly discreet on the meaning of massive retaliation in its application to total war, the implications of the doctrine are self-evident. Even if it were to follow the progressive deterioration of some local situation, a total war could be expected to start with a surprise attack on the enemy. We have already noted that the advent of long-range bombers, nuclear weapons, and intercontinental missiles gives us reason to believe that such an attack is a strategic necessity for both the aggressor and his intended victim. As Commander in Chief, the President would have to order American forces into action instantly and totally. "The trade of nuclear blows would be necessarily swift," General Twining said on January 28, 1956. "Unlike past wars, the peak of destruction would come at the very beginning instead of near the end of the war." Since the largest stockpile of nuclear weapons could be depleted in a few days, the decisive use of force would have to be made immediately; otherwise it would be practically useless.

The first phase of an all-out war would therefore be short and violent, yet no one pretends that a total war in the future would be rapidly concluded. Nor is it said that soldiers and ships would not be of any use. For the duration of a nuclear exchange, land and sea forces would be primarily concerned with every possible

39

attempt to survive. "Then would follow," said Admiral Carney on February 16, 1954, "a period when both sides would pick up the pieces, dust off the atomic residue, and make a reestimate of the situation." If the issue were still undecided, "tough people," to use Admiral Carney's words, would have to carry on, across radioactive ashes and waters, with whatever weapons were left. Considering the havoc that would result from atomic destruction of transportation facilities, communications, weapons stockpiles, and population, it is quite inconceivable that a country would be able to fight prolonged campaigns at the end of extended supply lines before a considerable amount of time had passed. Yet if a nuclear war is to end by force of arms, it must end on the ground. As President Eisenhower said on December 14, 1954, this could certainly not be done "in a hurried fashion." Here, he said, entered the philosophy of retaliation: "to make certain that no one could ever attack us and hope to gain by that kind of an attack."

Massive retaliation prepares for total war in that it attempts to deter it. The paradox of this strategy is that it is principally relevant to local or peripheral aggression. The administration's doctrine on local aggression has been stated in the general framework of collective security.[1] Now the principle of collective security has a negative and a positive meaning. As Mr. Dulles said on January 12, 1954, no one nation can, by itself, contain the power of the Communist world; likewise, any effort to achieve strength everywhere is doomed to failure. In a positive sense, collective security can achieve its deterrent purpose, for it is possible to develop an integrated force that will make it unnecessary for us (as Mr. Dulles said on December 8, 1955) "to spread our strength all around the world in futile attempts to create everywhere a static defense, nor need we crawl back into our own holes in the vain hope of defending ourselves against all the rest of the world." If an aggressor is not permitted to strike at places where his superiority is overwhelming and if he is not permitted to prescribe battle conditions that suit his purpose of world domination, then defense against aggression becomes a feasible objective, but only on the condition that less dependence is placed on local defensive strength and more reliance placed on global deterrence. Collective security thus comes to mean a collective willingness to respond vigorously with all suitable means and at places of the free nations' own choosing, and this means massive retaliation.

A discussion of the usefulness of local defenses logically leads to an important clarification of the concept of local aggression. It is true—as President Eisenhower said on March 17, 1954—that generalizations are always dangerous; war, he said, never shows "the characteristics that were expected; it was always different." The United States cannot commit itself to saying in advance what it would do under all kinds of circumstances, but it can establish categories of possible action in local warfare in order to warn an aggressor about the possible consequences of his action. The administration has established the categories that had to be established and has defined them with great care.

The United States might first encounter a completely local situation which is potentially dangerous for the maintenance of peace but not yet enlarged by the intervention of a major Communist power. As the President said on January 12, 1955, the local defenses which the United States tries to build up throughout the world must be able to put down internal rebellion; under normal circumstances, indigenous forces would be adequate in the situation. If the national government in the affected area could not quell the rebellion alone, American troops could be sent by sea or by air at its request, and the United States could supply tactical and logistical support on a temporary basis. Our intervention might thus be the stitch in time that forestalls a major disaster. Basically, this would be a police action, but the United States' stepping in would obviously raise the situation to a new level of diplomatic gravity.

President Eisenhower said on January 12, 1955, that our actions could "vary in severity from something of a very minor character on up." As was repeatedly the case in the Near East, police actions presuppose speed and demand highly mobile forces. The United States has ample power for dealing with a local emergency on the condition that the various elements of our strength are ready and free to be moved anywhere. As a deterrent, American power must be committed to defend, but it should not normally be engaged. Our armed forces "must regain mobility of action," declared the State of the Union Message of January 7, 1954, and our "strategic reserves must be centrally placed and readily deployable to meet sudden aggression."[2] This principle was applied when two Army divisions were withdrawn from Korea following the announcement of December 26, 1953, and more recently in our withdrawals from Japan. Massive retaliation thus implies a process of disengagement: our power should be nowhere in order to be everywhere.

Complementariness is another characteristic of ready power. Our strategy emphasizes "nuclear-air retaliatory power," the President said in the Budget Message of January 17, 1955, because this power is—and should be—"supplemented by other military forces of great strength, flexibility and mobility, and by the forces of our allies."[3] This statement is important, and it is also very precise. Our own conventional power and allied forces are said to be complementary to a massive retaliation capacity. This means that air-atomic power supplements the inadequacy of both local defenses and conventional power in general. It also means that under the umbrella of air-atomic power, local defenses ought to suffice in most situations. Mutual security's "essential ingredients are the deterrent power of the United States" and its "willingness to use that power in response to a military challenge," said Mr. Dulles on March 8, 1955. The deterrent use of massive retaliation would normally limit local warfare to conventional warfare. If the United States had to intervene, intervention would then be limited to a police action, and as the President said on March 23, 1955, "you don't send in A-bombs to restore order when a riot occurs." Therefore, the general effect of massive retaliation is that it tends to keep any local conflict limited in scope, that is, within the range of collective security, local defenses, and conventional warfare. This point has been generally overlooked.

The discussion just concluded has revealed that the notion of massive retaliation has a fifth and last meaning: dependence on the American capacity for massive retaliation. The reformulation of massive retaliation so understood has been under way for several years. As we have said, the administration's doctrine is based on the fact that it is impossible to build up adequate defensive forces all around the Communist perimeter. Because of developments in nuclear weapons technology, namely the availability of tactical and cleaner atomic weapons, a capacity for massive retaliation proper could be indirectly extended to other friendly countries. Not many nations can afford to create and to maintain the enormous war machine that massive retaliation requires, but the United States can choose to disinvest itself of its atomic monopoly by making nuclear arms available to some of its allies. Secretary of State Dulles wrote in the October, 1957, issue of *Foreign Affairs* magazine that it might now be possible to defend certain countries by nuclear weapons "so mobile, or so placed, as to make military invasion with conventional forces a hazardous attempt."[4] Invasion routes could be dominated by nuclear artillery, he wrote, and would-be aggressors could therefore not count on a successful conventional invasion. If atomic stockpiles—or other means to make atomic weapons available to U.S. allies—become a reality, as can be expected, the basis for massive retaliation will be spread, but, contrary to what Mr. Dulles seems to imply in his article, the strategy of massive retaliation will remain unchanged.

Mr. Eisenhower declared on January 12, 1955, that "when you resorted to force as the arbiter of human difficulty, you didn't know where you were going." Speaking generally, he said: "If you got deeper and deeper, there was just no limit except what was imposed by the limitations of force itself." This is to say that in spite of the deterrent of massive retaliation, a local situation might deteriorate or might be, from the very start, of such magnitude that the use of nuclear weapons becomes necessary. If that were the case, local aggression would move to a new level and become the object of massive retaliation proper.

Here again, important distinctions must be made. The object of our strategy is not to make aggression too risky to be tempting but to make it too expensive to be profitable. In the framework of massive retaliation, this result is achieved, as we have explained, by making the aggressor understand that he does more than expose the forces he has chosen to employ for his aggression, by depriving his other assets of a sanctuary status, and by extending the immediate area of the conflict. All of this points to grave decisions that would have to be made in the light of circumstances, and again, it is a matter, wrote Mr. Dulles in an article in 1954, "to which the aggressor had best remain ignorant. But he can and does know, in the light of present policies, that the choice in this respect is ours and not his."[5]

This strong phrase can be misunderstood and, indeed, was misunderstood. Both the administration and its critics have spoken at this point of the debate of "graduated deterrence." The notion makes no sense at all, and this explains some of the confusion about the categories of retaliation and the categories of warfare. In reality, it belongs to the aggressor to assume the risks involved in our retaliation. It belongs to us, Mr. Dulles declared to the House Foreign Affairs Committee on April 5, 1954, to make what he called "a judgment as to what would hurt the aggressor beyond his possibility of gain and, at the same time, not enlarge the conflict at our disadvantage." This means that the policy of massive retaliation provides for total deterrence but also permits "graduated retaliation." If we want to prevent local aggression from rising to levels of increasing seriousness—the categories of warfare—our will to deter must be total, and that is "massive retaliation." The initiative in expanding a local war is the aggressor's; for that reason, total deterrence is not inconsistent with graduated retaliation.

This doctrine is fully supported by an analysis of the various security arrangements which the United States has established on the periphery of the Communist empire. The nature of the commitments made by the United States differs for each area; they concern the North Atlantic Treaty Organization, the Pacific, and the Middle East.

In his article of April, 1954, Mr. Dulles emphasized that western

Europe was especially important to the United States. Europe's industrial capacity, he wrote, "represents so nearly the balance of industrial power in the world that an aggressor might feel that it was a good gamble to seize it—even at the risk of considerable hurt to himself." This is in contradistinction to most other areas, he said further, which offer "less value to him than the loss he would suffer from well-conceived retaliatory measures."[6]

For all practical purposes, the North Atlantic area belongs to America's vital interests. Article 5 of the North Atlantic Treaty states that

the parties agree that an armed attack against one or more of them . . . shall be considered an attack against them all; and consequently they agree that if such an armed attack occurs, each of them will assist the party or parties so attacked by taking forthwith such action as it deems necessary, including the use of armed forces."

Even in the missile age, this wording is very precise, and it combines flexibility with a strong commitment.

Mr. Dulles said in his press conference of March 16, 1954, that it was his opinion that the provisions of the North Atlantic Treaty gave to the President of the United States "the same authority to react as he would have if the United States were attacked." In fact, the actual American commitment to NATO goes far beyond the letter of Article 5. Although the United States is not obligated to do more than what "it deems necessary," American leaders have gone as far as it seems possible to go in their commitment. The strongest language ever used in the matter came from President Eisenhower, who declared, "in the most solemn terms," in Paris on December 16, 1957, that "the United States would come, at once and with all appropriate force, to the assistance of any NATO nation subjected to armed attack. This is the resolve of the United States—of all parts and of all parties."

It is also difficult to imagine that the United States would not keep its forces intermingled with European forces in the future. Any existing doubts on this point are perhaps a lingering effect of the European Defense Community controversy. In his article of April, 1954, Mr. Dulles said that massive retaliation did not mean that the United States intended to pull its forces out of Europe. Having in mind the ratification of the European Defense Community Treaty, which was still pending at the time, he added that American willingness was conditioned on the creation of what he called a "harmonious nucleus of integrated defense" in Europe. The rearmament of West Germany and her accession to NATO were approved in Paris on October 23, 1954, and the administration was prompt to pledge continued American participation in NATO. On March 10, 1955, President Eisenhower sent a message to the various prime ministers of the Western European Union and assured them that the United States was ready "to continue to maintain in Europe, including Germany, such units of its armed forces as may be necessary and appropriate to contribute its fair share of the forces needed for the joint defense of the North Atlantic area." The Presidential statement also included a commitment to consult on questions of mutual concern, including the level of forces to be placed at the disposal of the Supreme Allied Commander in Europe (SACEUR), and to deploy American forces in accordance with the mutually agreed-on strategy. This policy has not been changed by cuts made in American manpower. As far as NATO is concerned, these cuts were described by Secretary Dulles on December 18, 1956, as readjustments and streamlining.

The fact is that U.S. forces are now so deployed that they would be immediately involved in a war in Europe. NATO's strategy has been called a "forward" strategy, a term which well describes the Alliance's strategic objectives. The United States might possibly maintain a cordon of ground forces in western Europe as a token of its determination to hold the area; if the Soviets ever attacked, they would challenge the United States at once and thus unleash massive air-atomic retaliation. But on December 21, 1954, Mr. Dulles rejected this approach once and for all. He defined NATO as "a form of security which, while having as its first objective the preservation of peace, would also be adequate for defense, and which would not put Western Europe in a position of having to be liberated." A forward strategy means, therefore, that western Europe will be held. It also means that the defense line that the Alliance will attempt to hold will be on the threshold of the Treaty area. If Continental Europe were to be defended at the Rhine and the Scandinavian countries abandoned to their fate, there would be no forward strategy for NATO.

Since Western ability to hold the Iron Curtain front is decidedly doubtful in terms of land warfare, the forward strategy of NATO is bound up with its atomic strategy. It had always been evident that the enemy's superiority in numbers and conventional power would have to be overcome by superior firepower, yet it was only on December 17, 1954, that the North Atlantic Council, acting on the report of its military commanders, agreed to meet aggression in Europe with atomic weapons. The Council made it clear that NATO's strategy was massive retaliation. Mr. Dulles said in Paris on December 16, 1957, that this means, first of all, that "the major deterrent to Soviet aggression against NATO is the maintenance of a retaliatory power of such capacity as to convince the Soviets that such aggression would result in their own destruction." It also means, he said, that "the shield of NATO ground, sea and air forces is also an integral part of the deterrent."

The units of the U.S. Strategic Air Command stationed in the United Kingdom and North Africa are not integrated into NATO's structure, nor is British strategic air power a part of NATO. This situation is delicate, and it would not be wise to approach it head-on with formal statements of policy. Article 5 of the North Atlantic Treaty gives the two atomic powers of the Alliance as much freedom of action as they might desire. Our allies fear, with equal intensity, both an automatic atomic reflex by the United States in case of Soviet aggression and an American failure to act. Mr. Dulles said on November 19, 1957, that "the allies should be reassured on both counts." They ought to know that strategic weapons will be used if need be and that they will not be misused, yet, Mr. Dulles added, this does not involve "a veto on their part any more than an individual citizen has any veto over the action of the policeman on the beat. He is entitled to know that the circum-

47

stances under which the security force operates are such to give him reasonable assurance on these matters."

The problem of consultation with our allies is further complicated by the fact that we would have to use, for strategic purposes, bases located on foreign soil. Mr. Eisenhower indicated on March 24, 1954, that the United States had made arrangements for instant consultation with the United Kingdom and other interested nations in regard to the eventual use of these installations. In his article of April, 1954, Mr. Dulles recognized that American bases abroad had been constructed "only at the request of the host nation." Their availability in an emergency would depend, he said, "upon its consent, usually as a legal condition and always as a practical one." Consent to use these bases would not be granted, the Secretary concluded, "unless it was clear that their use was in response to open aggression and reasonably related to its scope and nature."[7] Cumbersome procedures of consultation and authorization would be as dangerous for collective security as they would for American security alone. As the President declared on December 16, 1957, "the mandate to consult must be applied in accordance with a rule of reason." There must be a capacity to react instantly "within the limits of known policy"; otherwise the consequences of delaying reaction might prove to be fatal to all.

The base for instant strategic retaliation will be broadened considerably when long-range, American-made ballistic missiles are put at the disposal of the Supreme Commander, Europe, as was decided by the NATO Council in December, 1957. On November 19, 1957, Mr. Dulles expressed the hope that the missiles could be placed on the Continent "under similar conditions to those which have already been negotiated out with the United Kingdom with respect to warheads." Atomic warheads would remain in the technical custody of American personnel, to be turned over to the Allies in case of war by the President under his Constitutional war powers, but the Allies would have an appreciable measure of participation in the handling of the missiles. The agreement between the United States and the United Kingdom announced on March 24, 1957, under which the United States would allocate intermediate-range ballistic missiles for use by British forces and stockpile nuclear warheads for the missiles (in American custody, of course), does not place this weapon under the authority of NATO's Supreme Commander, as will be the case for missiles to be placed on the Continent. This is in conformity with the general massive retaliation pattern of NATO, and it is hoped that this wise arrangement can be preserved in the future.

When the Atlantic Pact was signed, there was talk of building up a conventional force that would total ninety-six divisions by 1954. Although this goal was never attained, the strength of NATO today is not as much out of balance with Soviet power as is generally supposed. In the central German front, the United States maintains the equivalent of six divisions, Britain has four divisions but is in the process of reducing them, the French and the Germans have five understrength divisions, and the Benelux countries have three. In addition to this central "shield," almost thirty divisions are available in the flank sectors. Yet the Soviet Union holds more than thirty divisions in readiness in the German sector alone, and it is evident that the Western shield would not long deter aggression if it were not reinforced with tactical nuclear firepower. The U.S. Seventh Army is, for the moment, the only NATO field army that possesses a full range of nuclear weapons for its ground forces to use, while the U.S. Forty-ninth Air Division, stationed in the United Kingdom, is the mainstay of NATO's tactical air power. In northern and eastern Italy, the U.S. Army's Southern European Task Force provides atomic support to NATO's divisions in Italy; this force has been considered the forerunner of a number of atomic-support commands which the Budget Message of January 16, 1957, described as "particularly suitable as back-up for the ground forces of allied countries."

The NATO Communiqué of December 19, 1957, confirmed the fact that the Allies had decided to "establish stocks of nuclear warheads, which will be readily available for the defense of the Alliance in case of need." Since NATO had long counted on their use in case of war, there was nothing new nor secret in the fact that nuclear weapons, both tactical and strategic, were being stored in

Europe or carried by aircraft as a matter of routine. As we have noted, the new concept consists in spreading atomic capability. "Within this stockpile system," Mr. Dulles explained on December 16, 1957, "nuclear warheads would be deployed under United States custody in accordance with NATO defensive planning and in agreement with the nations directly concerned." In the event of war, Mr. Dulles said, "nuclear warheads would be released to the appropriate NATO Supreme Allied Commander for employment by nuclear-capable NATO forces."[8]

In reality, the new policy pursues a complex objective. The United States wants a greater exchange of military research and information, not only because we can benefit from effective scientific collaboration, but also because we waste precious time and manpower resources in unnecessary duplication, for as President Eisenhower noted, "the task ahead will be hard enough without handcuffs of our own making."[9] Our allies also need to know what adjustments will have to be made in their planes and missiles in order to accommodate the nuclear warheads that we would supply in case of war, and this, too, requires a greater exchange of information than we formerly had. Although we want to make possible the immediate availability of nuclear weapons in case of emergency, we have no intention of encouraging or providing assistance to any nation so that it can achieve an atomic-weapons capability. This principle was inspired by Congressional timidity, but if necessary, it can be abandoned in future negotiations.[10]

The Atomic Energy Act was amended in 1958 so that we could achieve these ends. It now permits the transfer of non-nuclear parts of atomic weapons and nuclear materials to any nation that has made "substantial progress in the development of atomic weapons." It also permits us to exchange with such a nation certain restricted information concerning nuclear weapons and to communicate or exchange certain restricted data concerning military reactors. To date, the United Kingdom is the only Allied power to have achieved a capacity for fabricating its own atomic weapons and their accompanying facilities. It is therefore the only country to qualify for the exchange of nuclear information under this section of the Act, which still prohibits the actual transfer of manufactured nuclear components of weapons. In a bilateral agreement signed on July 3, 1958, the United States agreed to sell a nuclear-propulsion plant for a submarine, along with the necessary nuclear fuel, to the United Kingdom—a first step toward increased co-operation.

The President can communicate to our other allies such restricted nuclear information—including design information—as is necessary for the development of common defense plans, the training of personnel, the evaluation of the enemy's nuclear capabilities, and the development of delivery systems. He is not permitted to transfer the non-atomic parts of weapons to a country—such as France, for example—that has not made substantial progress in developing atomic weapons of its own. Congress did not want our allies to receive what Senator Anderson called "do-it-yourself-kits" of information on how to make atomic bombs.

Although this policy will do little to remove misgivings, on the part of NATO's Continental members, about an Anglo-American monopoly of atomic weapons and vital information (it will indeed increase France's desire to become a full-fledged nuclear power—on the whole a desirable objective), it will spur the reorganization and integration of NATO's conventional infrastructure. The irritating question of who will unleash atomic retaliation in case of aggression remains unanswered. At present, no European country is willing to leave a decision concerning the use of atomic weapons to military commanders—meaning, of course, American commanders. The principle in force in this respect appears to be the NATO Council's decision of December 18, 1954, which reaffirmed the right of civilian authorities to decide when and how atomic weapons would be used in an emergency. The Council also approved the principle of a nuclear strategy as "a basis for defense planning and preparations by the NATO military authorities" but noted that approval did not involve any "delegation of the responsibility of governments to make decisions for putting plans into action in the event of hostilities." The Council thus failed to define the process of decision. Since NATO's strategic and tactical plans will be implemented in case of war, the apparent lack of a formal policy on the subject is the best policy.

It should be noted that a limited war in Europe is a contingency that appears to be theoretical, but this does not mean that it should be rejected. Mr. Dulles noted on December 10, 1957, that massive retaliation and limited war were not mutually exclusive, but he also acknowledged that there was no "final NATO doctrine on the subject as yet." The Berlin crisis might well put this doctrine to a test.

Lenin observed that "for world Communism, the road to Paris lies through Peking and Calcutta." The wording of this dogma is not vain. The United States has again been forced, against its will, to assume direct responsibility for the maintenance of peace in the Pacific area. This policy has found expression in a system of defensive treaties and declarations affecting the more directly threatened Asian countries.

American strategic thinking on the defense of the Pacific is dominated by the United States' world-wide responsibilities. Security in the Far East is endangered by international Communism, particularly by Red China as a world power. The Far Eastern security problem is further complicated by Asian neutralism and the squalid poverty of the Asian masses. Moreover, anti-colonialism is still a deeply motivating force in Asia, and for this reason, it was not possible for the United States to fit a security arrangement for the area into the framework of past colonial associations. The Pacific Charter, signed in Manila on September 8, 1954, dedicates all members of the Southeast Asia Treaty Organization to the task of upholding the principles of self-determination, self-government, and the independence of all countries—as the Charter states it— "whose peoples desire it and are able to undertake its responsibilities." For obvious reasons, the former colonial powers have shown a certain sensitivity in accepting increasing American influence, and their differences have generally benefited the Communists, who have learned that pressure tends to unite the Western powers in Europe and to divide them in Asia.

This situation has been rendered even more complex by the

fact that countries more directly threatened by world Communism are not parties to the collective security arrangement known as SEATO. The Indochinese armistice of 1954 originally created legal difficulties with respect to Laos, Cambodia, and Vietnam, which could not become parties to the Southeast Asia Treaty. On the other hand, the United States' allies refused to include Formosa in the collective security system. As far as the Indochinese states are concerned, however, a protocol attached to the Southeast Asia Treaty extended to them the benefits of mutual security. No similar arrangements with regard to Formosa have been made so far.

Since the United States does not possess territorial interests in Southeast Asia, it was stipulated that Communist aggression would be the only form of aggression that the United States would consider dangerous to its own peace and safety. Any other form of aggression would create only an obligation to consult. On the other hand, the United States has concluded bilateral security treaties with Japan, South Korea, Formosa, and the Philippines, and it is also a party to the ANZUS Pact, which binds it to Australia and New Zealand. The fact that it belongs simultaneously to SEATO and to those bilateral systems thus means that Pacific security is based upon both collective and bilateral treaties—once more, a flexible and skillful arrangement.

The heart of the Manila Pact, which created SEATO, is a declaration stating that "each party recognizes that aggression by means of armed attack in the treaty area . . . would endanger its own peace and safety." Each member agrees that it will "in that event act to meet the common danger in accordance with its constitutional processes." As Senator George put it on February 1, 1955, the approach used here reproduces "what Secretary of State Dulles has described as the Monroe Doctrine formula, which appears in the previous security treaties concluded by Mr. Dulles." This doctrine concludes that a Communist aggressor might be deterred from reckless action by a clear declaration that any aggression in the treaty area would be considered by the United States to be a threat to its own safety. It might be well to note that the formula gives the United States a flexibility of action even greater than the one enjoyed under Article 5 of the North Atlantic Treaty.

Unlike NATO, the Southeast Asia Treaty Organization has shown no intention of building up collective security forces to resist Communist aggression. Although a SEATO Council was established for consultation with regard to military planning, no member country has committed any element of its forces to form an allied command similar to the one existing in Europe. Mr. Dulles said on September 15, 1954, that American responsibilities were "so vast and so far-flung" that the United States would not serve the Alliance's interests by "earmarking forces for particular areas of the Far East, but by developing the deterrent of mobile striking power, plus strategically placed reserves." Forces stationed in the western Pacific area are able to strike at an aggressor, he added, "by means and at places of our own choosing. The deterrent power we thus create can protect many, as effectively as it protects one."

Our defense system in the Pacific is based on a chain of islands and is firmly anchored by major U.S. installations in Japan, Australia, and Hawaii. Guam and the Philippines are important strong points, while Okinawa, South Korea, and Formosa serve as advanced outposts. This peripheral strategy depends on the Seventh Fleet, strategic air power, and other forces in readiness for its effectiveness. On June 21, 1957, the United States agreed to a prompt withdrawal of all of its ground forces from Japan, and since South Koreans have, to a large extent, replaced American personnel in South Korea, it is more than evident that America's strategy in the Far East is massive retaliation. South Korea, Japan, and Vietnam are the only friendly Far Eastern countries with substantial ground forces, and except for the United States, no Allied nation has any real air power in the Far East. Local forces-in-being must be capable of maintaining internal order and coping with the early stages of aggression until reinforcements arrive and the Chinese mainland suffers strikes from the Strategic Air Command and the Navy's air arm. As matters stand, atomic weapons would almost certainly be used in case of major Communist aggression in the area. Speaking of Formosa, Mr. Eisenhower said on January 23, 1957, that tactical atomic weapons were regarded "as an almost routine part of our equipment nowadays, and you would almost have to use them, the way our forces are organized in that area." This applies a fortiori to the other countries which the United States is pledged to defend in the Pacific.

Such a warning is too serious to be disregarded by the Communists unless they have decided on general war in Asia. It is for this reason that Mr. Dulles outlined his "Three-Front" doctrine. The Secretary said on February 23, 1955, that "Asia is three fronts." It would be improbable, he said, that a war started by Red China "would be confined only to Formosa or South Korea. The forces on these two fronts exist as a common part of the forces deterring possible Communist aggression in Southeast Asia."

The paradox of the Three-Front doctrine is that the treaties which the United States has concluded with South Korea and Formosa are not formally interlocked with the Southeast Asia Treaty, though the United States is a party to all of them. Although Communist thrusts against Formosa or South Korea would not activate the Manila Pact, the Red Chinese could not attack in Southeast Asia without risking war on the other two fronts. To that extent, Chiang Kai-shek truly has been "unleashed." Since the Red Chinese would be over-extended if they had to fight on three fronts, the Three-Front doctrine serves to protect each of the three fronts from aggression.[11]

Of the various bilateral agreements with Pacific powers that have been concluded by the United States, the Formosa Pact demands special attention. It was initialed on November 23, 1954, and ratified by the Senate on February 9, 1955, a few days after the passage of Public Law No. 4, which is known as the Formosa Resolution. The terms of the American commitment follow the Monroe Doctrine approach. Article 10 of the Pact stipulates, however, that the parties "may terminate it one year after notice has been given to the other party." Article 6 limits the Treaty area to the islands of Formosa and the Pescadores, but it also states that

55

this area could be extended "to such other territories as may be determined by mutual agreement." On February 7, 1955, Mr. Dulles told the Senate Foreign Affairs Committee that it was the American view that "any agreement to extend the coverage of the China Defense Treaty to additional territories would in practical terms amount to amendment of the Treaty and should be submitted to the Senate for its advice and consent."

On June 27, 1950, President Truman ordered the Seventh Fleet to prevent any Communist attack on Formosa. "As a corollary of this action," he said, "I am calling upon the Chinese Government on Formosa to cease all air and sea operations against the mainland. The Seventh Fleet will see that this is done." The order remained in force, despite Chinese intervention in Korea. In view of the absurdity of this situation, President Eisenhower made cancellation of the order one of his first official acts of office. In his State of the Union Message of February 2, 1953, he declared that "we certainly have no obligation to protect a nation fighting us in Korea," but he also wanted to make it "crystal clear" that the new order implied no aggressive intent on the part of the United States.

On December 10, 1954, in a diplomatic exchange between the Chinese Nationalists and the United States, it was agreed that the use of force in the Formosa area would always be "a matter of joint agreement," except in case of an emergency action having the character of an "exercise of the inherent right of self-defense." It was further decided that "military elements which are a product of joint effort and contribution by the two parties" would not be removed from the Treaty area "to a degree that would substantially diminish the defensibility of such territories without mutual agreement." The restraint imposed upon Chiang by the Eisenhower administration ceased to be a "corollary" of our determination to defend Formosa, nor is the Seventh Fleet going to be used to "see that this is done."

It has been noted that with respect to international law, the status of Formosa is still unsettled. The Cairo Declaration, which stated the principle of Formosa's transfer to China, is no longer considered valid under international law. On the other hand, the treaty with the Nationalists was not considered as an instrument to resolve the question of Chinese sovereignty over Formosa. When it ratified the treaty, the Senate attached to the ratification an understanding that "the legal status of Formosa . . . and the Pescadores—whatever their status may be—is not altered in any way by the conclusion of this Treaty."[12]

The United States' commitment to use force in the Formosa area is subject to the Constitutional process, but it received advance implementation by exercise of Congressional authority when the President was granted standing powers that might be needed for the enforcement of our Chinese policy. As Senator George noted on February 9, 1955, the "essential" difference between the Joint Resolution and the Treaty is that "by the Treaty, the United States undertakes an international obligation whereas by the Public Law our action was unilateral and voluntary."[13]

Mr. Dulles noted on December 1, 1954, that the position of the offshore islands was "unaffected" by the Treaty. "Their status is neither promoted . . . nor is it demoted," he said. Public Law No. 4 authorizes the President to extend military operations beyond the Treaty area to "related positions" and to take any other measures "as he judges to be required or appropriate in insuring the defense of Formosa." As Mr. Eisenhower declared on January 27, 1955, any decision regarding American action towards the offshore islands will have to be made by the President, a decision "the responsibility of which he has not delegated." On September 11, 1958, the President said further that he interpreted the Resolution as requiring him "not to make absolute advance commitments" but to use his judgment "according to the circumstances of the time." According to Public Law No. 4, this is a military decision, and, as the President said on August 27, 1958, "you simply cannot make military decisions until after the event reaches you."

The wording of the Formosa Resolution was, of course, unfortunate, and it is responsible—to a considerable extent—for the difficulties encountered by the administration both in 1955 and in 1958. Instead of authorizing the President to extend military operations beyond the Treaty area, the Resolution should have author-

ized him to declare that the defense of the offshore islands was—
or was not—essential to the defense of Formosa. Such a formulation would have kept the United States above the situation but
would not have forced us to depart in the least from the present
substance of the Public Law, for under the present text, the President could not simply decide to defend "before the event reaches
him"—nor could he decide not to defend—thus leaving the initiative to someone besides himself.

Fortunately, the Communists saved the United States from em-
barrassment by consistently overstating their objectives. Thus far
they have not said that they wanted to push the Nationalists out of
Quemoy and Matsu; they want to push the Americans out of
Formosa. They used the offshore islands—as Mr. Dulles said on
September 30, 1958—"as the front edge of a wedge" which they
could drive in without stopping at the first obstacle, thus making
the situation quite clear for everyone concerned. For this reason,
Mr. Dulles declared on August 23, 1958, that it would be "highly
hazardous" for anyone to assume that an attack on these islands
would remain a limited operation.

On the other hand, the Nationalists were rightly concerned
about the effects of a Communist attack clearly limited to the offshore islands. President Eisenhower disclosed on August 27, 1958,
that the Nationalists had deployed "about a third of their forces
to certain of these islands west of the Pescadores, and that makes
a closer interlocking between the defense system of the islands
with Formosa than was the case before." And on September 4,
1958, Mr. Dulles declared that although the President had not
yet made any finding concerning the use of force in defense of
Formosa, he would not hesitate to do so if necessary. "We have
recognized," Dulles said, "that the securing and protecting of
Quemoy and Matsu have increasingly become related to the defense of Taiwan." He further warned that military dispositions
had been made "so that a Presidential determination, if made,
would be followed by action both timely and effective."

Since the disposition of forces in the Formosa area is a matter
of mutual agreement, there arose the question of why the United

States had accepted such a build-up of troops on the offshore islands. On September 30, 1958, Mr. Dulles described the situation as "one of acquiescence on the part of the United States, not of approval," adding that "we thought that it was rather foolish to put them there." On the previous day, Christian A. Herter reportedly said that the Nationalists' devotion to these islands was "almost pathological." And on October 1, 1958, President Eisenhower himself said that "as a soldier," he did not believe that it was a good thing "to have all these troops there." He added that "fundamentally anyone can see that the two islands as of themselves, as two pieces of territory, are not greatly vital to Formosa."

In making concessions during the crisis of 1958, the administration undoubtedly acted on the basis of diplomatic intelligence. The point was to break the deadlock by permitting the Chinese Communists to retreat without losing face. This tactical maneuver was not accomplished with great comity, but as far as can be ascertained, it represented no basic change of U.S. policy. As a matter of fact, any change in the administration's position concerning the offshore islands was not necessary; from its inception, it was as flexible as the Communists would allow it to be. Indeed, there is no tangible evidence that U.S. policy toward Formosa has ever been encumbered by considerations of honor or undue fidelity to our Nationalist ally. The guiding principle has been our national interest.

The objective of American policy was a diplomatic settlement that could be arranged without prejudicing too openly the rights of the Chinese Nationalists. The administration believed as President Eisenhower said on September 11, 1958, that "there are measures that can be taken to assure that these offshore islands will not be a thorn in the side of peace." Some agreement assuring at least a *de facto* cease-fire was necessary to insure, as Secretary Dulles said on September 9, 1958, that the "issues there will not be resolved . . . by violent, aggressive action which would risk world war." Dulles indicated on September 30, 1958, that an agreement of this sort could be made dependable by creating "circumstances" in which the Communists would feel it expedient to live up to it because of the "unpleasant consequences" that would result from a breach of promise. Ever since 1955, the United States has tried to obtain Communist approval of a renunciation of force, a principle that would involve neither a renunciation of political claims nor the pursuit of any objective by peaceful means. Since a renunciation of force would be reciprocal, it would formally bar Chiang's aggressive return to the mainland and would also permit a demilitarization of the offshore islands—and, quite conceivably, their abandonment if this could be done without appeasement.

In appeasement, it seems to be standard practice to demand concessions before it can be ascertained whether or not the enemy will accept them. The state of opinion is always such that it becomes a concession for the aggressor to accept his opponent's concessions. With respect to the offshore islands, the only point at issue seems to be whether or not Dulles should return to reason and become more flexible; the effect of increased flexibility on Communist behavior seems utterly irrelevant.

If the offshore islands "as of themselves" are not vital to Formosa, it is difficult to understand why they would be vital to the Communists, except as a tool with which to humiliate the United States. Since the United States accepts humiliation, the islands have become an important Communist asset. The situation being what it is because of circumstances of our own making, it is impossible to imagine how the islands could ever become a part of any real give-and-take process. Whether they are surrendered or not, it is safe to predict that debate on the subject will automatically and always return to its starting point, illustrating once again the self-evident truth that only courage permits flexibility. Lack of courage surrenders policy to appeasement, the most rigid and inflexible policy of all.

Our strategy for the defense of the Pacific cannot possibly satisfy the demands of all or even one of our allies. Some want American troops stationed wherever danger exists; others, who show no determination to rearm themselves, insist that they have a right to know what the United States would actually do to defend them against aggression. Such pressures should be resisted. The United

States ought to remain aloof from both friend and foe because to entangle ourselves with the unreasonable demands of others would destroy the fabric of collective security in the Pacific and, for that reason, benefit no one.

The formal basis of American policy in the Near East has long consisted of executive declarations concerning Arab-Israeli tensions. On May 25, 1950, for instance, the United States, France, and Great Britain stated that they would "immediately take action" within or without the United Nations to prevent frontier violations in the Middle East. On October 31, 1950, President Truman expressed, in a public letter to its king, the United States' deep interest in the continued independence of Saudi Arabia.

The Anglo-Egyptian agreement concerning British troops in the Suez Canal Zone was concluded in the summer of 1954. Following Israeli attacks in the Gaza area, President Nasser of Egypt attempted to obtain arms in the United States on terms that the administration would not accept. In September, 1955, he agreed to buy them from the Soviet bloc. The United States and Britain then presented proposals for financial assistance toward the building of the Aswan Dam, but Egypt saw fit to use inflated reports of Soviet aid as a bargaining weapon. Thereafter, her relations with the West deteriorated steadily. On July 19, 1956, with strong Congressional support, the United States withdrew the Aswan Dam offer, and on July 26, the Suez Canal Company was nationalized. At the end of October, Israel invaded Egypt, and after delivering an ultimatum to the belligerents, Britain and France began operations in the Suez Canal Zone. Moscow reacted furiously, threatening to hurl rockets at London and Paris. A United Nations force was established, and the area eventually returned to an uneasy *status quo*. Egypt continued her dubious course. Civil war in Lebanon and the revolution in Iraq in July, 1958, resulted in renewed tension, again followed by a precarious truce.

The events which preceded and followed the Suez invasion confronted the United States with a situation of unprecedented complexity. The whole region was in the grip of a resurgent nationalism which was, in fact, a revolt against past Western imperialism, economic and political feudalism, and centuries of national frustration. It went without saying that the United States was never opposed to Arab nationalism or to a genuine pan-Arab movement based on common interest. "There are plenty of good reasons why there should be greater unity among the Arab nations," said Mr. Dulles on July 31, 1958. The Secretary also pointed out that the United States was among "the early nations" to recognize the United Arab Republic when it was formed.

The history of nationalism rarely displays examples of behavior that call for lyric praise, and Arab nationalism is no exception to the general rule. With a complete lack of conscience, the Marxists hold that movements of "national liberation" are an "irresistible trend" and that any attempt to circumvent history is doomed to failure. The United States could not, of course, conform to such a deterministic view of Arab nationalism. The simple truth is that nationalism is a great force that can be used for either good or evil. As President Eisenhower said in his address of August 13, 1958, "change is indeed the law of life and progress," but it must give an opportunity to the aspirations of the Arab peoples themselves and be brought about, he said, "in ways compatible with international peace and security."

The fact is that Arab nationalism has not yet been used for good or guided into constructive channels that offer true promises of political stability and economic expansion. By and large, it has been employed as a screen for boundless personal ambitions—ambitions that are best fulfilled by unscrupulous means. The chief tool for building Arab unity has long been a common hatred for Israel. This is not an admirable feeling, nor is it realistic for the Arab nations to dream of obliterating Israel from the map without great risk to themselves. Still more disturbing are Nasser's efforts to identify the future of the Arab world with his own heroic ego. His revolutionary creed and the method he employs in subverting neighboring countries explain more than anything else—why the legitimate aspirations of the Near East have become entangled in Russian imperialism. The Arabs have no ideological sympathy for Communism, but they can gain so much by playing the great powers against each other that it would be futile to expect them to abandon the profitable game of power politics.

For her part, the Soviet Union follows, as usual, a simple approach: she nurtures every evil. Once a staunch supporter of Israel, she now uses cruel deception to abet the Arab fantasy of driving the Israelis into the sea; she supplies arms and fans delusions of grandeur; the Arab world is told that no bloc ought to be joined; that the Soviet Union will help unconditionally; that the West wants to impose again the yoke of colonialism in order to continue the spoliation of natural resources; no foreign bayonets of the colonizers will be able to prevent the revolution any more; no power can assume the right to interfere in the affairs of small countries; the people have a sacred right to arrange their affairs as they deem it necessary; the United States wants to entrench itself in Lebanon and use it as a springboard for aggression; on the other hand, aggression by a small power like Egypt against the United States is impossible.

Whatever sympathy the American people may have for the legitimate aspirations of Arab nationalism and whatever the policy the United States might wish to enforce might be, we have no choice but to put up a restraining influence in the Near East as long as it is both feasible and necessary. To encourage and to help the Arab people in their striving for independence and development is a valid objective of policy, but certain principles of international behavior must also be upheld. As President Eisenhower said in his press conference of August 6, 1958, "we do believe that freedom and the principle of liberty is indivisible in the world"; therefore, he added, "when freedom of the weak, the independence of the weak is threatened, the United States has a very deep responsibility; indeed, in its own self-interest, it must attempt to carry that responsibility." Another principle that must be upheld is what the President called in his message of July 15, 1958, "the right of all nations to work together and to seek help when necessary to preserve their independence." In addition, rampant nationalism threatens the peace; in his address before the United Nations on August 13, 1958, the President said that "aggression—direct or indirect—must be checked before it gathers sufficient momentum to threaten the world—aggressors and defenders alike." Finally, the strategic importance of the Middle East is such that to deny it to international Communism is foremost and vital.

None of the objectives of American policy in the Middle East is open to controversy; none is directly attainable. In view of the complexity of this situation, the most urgent requirement is a statement of purpose, a declaration without which every American move would appear as a hurried reaction to unexpected events. This is the basic purpose of the Middle East Resolution of March 9, 1957. The Resolution states that "the United States regards as vital to the national interest and world peace the preservation of the independence and integrity of the nations of the Middle East." To this end, economic and military assistance has been offered to the Arab countries by the United States. The Resolution further states that "if the President determines the necessity thereof, the United States is prepared to use armed forces to assist any such nation requesting assistance against armed aggression from any country controlled by international Communism."

In what they called "an attempt to direct the Resolution more to the basic causes of Middle Eastern difficulties," the Democrats refused to grant the President any authority which he did not already possess under the Constitution as Commander in Chief. They decided to water down the original language of the Resolution, which plainly stated that the President was "authorized" (under the conditions previously mentioned) to use force in case of armed aggression. Curiously enough, the Congressional amendment increased the scope of the Eisenhower Doctrine instead of reducing it, which was what the administration's critics truly intended to do. As amended, the Resolution was used by the administration as a basis for the landing of troops in Lebanon. As Mr. Dulles said on May 20, 1958, the Resolution "authorizes the United States to assist economically and militarily nations which want such assistance in order to preserve their independence." When Congress makes such a declaration by an overwhelming vote, Mr. Dulles said, "it places upon the President a greater responsibility to protect, in that area, the peace and interests of the United States than would have been the case had there not been such a declaration." In that respect, the Resolution was a mandate. "You cannot," said Dulles, "as a matter of legislative history assume that when you put a new sentence into a Resolution, that it is utterly meaningless."

This pointed and well-deserved remark shows that the United States is guided by two principles when it uses force in the Middle East as a matter of deliberate policy. If the independence of any Middle Eastern nation is declared to be vital to peace and the national interest, the United States does whatever it deems necessary for the preservation of peace. As the President said in his statement concerning the landings in Lebanon, American forces "will demonstrate the concern of the United States for the independence and integrity of Lebanon, which we deem vital to the national interest and to world peace." There exist here no self-imposed limitations other than the Constitutional process. The Eisenhower Doctrine follows here a rule of reason, and it is consistent with the United Nations Resolution of November 17, 1950, which brands any aggression, "whether committed openly or by fomenting civil strife," as "the gravest of all crimes against peace." However, the Doctrine is not formally consistent with the provision of the Middle East Resolution concerning open armed attack in the area.

Mr. Dulles emphasized in his press conference of September 10, 1957, that three findings have to be made before direct armed intervention by the United States—in case of armed aggression—can occur. "There has to be a finding by the President," he said, "that one of the countries was dominated by international Communism; secondly, there has to be an act of aggression by that country; third, there has to be a request by the country attacked for that aid." Under these conditions, armed intervention is not feasible in case of a legalized coup (like the one which occurred in Syria in 1957) or in case of a political revolution (as in Iraq). Aggression by Israel or against Israel is also beyond the scope of the Resolution. Such action is covered by a statement made by the President in April, 1956, in which he promised assistance to any Near Eastern state that was attacked.

Since the findings that have to be made in case of armed aggression are not likely to be met at present, it has often been said that the Eisenhower Doctrine is an illusory policy aimed at a shadowy objective. This empty phrase would not be mentioned here if it had not gained so much currency, thereby showing how little the public understands the art of diplomacy. The explicit objective of the Middle East Resolution is not illusory; any armed aggression abetted by the Soviet Union would be a major disaster; any policy aimed at deterring such aggression has a valid objective, and it succeeds as long as no aggression actually occurs. In recent years, the Soviet Union has repeatedly used what President Eisenhower called in his address of August 13, 1958, "ballistic blackmail." The pressure exerted on Turkey by the U.S.S.R. during the Syrian crisis of 1957 proves that the situation formally envisaged by the Resolution could very well be purposedly created by international Communism.

Since the finding that a country is dominated by international Communism is a matter of judgment by the United States, some Arab countries are bound to be more careful in their dealings with Moscow than they would have been otherwise. To that extent, the usefulness of the Middle East Resolution is better understood in relation to the situation that would exist if the American declaration had not been made. The real question is whether the evils of the area necessitate the restraining employment of American power. To jettison what is often called the sterile approach based upon a rigid opposition to Soviet imperialism would be to forsake the use of power. Aiming at a shadowy objective, like shooting at a man's shadow, is as good a way as any to show one's determination. By announcing its intention to cope with Soviet imperialism in the Near East, the United States simply revealed that American power had to be reckoned with east of Suez, and this is anything but an illusory policy.

It goes without saying that the doctrine of massive retaliation is eminently relevant to the present situation in the Near East. The various military establishments existing in the area would tend to limit any American intervention to what has been called a police action. On April 24, 1957, President Eisenhower declared that Jordan's independence was vital to the national interest, and the Sixth Fleet was deployed to back up his warning. Following the appointment of a pro-Soviet chief of staff in Syria on August 15, 1957, an airlift of arms to Jordan was announced, other vital shipments to Lebanon, Iraq, and Saudi Arabia were stepped up, and the Sixth Fleet maneuvered off the Syrian coast. A much more impressive show of strength was made the following year in Lebanon, yet it remained very limited in scope. Any situation that could not be coped with by the Marines and limited Army contingents would go beyond the scope of a police action. On October 16, 1957, Mr. Dulles warned that "if there is an attack on Turkey by the Soviet Union, it would not mean a purely defensive operation by the United States, with the Soviet Union a privileged sanctuary from which to attack Turkey." Excluding all-out war, this illustrates the maximum dimension of American actions.[14]

The Eisenhower administration has repeated only too often that the use of force always creates problems—without apparently resolving any. Anyone who has had to impose punishment knows that it is seldom difficult to determine whether or not the punishment is deserved; the difficulty is how and when to apply it successfully. As in the Far East, the problem encountered by American policy is not whether the United States must take a stand but how we should take it. If the occasion is offered, it should be eagerly seized. The Lebanese landings proved that the United States was willing to take risks for its friends and that it could move its power anywhere both rapidly and effectively. Correspondingly, Soviet threats were made less credible. It is entirely conceivable that in the near future, the Western strategic position in the Middle East will be reduced to beachheads on the fringe of the region. Since massive retaliation is a peripheral strategy, it should be possible to maintain a relative balance of power that could not be easily altered by military action or open intervention without considerable risks for the aggressor. Finally—when the situation is just drifting, as has repeatedly been the case—the use of power creates a new situation that is negotiable, even if the only negotiable factor apparently is the withdrawal of troops.

The most remarkable feature of the Eisenhower Doctrine is that it is an instrument of American diplomacy used to declare a policy unilaterally. This type of policy does not necessitate formal adherence by other nations, not even by those who might choose to benefit from it. The foremost objective pursued by the United States is that the Middle Eastern countries remain independent from Communism. They may, if they so choose, remain neutral and yet benefit from American aid and protection to an extent that they alone must determine. Never has the United States demanded that they stand up and be counted; this was well proved by the Lebanese situation in 1958. "Whatever our views may be," Mr. Dulles said on July 31, 1958, "we would not stay in Lebanon after we had been asked to withdraw by the duly constituted government. We might not think it was wise to withdraw, but we would withdraw under those conditions."

The same principle applies to the various forms of economic aid given to the Arab nations. In his address of August 13, 1958, President Eisenhower asked the United Nations "to ascertain whether an agreement can be reached to establish an Arab development institution on a regional basis." The task of this organization would be to accelerate economic development, and what is more important, it would be determined and controlled by the Arab nations themselves. In inviting the United Nations to patronize the creation of an institution that the United States could support, the administration departed from its past bilateral approach. This is important, of course, but it is also self-evident that the Arab world cannot simply jump from economic feudalism into industrial abundance. President Eisenhower said on August 6, 1958, that he had often heard the saying that "the Arab doesn't follow the desert, the desert follows the Arab." He knew, he added, that the people were impatient, but impatience is no more a virtue for nations than it is for individuals; it is often a revolt against reality. Furthermore, as Mr. Dulles said on July 31, 1958, "constructive economic developments really have to be dependent upon political stability. . . . When the principal personalities in a government are living in daily fear of murder and assassination, it's very hard to get their minds onto a problem of economic development for the next twenty years. They are more interested in the next twenty minutes."

American policy in the Near East is also determined by our NATO and SEATO commitments and by the Baghdad Pact, an organization reportedly established under American prodding in 1955. The United States refused to join with the United Kingdom in this organization because it had become a divisive factor in the Arab world. The commitment principle had to be reconciled with the legitimate fear of entanglement. However, the United States agreed to participate in the work of committees, and a military liaison group with the Baghdad powers was set up. The *coup d'état* in Iraq created the impression that the Baghdad Pact had become ineffective, but in reality, the situation in Iraq made it possible to assert, even more frankly than in the past, the true anti-Communist nature of the Pact. Article 1 of the Treaty provides that the signing parties will co-operate in collective security and will conclude special agreements to give effect to this cooperation. According to the declaration issued in London on July 28, 1958, the United States had decided "to cooperate with the nations making this declaration for their security and defense, and will promptly enter into agreements designed to give effect to this cooperation." This was to be done "in the interest of world peace and pursuing the existing Congressional authorization"— the Eisenhower Doctrine. In this way, the organization created from the Baghdad Pact, instead of being moribund, could begin its real life.[15]

It cannot be denied that U.S. policy in the Middle East is primarily directed toward preventing inner tensions from snapping. In its negative aspects, the policy is a holding operation; in the long run, it seeks to induce the Arab nations to build a durable peace. Its effectiveness cannot be ascertained, but its validity is beyond doubt. Nasser is no Middle Eastern Stalin, nor is he a modern Saladin. Old privileges will have to be liquidated and a new order constructed, and many years will pass before a genuine stabilization of Arab politics can occur. Moreover, the notion of "success" in our foreign policy requires further analysis.

Judgment of the success of a policy must first be made in terms of workable alternatives. If there are really no alternatives to massive retaliation, it is successful—for the simple reason that there is no other policy—according to the adage that the best can do no more. It should also be noted that success is directly related to the various tasks of national policy. If a nation achieves national survival when its continued existence is actually threatened, its policy has not failed. If the policy serves to deter open military aggression, its measure of success is greater. If it permits the restrained use of power while preventing an enemy from using an equal or perhaps superior power, the achievement is considerable indeed. All other tasks of policy are secondary.

Obviously, the success of U.S. policy cannot be ascertained by those whose minds are fixed on the horrors of its possible failure. Diplomacy progresses through alternating cycles of tension and relaxation; the future is and will remain uncertain. Those who vainly attempt to do away with the limitations that are inherent in all human endeavors are incapable of sound judgment. The Promethean dream of "peace in our time" is as dangerous as despair.

Like any other policy, massive retaliation has its own limitations. In his State of the Union Message of January 6, 1955, President Eisenhower said:

To protect our nations and our peoples from the catastrophe of a nuclear holocaust, free nations must maintain countervailing military power to persuade the Communists of the futility of seeking to advance their ends through aggression. If the Communist rulers understand that America's response to aggression will be swift and decisive—that never shall we buy peace at the expense of honor and faith—they will be powerfully deterred from launching a military venture engulfing their own peoples and many others in disaster. Now, this, of course, is a form of world stalemate.[16]

The President said on February 2, 1955, that he had used the word "stalemate" in a deliberate way. The cold war will continue; the growth of Soviet power cannot be checked. Both sides possess the power necessary for launching on the other a totally destructive attack, but their offensive capabilities are so great that neither could possibly hope to destroy the other without suffering complete destruction itself. What the President called "stalemate" has been referred to by others as "mutual deterrence." But how can one be "deterred" if he has no aggressive intentions? We have lost the easy, overwhelming superiority we once possessed, but nuclear stalemate works to our advantage because we seek peace.[17]

Nuclear stalemate is a diplomatic and not a military concept. It was inevitable that the Soviet Union would build up its air-atomic power as fast as it possibly could, and that has been very fast indeed. The U.S.S.R. has the means and the determination to achieve an over-all military lead over the United States, but as long as a stalemate situation is maintained, American diplomacy can keep the Russian leaders convinced that no matter how many divisions they maintain and in spite of their missiles and everything else, they cannot escape destruction if they ever decide to destroy the United States.

For the military, even absolute air-atomic power is not static—a power which, once attained, cannot increase or decrease. It is true that once absolute power has been achieved, to increase it still further ceases to be a matter of top priority. "There comes a time," Mr. Eisenhower said on March 2, 1955, "when a lead is not significant in the defensive arrangements of a country." If one has enough of a particular weapon, it is doubtful, the President continued, "that it is particularly important to have a lot more of it." As long as an absolute capacity remains on the other side, the enemy cannot hope to capitalize on a temporary gap in his adversary's defenses. In other words, a neck-and-neck arms race is no longer justified. And it is also true that if a country has actually attained absolute air-atomic power, a continuous build-up in conventional armaments will not increase its total security very much, even if such a build-up is desirable from the standpoint of flexibility. Otherwise the concept of stalemate—understood in a military sense—is a dangerous fallacy.

Progress must continue. Each side may have enough weapons to annihilate the other, yet there may be no stalemate. "There is nothing in history to indicate that stalemate is possible," said General Twining on May 20, 1955. "When great stocks of weapons are achieved, the ability to deliver them effectively then becomes the decisive factor." Offensive and defensive capabilities also come into the picture, for both change constantly. So does the equation of power. All of this remains so in spite of the fact that military technology does not change so radically that the progress achieved by one side does away with the other's ability to inflict unacceptable damage. The usefulness of technological progress is thus partially canceled in the short run, although progress remains vitally necessary.

The concept of atomic stalemate stems from the technical impossibility to achieve reliable nuclear disarmament, for there is no way to verify atomic stockpiles already in existence. Any agreement on nuclear disarmament—even if it could be combined with some form of inspection—would therefore not fulfill its first and major requirement. Consequently, American security must continue to rest on the retention of nuclear arms. Disarmament as an alternative to the balance of terror is ruled out. So is peaceful co-existence.

On February 2, 1955, President Eisenhower declared:

When I said stalemate, I was trying to describe where neither side is getting what it desires in this whole world struggle, but that, at least, have sense enough to agree that they must not pursue it deliberately and through force of arms; that is all.

This excludes the concept of preventive war. In his press conference of August 11, 1954, Mr. Eisenhower related Sir Arthur Conan Doyle's story of a monk who had left the Church for seven reasons, the first of which was that he had been thrown out. "They decided," said the President, "there was no use to recite the other six."

The President said on February 6, 1957, that "the likelihood of any nation possessing these great weapons of massive destruction using them in an attack grows less . . . every year. As their understanding of them grows, then the less the chance that they would go on an adventure that brought these things into play, because, as I see it, any such operation today is just another way of committing suicide."[18] For that very reason, many people see no future in massive retaliation.

On November 15, 1954, Senator Knowland declared that "atomic stalemate will result in ultimate Communist victory." When the whole world realizes that such a stalemate exists, the Soviet Union will start what Knowland called "Operation Nibbling." Bite by bite, it will absorb the neighboring countries. At that moment, said the Senator, "through the capitals of what remains of our anxious allies and with loud voices from the neutralists, as well as from sources in our country," an anguished cry will be heard: "Should we risk annihilation for Iran or Sweden or Formosa?" Softened up by inaction, the United States will eventually become what Knowland called "a continental Dien Bien Phu in the Communist world."

To assume that deterrence would so fail is to play Providence. As Mr. Dulles said on May 15, 1954, "no man has the right to assume that he sees the future so clearly that he is justified in concluding either that war is inevitable or that methods of conciliation are futile." The Eisenhower administration has not claimed that it has found some magic formula which will insure us against all possible forms of Communist encroachment. It has, however, expressed confidence that within the borders of the Communist empire, a silent test of strength is going on between the human spirit and a dictatorial system that can maintain itself only by force. The United States can—and must—therefore be strong in order to allow time and fundamentals to work for peace.

Communism cannot be talked out of existence; success must be

73

deserved. The Communist ideology is so contrary to all human values and its deeds are so patent that no one is excused from comprehending the nature of the challenge. It should be stated in principle that any blindness concerning the issues of our age is culpable. The very same principle demands, of course, that we support the foreign policy of the United States. Public opinion has the power to transform all human uncertainties into divisive controversies. By withholding its support, public opinion can destroy the efficacy of national policy. Our study of massive retaliation would not be complete without an analysis of public attitudes in response to national policy. Such an analysis will now be made.

PART TWO

The Massive Retaliation Debate

CHAPTER IV

"Remember Your Humanity"

THE DEVASTATING EFFECTS of nuclear weapons need little description. Be they set off by smaller battlefield weapons with a nominal force measured in thousands of tons of TNT or by the largest megaton weapons, all atomic explosions produce radiation, shock waves, light, and heat in varying amounts. In a total atomic war, hundreds of millions of people would lose their lives outright. The so-called fission-fusion-fission bomb—which uses elements of both the atom and hydrogen bombs wrapped in uranium 238—alone would create a fireball several miles in diameter in which all things, animate or inanimate, would be vaporized. Within a larger circle, destruction would be nearly total. Not only would human beings in the immediate area be subjected to a lethal dose of radiation, but dangerous radioactive fallout would spread several hundred miles downwind from the point of explosion, thereby contaminating thousands of square miles. In this manner, atomic weapons could be used for radiological extermination. To the millions who would die from shock waves and heat in the first moment must be added those who would suffer the delayed effects of atomic radiation; and genetic damage would reach the unborn and persist for many generations.

A more detailed description of all-out atomic warfare would only make the picture more horrible. Is it not true that a strategy based on the possibility of such slaughter is unlimited madness? A war that would destroy all of the great centers of human culture and place humanity on the threshold of new Dark Ages must flout the decent opinions of mankind.

Now massive retaliation prepares for these things. It leads to a thermonuclear holocaust. It is the policy of Dulles and Eisenhower. The United States has thus allowed its leaders to develop and to plan on the use of completely irrational weapons. The Pentagon generals shout for bigger and bigger weapons, and the Atomic Energy Commission dutifully manufactures them in its plants. America has surrendered its most sacred traditions. In a blind fear of Communism, the national interest has been deliberately placed above all other human considerations.

This is how public opinion has indicted massive retaliation *in toto*. It is repugnant to the moral aspirations of the American people. It is madness. In a total war, nuclear weapons would annihilate friend and foe alike. As its very name indicates, massive retaliation demands massive annihilation. The age of violence through which we are now passing has dulled our sense of values, but even if we were to put no faith in the power of moral force and make no attempt to conduct ourselves under the limitations of ethical conduct, we would still be faced with the inescapable fact that massive retaliation entails the threat of something that would be totally unacceptable, even to a Machiavellian politician. Sheer realism, as well as idealism, precludes the political feasibility of nuclear warfare.

The unquestioned conclusion to be drawn from all this is that if the human race is to be preserved at all, war must cease to be an instrument of national policy. Any major war in the future will be atomic, and atomic war means total destruction for all concerned. No truth could better serve the peaceful interests of a Christian nation like the United States, but does the administration understand this? It seems unbelievable that people with a Christian commitment would feel that if the other fellow carries a stick, they must carry a bigger stick in their hands. Such an attitude cannot be reconciled with moral principle in personal life. Why should it be acceptable in national affairs?[1] As Representative Cannon put it on April 29, 1954, the appalling destructiveness of modern weapons means that "we must not go to war. War, even if we win, is suicide."[2] And in 1956, Senator Lehman declared: "All of us are becoming aware that all-out war is an impossible solution for any of our international problems. There is simply no alternative to peace. The thought of war, using hydrogen bombs, is too shocking today to entertain, unless we have reconciled ourselves to the suicide of civilization as we know it."[3]

Let us repeat. According to the administration's critics, Mr. Dulles and his Pentagon supporters have all entertained the thought of suicide. The United States has threatened to use atomic weapons as a part of its official policy. Let us therefore continue the argument with the words of Walter Lippmann: "If there is no alternative to peace, then no one can go to the brink of war in the sense that he threatens to go to war. If war is not an alternative, then anyone who threatens war is either mad or is bluffing."[4] A war with the Soviet Union would lead to the utter destruction of the United States. Consequently, the Eisenhower administration is just bluffing when it threatens the enemy with a catastrophe hardly equal to the one America would certainly suffer if hostilities would ever actually break out. Such a threat is not credible.

Massive retaliation, then, is an empty phrase, a slogan formulated to replace a missing policy. Thomas E. Murray wrote in the May 6, 1957, issue of *Life* magazine that the "multimegaton H-bomb was born in a vacuum of military strategy. . . . The vacuum was filled with confusion." The United States was hurled, he claimed, "into the midst of absurdity." As Senator Lehman put it on April 12, 1954, the administration revealed "its habit of putting salesmanship ahead of statesmanship." One never knew where the glib slogan ended and a serious policy began. Mr. Dulles had raised the curtain on a dramatically new policy, he said, a policy that frightened the American people and shocked the rest of mankind; when criticism started, the explanations came in: massive retaliation was not a new policy; retaliation was not going to be massive or instant. "What it really was—or is," concluded the Senator, "still hasn't been explained."[5]

Adlai Stevenson declared on April 11, 1955, that it seemed "incredible to sober, thoughtful people that the government of the United States could be bluffing" on matters of such importance. Mr. Dulles never intended to do what he had said he would do; there was a yawning gap between his words and his actions. Yet these "sober, thoughtful people" could not get over the fact that Mr. Eisenhower had to go to Geneva in order to reassure the world of America's peaceful intentions. Mr. Dulles' bluff and bluster had delivered the United States into the hands of the Soviet propaganda machine, and the image which the United States projects over the world had been distorted out of recognition. Most of the world had reason to believe that America fully accepted the possibility of all-out nuclear war, to say nothing of preventive war.

These worries about American aggressiveness, widespread as they were assumed to be, were apparently not shared by the Communist leaders. As far as they were concerned, they had ample reason to believe that massive retaliation was—if not a case of outright bluff—at the very most a policy that still had to undergo a long debate before it became accepted national policy. The debate took place, and it killed any semblance of public acceptance.

In a celebrated study, William W. Kaufmann wrote that if the Russians decided to challenge our sincerity in these matters, "and they have good reasons for daring to do so, we would either have to put up or shut up."[6] They would not be deterred by such words as "massive and instant retaliation." Even when the United States had an atomic monopoly, the Chinese Communists attacked in Korea; and the Soviets blockaded Berlin. How, then, could the loss of this monopoly be a force for peace? The growth of Soviet power, wrote Paul H. Nitze, "does not tend to inhibit action by the Soviets. It merely inhibits the possibility of action by ourselves."[7]

Nothing more can be said. The critics' argument has ended; it has completed a full circle. The stark stupidity displayed by partisanship in this instance cannot be hidden. Massive retaliation has been simultaneously described as bluffing and madness. Mr. Dulles really plays Russian roulette with the lives of all of us; he does not mean what he says; his reckless aggressiveness has distorted the picture of a peace-loving America, but it has not impressed the

Communists. This means that for its critics, U.S. policy cannot be anything but suicide or a vain threat. Massive retaliation has been deliberately crushed in the pincers of nuclear madness and nuclear bluffing.

These thoughts have implications that are exceedingly serious. The very people who accused Mr. Dulles of making reckless statements are the first to proclaim that consistency and popular support are essential to the success of any policy of deterrence—a consistency and support that they deliberately sabotage. In his study of massive retaliation, Mr. Kaufman asserts that the prestige which accrued to the United States after World War II is "the prestige that invariably accompanies enormous wealth and power rather than the prestige of boldness, sternness, and consistency."[8] A policy of deterrence which is not fully supported by opinion is likely to succeed only "in deterring the deterrer."[9] In the same breath, Mr. Kaufmann says that "the outcry against massive retaliation has stemmed from more than fear and partisan politics; it has been a reaction against the despair, the futility, the recklessness that the doctrine implies."[10] Yet he also says that "the more grimly determined we appear to meet these contingencies with massive retaliation, the less likely they are to arise."[11] And he states, with the same dogmatism, that "we should be prepared to seize every favorable opportunity to demonstrate how serious are our deterrent intentions."[12]

How so many conflicting statements can be made in so short a space by a responsible scholar is a mystery that we do not pretend to explain. By means of a corrosive intellectualism, Mr. Kaufmann attacks the policy of deterrence at its most delicate point and then justifies his repudiation of that policy with the destruction which he himself has wrought. Whether the process is honest from the standpoint of scholarship, we do not know. To the extent that it strikes at the most sensitive part of the doctrine of massive retaliation, it endangers the security of the United States.

Massive retaliation certainly means assuming the risk of national destruction. The days when the American people could enjoy total security or assured victory in war are gone forever.

Let us remember, however, that there is, as President Eisenhower said on September 30, 1953, a tragedy "greater than winning a war," and this "would be losing it." "There are basic moral values and vital interests for which we stand," said Secretary Dulles on January 17, 1956. "The surest way to avoid war is to let it be known in advance that we are prepared to defend these principles if need be by life itself." If these basic values and interests have to be defended—"if need be by life itself"—the principle that there is no alternative to peace must be qualified. Does one accept as a valid objective of policy the concept of a continued national existence (in a sheer physical sense), or does the concept of national survival imply the survival of the values for which the United States stands? The atomic age has rendered this alternative both concrete and unavoidable. Whether it likes it or not, American society has to face it. Loose talk about war being suicidal can obscure—but it does not eliminate—the necessity of this fundamental decision.

If it were true that massive retaliation as a strategy has failed to deter Communist imperialism, this hypothetical fact would be susceptible to one conclusion and one conclusion only: that it is imperative that Communism be deterred. The greater the risk, the more urgent deterrence becomes. Mr. Dulles expressed a simple truth when he said on April 11, 1955, that "in this connection we should remember that, while modern developments have made war more terrible, they have also made the consequences of retreat and surrender more terrible." The more reluctantly public opinion supports its government's deterrence policy, the less efficacious any warning and the more necessary further deterrence become.[13]

On this precise point, American partisanship has succeeded in inverting the situation almost completely; the necessity to deter has been turned into proof that American deterrence has failed. In his speech of March 8, 1955, for instance, Secretary of State Dulles noted that Chinese Communist propaganda portrayed the United States as being merely a "paper tiger." In a public letter, John Carter Vincent, a noted diplomatist, wrote that the "tigerish roars emitted by Mr. Dulles during recent years . . . have done much to earn him, not the United States, the title of 'paper tiger.' "[14] This illustrates how every warning and every phase of diplomacy can be described as futile, tigerish roars, with no other proof of their alleged futility than the necessity to roar.[15]

Public opinion has transformed the present stalemate between the Communist world and the free nations into a diplomatic liability, but in spite of all the contortions of a subversive intellectualism, the reality of American statesmanship is unchanged. It is not the deterrer who has been deterred, but all potential aggressors. As the President said in his address of April 5, 1954, "the men in the Kremlin" have been deterred. "As long as they know that we are in a position to act strongly and to retaliate, war is not a decision to be taken lightly. . . . Of all those sobering effects none is greater than the retaliation that would certainly be visited upon them if they were to attack any of our nations or any part of our vital interests aggressively and in order to conquer." Could this simple truth be beyond the grasp of the cynical intellectual?

What have the great prophets of scholarship offered as an alternative to massive retaliation? This is the real test of their sincerity. They pretend to know, better than anyone else, what devastation would result from nuclear war. They claim to be the realists of the age, yet for them, realism is nothing more than concentrating on the destructive potential of atomic weapons. They assert that it is sheer illusion to expect that a future war would not be atomic. Nor are they neutral in feeling. But a policy? They have none.

These people are satisfied to appeal as human beings to other human beings. "Can *we* not forget our quarrels?" they ask. The words of Bertrand Russell's manifesto of July 9, 1955, are significant. "Remember your humanity," he wrote, "and forget the rest. If you can do so, the way lies open to a new paradise. If you cannot, there lies before you the rise of universal death."[16] "It was no accident," said Adlai Stevenson on October 15, 1956, "that the instinct of survival which is common to all men and to all nations is slowly but surely compelling the most practical and hardheaded statesmen to give increasing heed to the prevention and abolition of war." On October 26, 1956, Mr. Stevenson spoke of President Eisenhower's stubborn insistence that we place our security in the deterrent effect of a lead in nuclear technology. "We were saying the same things years ago," he said. "The Russians caught up with us; they'll do it again. . . . What does the administration propose then?" The cobalt bomb or a weapon that can shake the earth's axis? "This is madness," he concluded, "this policy of trying to preserve the peace by a preponderance of terror. . . . No, I say the way to peace is not through fear and ever more terrible weapons— it is through faith and confidence and rising standards of living among the have-nots—the millions of people who tremble on the sidelines of this mad arms race in helpless terror."

Viewed in this light, massive retaliation and all preparations for nuclear war are acts of hostility against mankind, and no co-operation should be given to this insane and unending race. Man's sovereignty comes before the sovereignty of governments, and if the nations of the world pay no attention to man's sacred rights, it becomes necessary for the people of these nations to restrain and to tame their governments. The appeal to humanity thus became an open call to rebellion, not the rebellion of enslaved people against their masters but the rebellion of free peoples against their freely elected governments.

It was only logical for the rebels to throw themselves headlong behind a movement for the cessation of nuclear testing. According to them, the objective of nuclear testing was the development of ever more terrifying weapons that could not be tested without creating world-wide radioactive fallout and unmeasurable hazards to man's future. But the latter point was not easy to prove, nor was it possible simply to do away with the hard realities of our age. The proponents of a test ban had to prove that it was safe for the United States to stop testing nuclear weapons, and since they were primarily interested in the abolition of war, they also had to prove that a test moratorium would lead to effective disarmament. The whole issue soon became too complex for public opinion to handle; having lost its original simplicity, it turned into a hotbed of confusion and contradictions.

What, in reality, was the objective of nuclear testing? Here again, the opposition did not bother to answer the question with due clarity. In 1956, for instance, Mr. Stevenson was satisfied to identify himself with proposals that had been made long before and by many people, namely, that the United States discontinue testing large hydrogen weapons and concentrate on nuclear weapons of smaller yield. He did not propose that atomic testing as such be discontinued. Rather, he said that the hydrogen weapons already in our arsenal were large enough for any conceivable military purpose, and he spoke as if the administration were so infatuated with weapons too terrible ever to be used that it had decided to continue what Senator Gore called on October 18, 1956, "the heedless testing of bigger and ever bigger bombs."

No one in his right mind could ever have pretended that this was the administration's policy on nuclear bombs. "We know we can make them big," President Eisenhower said on April 25, 1956. "We are not interested in that any more." The objective of further testing was to perfect a more compact weapon for military use, more specifically, a missile warhead. "It is a little bit of a paradox," the President remarked, to urge "that we work as hard as we know how on the . . . missile and that we stop all research on the hydrogen bomb." On June 5, 1957, the President said that nuclear weapons would be included "as almost certain weapons of war in any future global thing" and that the United States would be "foolish indeed to be behind anybody else."

Continued testing has also been justified by the development of weapons that are relatively free from fallout, the so-called "clean" weapons. Hydrogen bombs were made less "dirty" by means of a revised structure (the elimination of the casing of uranium 238 used in 1954) and by using air bursts rather than surface shots. The success of American research in this direction was first announced by Admiral Strauss on July 19, 1956, and was confirmed by the President on June 5, 1957, when he said that fallout had been reduced by "nine-tenths." On June 26, 1957, Mr. Eisenhower spoke of a fallout reduction of 96 per cent and added that he had been advised by his scientists that "with more time," they could eventually produce "a completely clean bomb."

Partisan criticism has scoffed at the idea of a clean hydrogen bomb. Espousing, apparently, Khrushchev's philosophy that even a clean bomb would do dirty things, Senator Humphrey said on July 19, 1957, that the talk about making a clean bomb is the kind of language that "makes us look ridiculous" all over the world. It is, he pontified, "an absurdity of monumental proportions. . . . If it ever came to all-out war with large nuclear weapons it would be a war to the very death, and the largest and dirtiest and most terrible weapons would be employed." It is "common knowledge" that our military forces would use fallout contamination in the prosecution of a war in order to isolate entire areas. Any talk about a clean bomb gives the impression that the United States possesses what Representative Holifield called a "humanitarian hydrogen bomb."[17] As long as the weapon is triggered by fission, there will be fallout.

The manner in which public opinion took offense at the notion of a clean bomb is revealing. Everyone understood from the start, of course, that the issue was a cleaner weapon or, as the President said on June 5, 1957, that the hydrogen bomb, "in proportion to its size," was "probably one of the cleanest." The sincerity of hurt feelings was well established when Mr. Eisenhower mentioned on July 3, 1957, that he was thinking of sharing with the Soviet Union and other countries the knowledge of how to produce cleaner bombs. Although the President displayed in this instance what is often called "constructive leadership" and a sense for new ideas, the opposition instantly reversed all of its positions. The value of cleanliness was to make the bomb a more valuable weapon; the secret should be well guarded from the Soviets. "Before we agree to give them any information," said Senator Mansfield in a public interview on July 4, 1957, "we certainly should have an iron-clad agreement, backed by escape-proof inspection arrangements, to do away with the building of the bigger bombs and a disarmament plan which would cut down defense expenditures for all countries."[18]

If the purpose of nuclear testing was not to develop more terrible weapons, Mr. Stevenson's reasoning had floundered. The argument gingerly turned to a new approach which seemed more promising. It was said that the testing of nuclear weapons created hazardous radiation, thereby endangering the future of mankind. Is this true?

The general public has experienced certain difficulties in understanding the various types of fallout. We shall therefore discuss them briefly.[19] Now a nuclear device with a yield of one megaton, for instance, releases 50 per cent of its energy in the form of blast, or shock; some 35 per cent of the energy occurs as thermal radiation, while 15 per cent takes the form of nuclear radiation. Two-thirds of the nuclear radiation forms what is called "residual radiation." It is this radiation with which we are concerned. Radioactivity is induced directly in the environment of a nuclear explosion by the burst, and although it is present, it is not said to constitute a testing hazard. This is not true of the radioactivity that is produced in the weapon itself and later spread in the environment by fallout.

In a surface burst, a large amount of dirt and debris is mixed with the atomic cloud, and a great deal of radioactivity is absorbed by the larger particles, which are bound to fall out locally. As the height of the burst is increased, less radioactivity is dispersed on the ground near the point of detonation. That which is carried aloft into the troposphere is deposited on the earth's surface in a matter of weeks by rain, snow, and moisture along the belt of latitude in which the explosion occurred. Particles of very small size are pushed into the stratosphere, where they are mixed and transported. Although they can remain airborne for years, these particles will eventually be removed from the stratosphere and will then fall very quickly, just as tropospheric fallout does. It is universally known that stratospheric fallout occurs everywhere on earth and that there is a concentration of fallout in the northern portions of the northern hemisphere. The non-uniform descent of stratospheric fallout is attributed to the tropopause breaks. It is further aggravated by non-uniform removal processes, such as rainfall or snowfall.

Of the more than two hundred types of isotopes produced by nuclear fission, cesium 137 and strontium 90 are the only two that have given mankind real anxiety. Although cesium 137 falls in amounts equal to strontium 90, vegetation takes so little cesium from the soil that major concern has shifted to strontium.[20] The latter is produced in quantity by fission reaction; its similarity to calcium gives it a bone-seeking property.[21] The concentration of strontium 90 in the soil of the northeastern United States has increased considerably. When the debris from the fifty megatons of fission produced by the first five years of nuclear testing will have settled, the concentration of strontium 90 might attain levels as high as forty-five millicuries per square mile for the above-mentioned region.

Once removed from the atmosphere, strontium 90 becomes soluble on contact with most soils; it cannot be leached by water. It is taken up by plants and eventually finds its way into the human diet. It can be stored in the human skeleton at the sites of active bone growth and bone-tissue reforming. However, at each level of assimilation—from soil to bone—there exists a measure of discrimination in favor of calcium and against radiostrontium. Metabolic processes in humans and animals are favorable to such a discrimination. When humans obtain calcium from a diet that does not contain milk or milk products, the strontium-to-calcium ratio is 0.25 to 0.30; when milk is the source of calcium, the ratio is about 0.55. This difference is explained by the fact that there is seven times less strontium per gram of calcium in milk than in the fodder from which the milk was produced. When combined, these different factors give an average discrimination factor of 8.0 in favor of calcium.[22]

What counts, of course, is the total amount of strontium which finds its way into the human skeleton, not the manner in which it got there. The maximum concentration that will result from nuclear testing up to mid-1957 may one day reach a total of five micromicrocuries of strontium 90 per gram of calcium, a dose that could be expected to deliver half a rad to the skeleton during a lifetime. This amount compares with a normal skeleton irradiation of seven to thirty rads. The amount of strontium irradiation would thus be from 1.5 to 6 per cent of the dose that is due to natural and unavoidable causes.

What evil consequences are to be expected from radiation? Genetic effects must here be distinguished from somatic hazards, such as leukemia, bone cancer, and a reduced life span of life. Certain principles concerning genetic damage resulting from radiation have been agreed upon. There exists no safe level of radiation in the sense that there exists no level of radiation below which no genetic effects could occur. Any amount of radiation, however small, which reaches the gonads of an individual who may later reproduce involves a risk proportional to the amount. Moreover, mutations are almost always recessive: they damage the genetic pool. Mutations that produce only a minor impairment might persist much longer than those which cause a major impairment and could affect a correspondingly larger number of persons. In this manner, a mild mutation can be as damaging as a more serious one. There is no threshold and no recovery; the proportionality between the amount of radiation and the number of mutations holds, regardless of the intensity or the spacing of radiation doses. With respect to future generations, it would make little difference whether one individual receives ten roentgens or ten persons received one roentgen or one person receives one roentgen at ten different times during reproductive life.[23]

Genetic damage resulting from radiation will be spread over the whole future of mankind; only a small fraction of it might appear during the first succeeding generation. Can it be measured? In reality, mutations occur in haphazard fashion in widely scattered and untraceable individuals. Assuming that there will be a certain number of natural mutations and assuming further that all of them will be due to background radiation, one can say that mutational damage would be increased by 3 per cent if the fallout rate is one-tenth of a roentgen per thirty years. Some scientists are brave enough to quote actual figures concerning embryonic deaths and genetic mishaps. Even so, any such reasoning is statistical and is based upon carefully stated assumptions. That is to say that deductions concerning the genetic effects of fallout would be completely meaningless if they were taken independently—that is, without certain assumptions—or if they were treated as inductive findings.

It has been established that strontium 90 is a rather insignificant source of radiation compared with natural and medical sources and that it is not likely to cause much genetic damage. Radio-strontium emits beta rays, and beta rays cannot penetrate tissues more than half a centimeter. One is therefore completely safe in concluding that present fallout will increase genetic damage only by a fraction which might never become truly measurable.[24]

In his statement of October 30, 1956, Mr. Stevenson asserted that genetic damage caused by radiation was of relatively minor concern compared with pathological damage from blood changes and cancer. The relationship between genetic mutations and radiation has been proved scientifically, but any estimate of the somatic damage that could result from radiation is conditioned by the acceptance of the theory that the incidence of cancer is proportional to the amount of radioactive material in the body. To say the least, Mr. Stevenson showed great courage in identifying himself with this theory. Let us repeat, however, that the theory of a proportional relation between radiation and cancer has not been proved. This ignorance is a part of our general ignorance concerning the causes of cancer. The minimum dose of radiation (on record) that has produced a bone tumor in man is two thousand rads.

All reports from reliable sources—including the United Nations Scientific Committee on the Effects of Atomic Radiation—have pointed out that as far as leukemia and bone cancer are concerned, there is no certainty that fallout would produce any additional cases of either disease. It is therefore scientifically sound—unless proved otherwise—to assume that there exists a threshold of susceptibility to radiation damage. The existence of a proportional relationship can be similarly assumed. We can say, for instance, that 10 per cent of normal leukemia and bone cancer cases can be attributed to normal radiation. Since the relation between normal radiation and fallout radiation has been rather well established—and on the basis of the above-mentioned assumptions and other scientific data—it has been concluded that the radiation from nuclear tests up to mid-1957 might produce fifty thousand additional cases of bone cancer and leukemia during the next thirty years.[25]

Representative Holifield declared on March 29, 1954, that "if the people of the world would know the truth, the truth will have a chance to make them free." With a better understanding of the atomic age, he said, "there would be a surging and irresistible demand for international peace. Such a demand would compel the political leaders of the nations of the world to sit down at the conference table and settle their differences peacefully."[26] So far, the "truth" has produced only confusion and anti-American emotionalism. As far as American public opinion is concerned, it has seemingly looked upon the United States government as an obscurantist core of reaction which the people have a responsibility to dissolve. The administration allegedly denied the existence of any risk, but a subtle change has taken place, for the administration now recognizes that it is necessary to gamble with the possibility of some radiation damage in order to secure the survival of all. What a resounding victory for democracy in action!

For a long time, the Atomic Energy Commission merely whispered information about fallout. Now—although one does not know how many frightening facts are still buried in secrecy—much information has been put forth.[27] Who can say that Mr. Stevenson was wrong when he protested, with "all the force in my being," against the administration's policy of hiding the facts? The public's pressure was once dismissed as Communist propaganda, but now the burden of proof lies on those who want to continue testing. The people thus educated their government, but then the foundation of democracy is faith in the people and in the soundness of their spontaneous judgments.

This jargon has become a part of the patterns of a society which would gladly drive its members into moral despair, lust and material enjoyment while focusing its attention on a single limited evil which has become a necessary part of our destiny, all on the assumption that one "unnecessary" human tragedy is one too many. No responsible person has ever denied that radioactive fall-out is undesirable or that testing implies no risk at all. Public opinion stubbornly clung to the view that because radiation hazards were unmeasured, they were unmeasurable. The fact is that scientists do agree on fallout measurements and that fallout radiation dosage is very small compared with other sources of radiation.[28] The political choice which the United States had to make was simple: Were we willing to risk annihilation by surrendering progress in nuclear armaments in order to eliminate a relatively minor and well-controlled risk.[29]

As the President said in his press conference of June 5, 1957, the American people ought to be "concerned just as much . . . with the defense of the United States" as they are with the suspension of nuclear testing. The question which the government had been studying for many years, said Mr. Dulles on November 29, 1955, was "whether or not a suspension of testing could be made dependable and in the interests of the United States." Knowing how little appeal the concept of national interest held for American public opinion, the Secretary added that when he said the United States, he meant to refer "not only to our national interest, but the interest that we have in protecting peace and freedom in the world." The opposition retorted that atomic testing could have been discontinued long ago for two reasons.

The administration's critics first asserted that a test moratorium was safe because it was "self-enforcing." It was possible, they said, to curb the hydrogen bomb without having to rely on Soviet good faith. The explosion of a hydrogen bomb could be detected so accurately that it would be possible to determine almost immediately the intensity of the blast and the materials that were used to manufacture the weapon. "One can just barely sneeze aloud, and the world will be able to detect it," Senator Anderson declared on June 17, 1957. "We do not have to worry" about the testing of hydrogen weapons because "there is no possibility it cannot be detected."[30] If there is self-enforcement, there is no need for control measures or for agreements; we just stop testing, and that is all. If the other nuclear powers do not follow our example, we should "reconsider our policy," said Mr. Stevenson on April 21, 1956. It was as simple as that.

As a second proof that testing could be discontinued, the opposition pointed out that a test moratorium was safe because it would not jeopardize our position in nuclear weapons technology. In his statement of October 30, 1956, Adlai Stevenson claimed that a test suspension would freeze the development of nuclear armaments and thus "prevent the Russians from catching up . . . so long as the agreement is in force." In a similar vein, Senator Humphrey wrote in the August, 1958, issue of *The Progressive* that a ban on testing would "check the arms competition—which is in large part a technological competition—at a key point, the development of nuclear weapons."[31]

The critics of the administration had to emphasize the second point in order to prove their first assertion, namely, that a test suspension was a meaningful disarmament measure. By the same token, they gave the lie to their claim that further testing had no real usefulness. Moreover, it was hard to believe that the Soviet Union would accept a frozen position of relative inferiority—which indicated the need for some enforceable agreement on suspension.

One need not be a great prophet to predict that the usefulness of further testing is bound to decrease very sharply and soon become outbalanced by its physical and political disadvantages. If our scientists thought they had learned "the things they wanted to know," said Mr. Eisenhower on April 9, 1958, he would "very seriously" consider announcing the discontinuance of tests, "not as part of an agreement or anything else, but as a unilateral statement on our intentions." The day this statement is made, it will be said that our leaders have finally caught up with the Stevenson vision.[32]

Adlai Stevenson's vision was somewhat obscure, as we have seen, and he did not explain how a cessation of testing would lead to disarmament. For many years the Soviet Union successfully played with the idea that stopping tests was an "easy" and "clear" start toward disarmament. Suspension carried no "complications."

As Khrushchev said on August 29, 1958, if the United States and the United Kingdom "really" wanted a complete cessation of atomic and hydrogen tests, they should have discontinued them immediately. "Everything else" could be discussed and agreed upon at some "later" date.

The rebels' language was not much different. "There must be a beginning, a starting point, a way to get off the dead center of disagreement," Mr. Stevenson said on September 29, 1956. It was not enough to say, "Well, we have tried and failed to reach agreement with the Russians." Mr. Stevenson's doctrine was that "this is one time we cannot take 'No' for an answer." And if the Russians refuse to go along, "well, then at least the world will know we tried." Senator Fulbright spoke the same language when he said on June 17, 1957, that "if the cessation of testing of large bombs is in itself a good thing, why should not that be the first step? If we can take a step in this field, would not that tend to inspire confidence in the next step?"[38]

It is difficult to imagine a doctrine more divided against itself. It blandly asserts that a test suspension is a single-item matter that should not be linked to other disarmament proposals, and it asserts, with the same dogmatism, that suspension would constitute the first step toward a prohibition of nuclear arms production and eventual disarmament.

Mr. Dulles said on June 10, 1958, that to call a test suspension a disarmament measure was "a misnomer." "All it means," he said, "is that the arsenal of nuclear weapons that you have is accumulating without any exact knowledge as to what the consequences of their use would be." In its devastating simplicity, this statement shows the fallacy of the "first step" philosophy. In order to lead to disarmament, test suspension must be linked to other disarmament measures in a single package and must be controlled. As the President said in his press conference of June 5, 1957, the administration has tried again and again to make the abolition of testing what he called "a part of a general system of disarmament —controlled and inspected disarmament." If this can be achieved, he added, "we will be glad enough, and very quickly, to stop tests."

The first step toward disarmament should include, said Mr. Eisenhower on June 26, 1957, besides monitoring stations for the enforcement of the suspension itself, an agreement to cease production of fissionable materials for weapons purposes, limited aerial inspection, and a beginning in the general reduction of armaments. The administration did not demand the abolition of nuclear weapons, since there is no reliable method of detecting fissionable materials already in existence. Nor did the administration make test suspension dependent upon what Mr. Dulles called on June 25, 1957, a "coincident cut-off" of production of fissionable materials for weapons. Test suspension was to be dependent, he said, only "upon a coincident agreement for a future cut-off." By defining what the Secretary of State called on June 10, 1958, "conditions precedent" and "conditions subsequent," the administration attempted to maintain a relationship between test suspension and disarmament.

Ever since 1945—and more recently in 1957—the Soviet Union has refused to agree to anything that would facilitate disarmament. On the day following the boastful announcement that it had successfully fired an intercontinental missile, the Soviet Union accused the Western powers of having torpedoed the disarmament talks, and the work of the United Nations subcommittee came to a complete halt. However, Mr. Dulles said on January 10, 1958, that he thought a resumption of disarmament talks was "highly likely," despite the fact that at that moment, the Soviet Union had broken "all lines of communication." The pressure of world opinion is so great, he said, that "talks will be resumed." And the administration repeatedly declared its willingness to consider alternative proposals if there was any indication that these would offer a profitable line to pursue.

The Soviets broke the deadlock by making, as usual, weird announcements and charges. On March 31, 1958, they announced a conditional suspension of testing. On April 2, 1958, Mr. Eisenhower dismissed the Soviet announcement as "a gimmick." This sober appraisal was taken as proof that the administration was fundamentally opposed to disarmament although it claimed otherwise.[34] The Soviets also trumpeted charges that American planes

95

were menacing Soviet territory in the Arctic and elsewhere, thus proving the soundness of the Arctic inspection system proposed by the administration but dismissed by Khrushchev as "quite comical."

A meeting of experts on the monitoring of a test suspension was successfully held at Geneva. Since the principle of control had been agreed upon, the United States and the United Kingdom announced, on August 22, 1958, that they would stop nuclear testing for a year if the Soviets would agree to confer on controls at the diplomatic level. The rebels hailed this announcement as a worthy and belated concession to realism. They professed to rejoice over the fact that the administration had agreed to "break the package"; they claimed that U.S. policy had undergone a fundamental change. They soon discovered, however, that the administration's offer was qualified. As Mr. Eisenhower declared on August 27, 1958, "the principle of the policy has not been abandoned at all. . . . We have not changed our general program or plan." The United States had insisted not that all phases of a disarmament program should be accepted and started at the same time but, as Mr. Dulles had said on June 10, 1958, "that we should start perhaps at different times but with the understanding that there would be a freedom of action if progress was not made in some of these other fields." The Soviet Union soon resumed testing, however, and the confusion became as complete as it had been before.

New concessions have been made by American diplomacy. Since the Soviets claimed that a ban on testing on a year-by-year basis was "nonsense," the United States and the United Kingdom dropped, on January 19, 1959, the requirement that any discontinuance of testing had to depend on explicit progress in the formulation of major disarmament measures. The principle long held by the Eisenhower administration had thus been reversed. The move was timely, but it did not satisfy the U.S.S.R., which continued to use the crudest of notions to torpedo the success of the talks. Control posts in Red China were said to be unnecessary since Red China did not possess atomic weapons and necessary as far as they would entail recognition of the Communist regime by the United States. As the State Department statement of January 24, 1959, pointed out, the Russians demanded a veto on any action of the proposed control commission to carry out inspection in the field. They wanted to dominate the commission in order not to be "at the mercy of an automatic Western majority" within the commission. They finally proposed a system of "self-inspection" under which nationals only would man the control posts, with a "few foreign controllers to check them." In other words, the West failed to take into consideration "the security" of the Soviet state. Americans wanted "to poke their nose in everything." They wanted to transform the control posts into "towers of Babel." The West truly intended "to fake evidence of tests" in order to cast "slurs on the reputation of the U.S.S.R."

Whatever the ultimate outcome of the talks at Geneva may be, one thing is assured: the attitude of public opinion has not changed, nor could it be expected to change whatever the Soviets do or will do. It is the Eisenhower administration which misleads the people. It has misled the people about the "clean" bomb. It has misled the people about the pollution of our children's milk. It is lying now about underground tests.[35] For the Soviets, it will suffice to assert that they favor disarmament and that they leave the question of peace to the United States. It will suffice because public opinion will continually complain about the administration's *intransigeance* and its cumbersome packages. If the Soviets invent some new trick, Mr. Holifield will again ask the question he asked on August 22, 1958: "When, in the name of God and preservation of humanity from nuclear suicide, will we learn to lead instead of reluctantly follow world opinion? When will we punch instead of timidly counterpunch?"[36] Any condition attached to our proposals will be denounced as a reflection on our sincerity; it will be described as a tragic continuation of the futile and abortive Dulles philosophy, which has failed to establish our true picture before public opinion. There will be no other concept of leadership than to yield to a concerted and Soviet-inspired movement of opinion: to punch and to do away with Dulles.[37] As Walter Lippmann wrote in the *New York Herald Tribune* of December 24, 1957, the policy of not wanting to negotiate, "which is incarnate in Mr. Dulles personally," carries within itself the "built-in certainty that the United States will accept the onus in the eyes of mankind of having made it inevitable that all peace proposals come to nothing." Whom the gods would destroy they first make mad.

In contradistinction, Soviet propaganda will be described as flexible, persuasive, and non-doctrinaire because it will aim "at men's minds" and be unencumbered by rigid strategic concepts. As the President sadly remarked on March 26, 1958, the Soviets will not be "handicapped" by any attempt "to observe fact and truth." Sitting as an impartial arbiter between East and West, James Reston will repeat at every opportunity that the administration is confused and resentful of criticism. Walter Lippmann will accuse Secretary Dulles anew with words used by everyone every day, and his slogans will be found provoking and constructive. If the U.S.S.R. rejects some new package, it will again seem that the Soviets might agree to some specific proposal if only it were separated from the whole and discussed on Soviet terms. To cling to a program after its acceptance has become hopeless would be incomprehensibly obtuse; it is like expecting a baby to walk two days after his birth. Soviet *intransigeance* will never reflect obstructionism; it will merely reveal a national tendency to take matters more slowly. Stalin's dictum that "sincere diplomacy is no more possible than dry water or wooden iron" will again be applied equally to the Soviet Union and to the United States. Each time the Soviets seem to move toward agreement, the United States will deliberately attach to proposals already made some new condition that will make agreement impossible. On June 17, 1957, Senator Anderson depicted the history of disarmament negotiations in terms of a drinker who knew a lovely lady and wanted to marry her. She would not marry him unless he stopped drinking; he would not stop drinking unless she married him. So do the Soviet Union and the United States behave. In the eyes of opinion, they are both equally to blame.[38]

CHAPTER V

"Turning Brush Fires into a Thermonuclear Holocaust"

THE DOCTRINE of massive retaliation applies to local aggression even more than it does to all-out war. The Eisenhower administration has constantly emphasized that the threat to American security is many sided; it has never subscribed to the theory that the United States' ability to deliver massive atomic retaliation is, by itself, adequate to meet all of our various strategic needs. As we have seen, U.S. strategy does not rely exclusively upon one weapon or even one service, nor is it anticipating only one kind of war. As Admiral Radford said on March 9, 1954, America "could become a prisoner of its own military posture if it had no capability, other than one to deliver a massive atomic attack."

Local aggression must be opposed decisively yet with rational means; it should never be enlarged to our disadvantage. This means that an aggressor must be made to suffer beyond his possibility of gain and no more. In his article of April, 1954, Secretary of State Dulles wrote that "it is important to have the flexibility and the facilities which make various responses available." The United States must have the means, he continued, "for responding effectively on a selective basis when it chooses. It must not put itself in the position where the only response open to it is general war." Mr. Dulles expressed himself even more clearly when he said during his press conference of July 18, 1956, that our theory of deterrence is to limit war—in the use of targets, weapons, and areas—to the minimum needed to deter and to repel aggression.

We repeat this doctrine here because the critics of massive retaliation have obstinately denied that it is a strategy of selective
retaliation. They have insisted that it will not stem Communist
aggressive attempts short of an all-out war. On March 6, 1954,
Mr. Stevenson expressed his misgivings as follows: "All this means
—if it means anything—is that if the Communists try another
Korea we will retaliate by dropping atom bombs on Moscow or
else we will concede the loss of another Korea."

This slick formula seems to imply that the administration will
react to local aggression by dropping nuclear bombs, not at the
center of the trouble, but at its source. In other words, it implies
that the administration is unwilling to keep local hostilities limited. "Now we are making clear to the Communists," said Senator
Kennedy on January 24, 1954, that an act of aggression will be met
"by retaliation by the United States on the home territory of China
and Russia."[1] Their homelands will cease to be a sanctuary from
direct atomic attacks by the Strategic Air Force of the United
States, and, according to the administration's critics, this would
mean general war.

It is well known that neither Mr. Dulles nor anybody else in the
administration ever said any such thing. The revealing fact in all
this is that American statesmen of stature have seen fit to identify
themselves with an exceedingly crude version of the administration's doctrine. Senator Knowland said on January 22, 1954, that
these individuals had built a straw man which they claimed was
Dulles'.[2] Quixotic attacks were made on an imaginary doctrine
and the results were bound to be startling.

The terms of the problem were inverted by partisanship. In his
address of March 6, 1954, Mr. Stevenson pretended that the decision to rely primarily on a nuclear strategy had imposed upon the
United States the alternative of inaction or national suicide. "Are
we leaving ourselves the grim choice of inaction or a thermonuclear holocaust?" he asked. "Are we indeed inviting Moscow or
Peiping to nibble us to death?" By asking this very question, Mr.
Stevenson agrees that the purpose of local aggression—from the
Communist standpoint—is to nibble the United States to death all
over the world in little wars and ill-defined situations. But if this

be the case, nibbling aggression is a very serious process, and it justifies the taking of correspondingly grave risks. The critics of massive retaliation admit that the progressive strangulation of the free world by peripheral Communist advances is a matter of life and death for the United States, and yet they hold that it is not worth threatening to retaliate massively and decisively at times and places of the United States' own choice. They say that in the hypothesis of local aggression, massive retaliation entails the taking of too great a risk, that bluffing will be followed by piecemeal surrender and, eventually, death. But if death is the outcome, the risk is not too great, and to that extent, the validity of massive retaliation remains unchallenged. As Vice-President Nixon said on December 6, 1956, "in the atomic age, there is no place for military aggression. . . . The nation that starts a little war today may set off a chain reaction that could destroy our civilization." Creeping aggression cannot be tolerated. It must be deterred.

Obviously, the partisan argument has backfired. In an abrupt change of direction, the administration's critics now retort, along with Dean Acheson, that "if it is said that we cannot afford another war like Korea, the answer is that such a war is the only kind that we or anyone else can afford."[3] This phrase is a striking example of intellectual bad faith, for Mr. Acheson is merely playing with words. When it is said that a new Korea cannot be afforded, the claim is not that the United States does not possess the resources with which to fight another limited war, as we did in Korea, nor is it pretended that a total atomic war would not be a total tragedy. The issue is that a new Korea is now too dangerous to be afforded. The overwhelming danger of local aggression in the present state of affairs is that it could lead to the holocaust which Mr. Acheson —and every responsible person for that matter—wants to prevent.

Dean Acheson's language is not the language of statesmanship. Does he want the United States to announce that it can well afford another Korea? Should the administration publicly proclaim that it has imposed upon itself the obligation to fight aggression on the aggressor's terms? What sense does it make for an American statesman to pretend that massive retaliation has "invited" the Communists to resort to local aggression or to repeat again and again that the Communists are "now able" to calculate that America will not risk general war over some "small" aggression in the world? This illustrates anew how atomic madness and atomic bluffing are constantly played against each other by partisanship. The Communists will not be deterred from local aggression, but the United States will be paralyzed in inaction. The Soviet Union can well afford to take the risks of massive American retaliation for some limited stake in Asia or the Middle East, but American public opinion describes the United States as a domineering bully whose words, instead of being credible, invite the aggressor (a successful and fearless plotter) to continue on the road to world domination. It is America that has frightened itself by its own threats; it is the deterrer who has been deterred. Partisanship has not permitted the administration to link Communist imperialism as a whole to local aggression, but it has granted the Soviet Union all rights to do so. What the Soviet Union can do, the United States apparently cannot do.

In this manner, the critics of massive retaliation have maneuvered themselves into a pitiful dead end. They defend a concept of massive retaliation in reverse. Only an intellectual clique is foolish enough to amuse itself with such self-defeating ideas. Thus far the relevance of massive retaliation to local aggression is still unchallenged. "As in the case of all-out war," said Donald Quarles on August 4, 1956, "if the Communist leadership were tempted toward limited aggression, but were faced with the plain fact that the United States stood ready to use its best weapons to defend its vital interests, they would have to conclude that such aggression would be unprofitable." To say the least, this reasoning is rational, and it is also supported indirectly by historical evidence. The drift away from realism, which started after World War II, could have lasted through a whole period of crippling aggression, but it has been brought to an end.

Having failed to prove the inadequacy of the massive retaliation policy to deter local aggression in principle, the debate now turns to problems of military strategy proper. First, how will local aggression be opposed? It is granted that the administration has never intended to turn local situations into a global war as a matter of deliberate policy, and it is no longer denied that local aggression must be approached in the light of a global Communist strategy of world domination. However, it could be that the present nuclear strategy has, *de facto*, placed the United States in an incapacity of waging local hostilities without "enlarging" them. Reliance on air-atomic power might have crippled the United States' ability to cope with local aggression as such. Massive retaliation limits the means for retaliation; it is a strategy that is completely lacking in flexibility. In contradistinction, the Democratic policy of containment did not suffer from this essential drawback. It was a "flexible policy," said Senator Gore on January 22, 1954, "which could take different forms as situations required."[4] Atomic weapons, even if they were possessed in a monopoly, said Adlai Stevenson on March 6, 1954, are "no answer to all the complicated aspects of this worldwide struggle."

The actual success of the policy of containment is, to say the least, a debatable issue. Its alleged flexibility might well have arisen from the fact that it was not a global policy. To explain the absence of an over-all strategy with the "complications" of the international situation is an abdication of policy. Complicated as it certainly is, the problem of security in the atomic age can be resolved, and a solution must be found.

In this way, the debate is finally forced out of generalities. If alternatives to massive retaliation can be found, they must be presented. At this point of the debate, the critics of massive retaliation are divided. One school of thought upholds the concept of rational nuclear armaments and rational nuclear warfare, while a second group, to be discussed later, clings to the idea of conventional warfare. Atomic Energy Commissioner T. E. Murray testified on April 12, 1956, before the Subcommittee on Disarmament of the Senate Committee on Foreign Relations that the theory of rational nuclear armaments

means that decisions with regard to the size and type of nuclear weapons to be placed in stockpile should be made in the light of two principles. There is the military principle that the weapons we manufacture should be demonstrably useful for the purpose of actual war. And there is the higher principle that the use of force in warfare is subject to the dictates of the moral conscience.[5]

The nuclear stockpile should cover the entire spectrum of nuclear yields, for the United States must be able to meet the whole range of likely Soviet military actions. Since our supply of larger megaton weapons is assumed to be adequate for all military purposes, Mr. Murray's doctrine places a strong emphasis on weapons of a smaller yield. "Increasing concentration should be set," he said, "on the stockpiling of a wide range of very small weapons" in large numbers. When he said "small weapons," he meant weapons with a yield range of a few kilotons; by "large number," he meant "tens of thousands of weapons in this range." These smaller weapons would form, he added, a "broad and solid base upon which could be superimposed a stockpile in the image of a pyramid of intermediate and large size weapons." A stockpile so composed could support a strategy of discriminating use of force against all kinds of military aggression. The Commissioner concluded that "with this diversified nuclear armament, possessed in abundance, American and allied military forces of reasonable size would be equipped to handle all the various wartime contingencies that might arise."[6]

This doctrine sounds so much like everything the administration has always said that to turn it into a criticism of massive retaliation would be a remarkable feat, but it has been done. Ever since tactical atomic weapons came into being, the administration has stressed that atomic weapons can be discriminating and that their effects can be confined to military targets. When the President and Mr. Dulles spoke of tactical atomic weapons in March, 1955, public opinion pretended that the days of massive retaliation were over and that it had been officially replaced by a new policy, namely the policy of "graduated deterrence," which meant the rational use of atomic weapons in warfare. In October, 1957, Mr. Dulles published an article in which he stressed the capabilities of tactical atomic weapons for the defense of western Europe, and again it was said that the administration had formulated a "new" policy and had discarded massive retaliation. We know now that the administration's policy was "new" only to the extent that the administration's critics had misconstrued U.S. strategy.

It is true that the administration has never officially announced how many smaller atomic weapons have already been stockpiled. Little, if anything, has been said publicly about the Atomic Energy Commission's planning in the production of fissionable materials. It has been said that an increased production of plutonium is necessary in order to accelerate the flow of smaller and cleaner weapons in our arsenal. However, for lack of evidence, the public cannot say whether the number of low-yield warheads is adequate for meeting the increased demand for tactical weapons.

It is interesting to note that this missing link—the lack of information about the number of tactical warheads already stockpiled—makes up the entire difference between Murray's doctrine of rational nuclear armaments and the administration's repeated concept of rational nuclear warfare. Without the smaller warheads, nuclear warfare cannot be conducted rationally. But are the warheads really missing? Does public opinion feel that it has a right to be told how many atomic bombs have been produced by the Atomic Energy Commission? Although this claim is implicit in Mr. Murray's criticism, he dares not express it, for if he did, he would expose himself to ridicule.

It seems self-evident, then, that with the passage of time and with increasing nuclear stockpiles, the production of fissionable materials will indeed move towards smaller weapons rather than larger ones. This rule of reason is the wide-open door through which the Commissioner so dramatically forced himself.

Let us be careful, however, not to obscure the main issue. Mr. Murray and his supporters are in favor of limited atomic warfare. In his testimony of April 12, 1956, he said that "limited nuclear war is a possibility that our conscience can face and accept. It is also a possibility that is inherent in the present state of international tensions. . . . Wars in the future will be nuclear wars." Although all-out nuclear war is no more acceptable than suicide or murder, he continued, nuclear war does not, by itself, need to be all-out atomic war. In the report he made upon leaving the Atomic Energy Commission, he disassociated himself from the doctrine which holds that the "use of small atomic weapons means stepping on an escalator that inexorably leads to the depths of total nuclear war." He claimed that "this crude belief is unwarranted."[7]

Mr. Murray's position is so close to the administration's doctrine that one wonders why it cannot be discussed soberly, without implying that the United States is in favor of a war of annihilation. Referring to the last war's obliteration bombings, he declared that from the Civil War and the Casablanca Conference of 1943 all the way to the use of the atomic bomb against Japan, unconditional surrender had become an objective of American policy in war— an accusation that was widely endorsed by millions of Americans. From the exalted and mystifying position he occupied in the government, he warned that the totality of destruction already implied in unconditional surrender had become an attainable possibility and declared that this trend in American policy toward the totality of war had to be reversed. As free persons, we can choose to curb the maddening logic of war and overcome what he called "the seduction exerted by a technological open end." Although he himself pointed out that "it would be fatal to permit ourselves to drift into the habit of thinking about nuclear war only in all-out terms," he finally referred to "an inversion of values" and the "widespread ignorance of the realities of the nuclear age which still strangely exists on all strata of American opinion, from the highest to the lowest."

The neurotic attitude of national self-incrimination is not the only revealing fact in this part of the debate. The concept of rational nuclear armaments, as defined by partisanship, presents certain dangerous features which are not part of massive retaliation. Obviously, the apology for rational nuclear war made by Mr. Murray goes too far. It overlooks both the still gigantic yield of the smallest nuclear warheads in existence and the political limitations of nuclear warfare. There mysteriously creeps into the public mind the notion that there is some way of reducing the yield of nuclear weapons to a more reasonable minimum, an idea that is not founded on facts. The confusion about the matter is thereby increased. It is true, of course, that (as opposed to the "absurdity" of a megaton weapon) a tactical warhead appears rational, but is this true when the same weapon is compared to conventional armaments?

Mr. Murray's proposals do not go to the root of the problem. They are politically dangerous in that they undermine the comprehension of the administration's strategy for local aggression. Let us recall that the administration has made here a paramount distinction of various degrees or levels of retaliation. It has first spoken of a truly local situation that could be met with a mere police action, in which case the use of any nuclear weapon is out of the question. The administration has also spoken of a local war sufficiently grave to justify the employment of nuclear weapons and, finally, of a local war that would involve a direct, if not total, clash between the United States and a major Communist aggressor. In the two latter cases, the argument for the smaller atomic weapon is not as clear as Murray claimed it to be. Under certain conditions, the exclusive use of small warheads might be just as irrational as the indiscriminate use of megaton weapons. It is certain that the United States should have available all sorts of weapons, but the type and the degree of retaliation can be determined only by circumstances. We shall now turn to an analysis of this particular problem.

Most of the critics of massive retaliation as a means of deterring local aggression have unsuccessfully attempted to keep clear of nuclear warfare altogether. "Anything that has to do with atomic energy is potentially dangerous," said Senator Mansfield in June, 1955.[8] Once they are used, nuclear weapons will unleash a wave of horror and distrust; they will snowball into the use of thermonuclear bombs. The Soviet Union has developed a full array of atomic weapons, and if we ever use atomic weapons, we must expect retaliation in kind.

Viewed in this light, even graduated retaliation or rational nuclear warfare is a mirage. There is no such thing as limited atomic warfare. Even tactical atomic weapons are not as precise as the administration has "claimed." There will always be civilian installations and population centers near military targets; there will always be local fallout. It is wishful thinking to assert that tactical atomic weapons have achieved "conventional" status in military forces. The only ultimate weapon is the fighting man with his feet on the ground, and it is the fighting man that has been sacrificed to massive retaliation. America has so reduced its conventional forces that it will have to use atomic weapons in a future war, regardless of the consequences. In contradistinction, the U.S.S.R. is the only major force in the world today that possesses both a completely new arsenal of weapons-in-being and the capability of fighting either a nuclear or a non-nuclear war, big or small, on any kind of terrain or in any climate. The United States should also possess these factors. We must maintain the dual capacity to wage total atomic war if necessary or victorious small wars without having to use atomic weapons.

This doctrine creates a host of delicate problems, which, for the sake of clarity, will be treated as parts of two general questions, namely, the question of deterring local aggression and that of actually fighting it when and where deterrence has failed.

One knows how often the critics of massive retaliation have pointed out that atomic weapons did not deter the rape of Czechoslovakia or the blockade of Berlin. As Senator Jackson said on February 16, 1954, "atomic retaliation for which we had a monopoly in 1947 did not stop guerrilla warfare in Greece. It did not stop the Korean war."[9] Nor did it bring the Indochinese War to a successful conclusion. This must serve, it is said, as a reminder of the probability of limited aggression occurring under the umbrella of atomic deterrence.

Czechoslovakia, Berlin, and Korea certainly proved that the United States did not, at the time, have a policy of deterrence, as was made so strikingly evident by the misuse of our atomic monopoly. Beyond that, Senator Jackson's reasoning leads to no precise conclusion. The point at issue is not whether our present conventional forces are a part of the deterrent we maintain against aggression. The conventionalist argument must prove that local aggression can be deterred only by what General Ridgway called military power "real and apparent to all concerned." Wherever war can break out, he wrote to Secretary Wilson on June 27, 1955, "a strong position of tangible free world strength must be maintained."[10] Our bombing force is stationed too far away, and the American soldier in uniform should always be near at hand as a symbol of might, a symbol of success and friendliness, like the policeman on the beat.

If proved, this doctrine would seriously challenge an essential part of the administration's strategy. On March 16, 1954, for instance, Mr. Dulles said that the free world does not have "to depend upon having in place forces in being sufficient to stop an attack in its track where it could occur because you rely primarily upon deterring that attack, not necessarily upon being able to stop it." According to the administration, local defenses always need the backing of American power, but this does not necessarily mean American ground forces. It is not enough to speak of the American soldier in uniform as a symbol of success and friendliness wherever he is. The fact is that the conventionalists have experienced great difficulties in the formulation of a strategy of deterrence by conventional power alone. They say that American power will deter aggression whenever such power is "real," "tangible," and "apparent." A fleet task force would illustrate "apparent" power (in the conventionalist sense) by proving to the would-be aggressor that we are willing to commit force in a situation, but would it be "tangible"? The landing of Marines in Lebanon was both "apparent" and "tangible," but the limitations inherent in the actual commitment of force might not have convinced the Soviets that American power in the Middle East was "real." The conventionalists assume, in other words, that power is "real" when it is actually engaged and that it is "apparent" and convincing because it is "tangible." Since power is real only when it is adequate, it is quite evident that the conventionalist argument begs the question.

The critics of massive retaliation have spoken of what Senator Gore called on January 22, 1954, "the presence of American forces in strength . . . to bolster the will to resist."[11] General Ridgway also spoke of this on February 23 ,1955, before the Senate Armed Services Committee. He said that it could not be a mere coincidence that the Soviet bloc has never risked aggression in any area where American forces are deployed. In a letter to Secretary Wilson, he wrote that "weakness in the strength of ground forces anywhere in the free world invites aggression in those areas." Others have repeatedly said that the United States cannot afford the risk of "withdrawing" its forces, thereby creating a "vacuum" into which, as experience has proved, the enemy is "likely" to move. Withdrawal would be justified only if American troops could be replaced by adequate local forces. Now there is little evidence, it is claimed, that friendly forces are being built up to the point where they could readily "replace" American troops overseas.

This discussion should be considered a classic example of how partisan criticism often proceeds in the United States. The critic quickly jumps from one shaky concept to another, without ever letting the weight of the argument rest on any of them, and then comes to a conclusion that has no real connection with its logical antecedents. In this instance, the conventionalist has spoken, in rapid succession, of troops and tangible American power, of vacuums, withdrawals and local defenses. Each of these terms needed explanations, none were given. If a definition of deterrence were to be construed on the foregoing basis, it would read as follows: Communist imperialism is to be deterred by the American dough-boy as stationed around the world at the time when Mr. Dulles began to speak of massive retaliation and before Secretary òf Defense Wilson started to pull down the conventional strength of America under orders from Wall Street.

This illustrates the pitfalls into which the conventionalist argument has fallen. The irony of the situation is that no strategy would be found more unpopular with the very people who support it than a strategy which requires the commitment of American manpower. In every international crisis of the recent past, the first and quasi-instinctive reaction of public opinion has been that there should be no commitment of American manpower. The isolationist cries that the gallant youth of America is about to be sacrificed on the altar of the one-worlders. In 1954 and again in 1955, in 1956 as well as in 1957 and 1958, Senator Morse spoke of the shiploads of coffins soon to be delivered at American ports and appealed to mothers to rise against the administration and to oppose intervention in Indochina, Formosa, and the Middle East. Many reasons have been invoked, but the common denominator is that there should be no commitment of troops.

The administration seems always inclined to send American troops to the wrong place, at the wrong time, and for the wrong war. If the place is Indochina, this is "not where such a war would be fought anyway," said Senator Morse on April 19, 1954.[12] Senator Kennedy had said on April 6, 1954, that "for the United States . . . to send troops into the most difficult terrain in the world, with the Chinese able to pour in unlimited manpower," was madness. It would be a "hopeless situation," he said.[13] Even the two hundred American technicians stationed in Indochina in the spring of 1954 were two hundred too many. "Step by step, we are moving into this war in Indochina," said Senator Stennis on February 9, 1954, "and I am afraid we will move to a point from which there will be no return. . . . The situation is grave. We must either go in or stay out."[14]

What was said of Indochina can, of course, be said of any other country. Every terrain will be the most difficult in the world at the moment when we must consider sending troops into it. The problem will always be either to go in or stay out, and the Communists will be capable of sending in unlimited manpower anywhere or everywhere. The conventionalist pretends that the United States has deployed its strength in areas where aggression is not likely, as in western Europe or Korea. At places where aggression truly threatens, in Southeast Asia or Iran, there are no American troops, nor does the United States have the means to move its strategic reserves into position wherever it might become necessary.

Since American troops cannot be withdrawn without creating a vacuum, what does the conventionalist propose to do about them? Would the Chinese Communists show more restraint if the United States kept three divisions in Korea instead of two? Would NATO be stronger if seven American divisions were stationed in Germany instead of six? Would General Ridgway pretend that without massive retaliation any amount of conventional forces would provide adequate deterrence? Does he mean that the administration ought to place a token force in every country on the periphery of the Communist empire to wave the flag in case of aggression? Would he place an Army division in Iraq? Or Laos? Or Syria? These questions and many others have not been answered—nor can they be answered—by the conventionalist. By pretending that the United States has no strategy at present, the critics of the administration have pushed themselves into a situation in which they cannot possibly present workable alternatives to massive retaliation. This is the root of the problem.

"The position of Mr. John Foster Dulles . . . is essentially a prepare-for-one-type-of-war policy," said Senator Jackson on February 16, 1954.[15] The United States has been so preoccupied with preparations for all-out war with the Soviet Union that it has limited the means available for the cold war to what General Ridgway called in his letter to Mr. Wilson "those which are essentially by-products or left-overs from the means available for general war." "We do not have, nor does the administration intend to have the ground forces . . . to deal with limited operations, should they be necessary," said Dean Acheson on September 26, 1956. Since the only force that the United States can "afford" to use is limited force, a nuclear strategy is not credible to the potential aggressor. "It is not credible," Mr. Acheson said, "that many occasions are serious enough to lead . . . to use atomic weapons." Massive retaliation has been "merchandised to the American people as the total basis of . . . security," declared Senator Lehman on May 16, 1954. "No, the recent effort to sell that slogan to the American people was a total fraud."

It is not difficult to see the error in this line of reasoning: atomic strategic bombing has been identified with massive retaliation and nuclear warfare. This is the "fraud." The conventionalist asserts that the administration has sacrificed, on the altar of economy, our capability of fighting non-nuclear wars because it pretends that we have placed all of our eggs in the Strategic Air Command's basket. This assertion is untrue. We deceive ourselves if we say that 35,000 planes, 900 ships at sea, and 2,500,000 men under arms are "left-overs" and "by-products" of the means available for all-out war. Whether they are maintained for general war or not, these forces are available, and they are considerable. Furthermore, with the advent of smaller and cleaner nuclear weapons, the atom has become an egg that can be placed in many baskets—in the Army's basket just as well as in SAC's. Admiral Radford said as early as December 14, 1953, that "today atomic weapons have virtually achieved conventional status within our Armed Forces. Each military service is capable of putting this weapon into military use."

It is self-deceiving to pretend that even the largest army in the world would have deterrent value without massive retaliation. It is also fraudulent to pretend that little wars are so different from big ones, even in the atomic age, or so urgent that the United States ought to be "100 percent ready to meet every little trouble that could arise," as President Eisenhower put it on December 15, 1954. The administration has tried to develop a long-range program that "met the over-all needs in the best way." As Commander in Chief, the President said, he would "rather improvise and resort to expedient in little wars than he would in big wars. He would rather cast and mold his security arrangements to meet the great threats to the United States, and take the others, as far as he could, in his stride."

It would be perfect strategy, of course, for the United States to station troops at every place where trouble might arise, but no one can say that this is feasible. The forces now maintained by the United States should therefore be considered a successful deterrent because they are "fully adequate to perform all essential tasks in the initial stages of a shooting war, global or otherwise, and they constitute an ample base which will permit a rapid and orderly buildup when and if that should become necessary."[16]

We cannot expect this doctrine to be convincing to the critics of massive retaliation, who have now raised several new issues. What would happen, they ask, if the Soviet Union would ever agree to outlaw the use of atomic weapons in warfare? The answer is quite simple. For many years, the U.S.S.R. has used the protests of the American people against atomic weapons in an attempt to convince the world that a legal ban on nuclear war is a necessity, this in order to increase the Communist preponderance in conventional armaments. These proposals have been rejected by the United States because of the Communists' reasons for making them. Is it unreasonable to expect that the present administration will never agree to a disarmament system that would expose the United States to defeat?

It is said that atomic tactics have never been tested. If they were ever used, the initiative for launching the first atomic war would rest with the United States. The idea that atomic tactics are unproved is a poor play upon words. They are said to be unreliable for no other reason than that they have not been truly tested. They have not been tested because we have never had to use atomic weapons (which proves the success of deterrence rather than its alleged failure) and because the realities of the atomic age are new. The atom has revolutionized the whole art of warfare.

Neither the fact that atomic warfare is unproved nor the fear of having to take the initiative in the first nuclear war in history is proof that tactical atomic weapons will not be used in a limited war. If two parties are armed with both rifles and bows and arrows, one cannot infer from the inequality of the two weapons that the greater power of the rifle would preclude its being used. The only sensible conclusion seems to be that the parties will either use their rifles or not fight at all. It is not safe to affirm that a general appreciation of the consequences of nuclear warfare will create on both sides a common unwillingness to use atomic weapons. Here again we are tricked by words. This general unwillingness is unwillingness to go to war, and that is deterrence. Let us recall that when disarmament is discussed, partisanship flatly assumes that atomic weapons will be used in any future war. In this light, is it consistent to pretend now that they would not be used?

As far as the responsibility for unleashing a nuclear war is concerned, it ought to be put squarely on the aggressor. The administration's critics speak as if the rational use of atomic weapons were a crime greater than aggression itself. It is unfortunately self-evident that if American public opinion refuses to understand that atomic weapons can be used discriminately, the United States might never have the determination to use them.

A new problem has arisen. In recent years, the United States has constantly assumed new obligations in Asia and the Middle East. "Yet, simultaneously," said Senator Lehman on June 20, 1955, "with the assumption of additional great responsibilities, we have constantly weakened our defenses and lessened our ability to meet the responsibilities which we have assumed and to which we are solemnly committed."[17] And General Ridgway wrote Mr. Wilson that "no one knows when those ominous sight drafts may be presented for payment. No one can tell at this time the form or scope of performance these commitments may require of the United States. . . . Present United States military forces cannot support fully America's diplomacy. If military power is to support diplomacy . . . it must be capable of being applied promptly, selectively and with the degree of violence appropriate to the occasion."

The United States has been accused by American public opinion of "pactomania." This new self-accusation reveals the atmosphere in which the whole massive retaliation debate has been conducted. The failure of deterrence has been postulated, although it was this very thing that had to be proved in the debate. Treaty commitments have been likened to a bank credit, which, if overextended, can cause bankruptcy. A commitment, so-called, is identified with the sending of a contingent of troops to a treaty area or the building of a strong army—again, the very point that had to be established. "New" commitments are referred to as additional imperialistic ventures, as if the fear of overextending ourselves would justify abandoning this or that country to its own fate and holding to what the United States still controls.

The truth is, of course, that the various treaties concluded by the

Eisenhower administration are not new obligations; they represent the substitution of clearly defined relationships for ill-defined ones. The United States faces the same enemy everywhere. It is therefore feasible to devise a central and indivisible strategy which will make it clear to the potential aggressor that it is the commitment made by the United States, rather than local defenses, which constitutes the deterrent. Not even in western Europe does one find enough power-in-being for coping successfully with major Communist aggression; a fortiori is this true of Asia and the Middle East, where the defensive perimeter is so vast that it is not feasible to maintain a sizable contingent of troops, even if this approach were politically or juridically feasible, which is not the case. These facts make it quite clear that the seriousness of American intentions must be well understood and that American public opinion must not pull down, in a conscious and methodical manner, every policy put forth by the United States.

In view of our commitments, it is vain to assume that the Soviet Union may decide to try to get away with limited ventures on the theory that President Eisenhower would have to decide, after long and serious study, whether such a place as, say, Beirut is worth thirty million American lives. The truth is that a decision not to intervene might prove to be just as difficult to make as a decision to intervene. It is enough to say that warning has been given and that it has been effective. It is not necessary for the United States to answer in advance such a question as what would happen if Communist China would attack Laos, nor should we act as if American policy were of so little consequence that it has to be detailed in every situation in order to become credible. As Senator Capehart said on April 25, 1956, "what are the critics complaining about? Are they complaining because we are not at war somewhere? Is it their idea of maintaining peace . . . that we must be fighting somewhere? Are they disappointed that there is no war in Korea or Formosa or that there is not a great deal of shooting going on?"[18] These are simple but pertinent questions.

The critics have the right, however, to ask what would happen if—assuming the failure of deterrence—aggression would have to be fought. The conventionalist pretends anew that the United States is so committed to air-atomic power that it does not have the means to fight local aggression without resorting to atomic weapons. Now using atomic weapons in a local war, said Senator Douglas on January 22, 1954, is "more or less like using a 155-mm. shell to destroy a swarm of mosquitoes."[19] According to General Gavin, it is more or less like using a "tank to catch a pickpocket."

These comparisons express the two dimensions of the problem. The "155-mm. shell" concept conveys the impression that the weapon is far out of proportion to its target and is therefore cruel and inhuman. It also implies that no matter how potent it might be, an atomic weapon would not stop an aggressor in a local war. It goes without saying that even tactical atomic weapons could be used in a cruel way, without any real military justification, but this is not the question. The critics implicitly assert that the administration's strategy of massive retaliation necessarily calls for such a reckless use of the atomic bomb. It is in this way that the question should be stated, and when it is thus expressed, its fallacy becomes obvious.

Time and again the problem of local aggression is discussed as if the present administration had said nothing on the subject. Weighty volumes are written, but their authors do not bother to quote from authoritative statements made by both Mr. Eisenhower and Mr. Dulles, and still less, of course, do these authors attempt to refute the administration's policy concerning limited war. Having failed to make even a limited effort to understand it, the critics simply assert that there is no policy at all on the matter.[20]

This is not so, as we well know. If some local situation is comparable to the whirling of a swarm of mosquitoes, the administration speaks of a police action; atomic weapons do not enter into the picture at all. The opposition cannot seriously claim here that American defenses have been geared to nuclear weapons to such an extent that the United States is not ready to fight a non-nuclear war. The argument would then mean that a swarm of mosquitoes is no match for the Marine Corps or the United States Navy.

Does one mean by "mosquitoes" a sudden and disorderly rush of Communist hordes pouring manpower into some local situation and quickly overpowering a small American force in spite of all its modern weapons? An invasion of this kind would, of course, go immediately beyond the range of a police action. Conversely, a rational use of nuclear weapons would be justified, both militarily and morally, and one could no longer speak of purposeless and wasteful destruction. The question, then, is whether nuclear weapons would be effective. Now the effectiveness of tactical atomic weapons against certain targets—such as naval concentrations, airfields, and supply depots—is not open to question. The scope of the debate is therefore reduced to the following issue: Would tactical atomic firepower stem an invasion and bring the resulting conflict to a successful end?

This particular question has been emphatically and almost universally answered in the negative. It has been said that tactical nuclear weapons would have no usefulness in terrain like that of Korea. Referring to the Korean War, Representative Sikes asserted on April 28, 1954, that "we were not saved by atomic weapons, not by superweapons, but by heroic exertions and by hastily rebuilt conventional ground forces."[21] There is no example in history, or so it is said, of a nation that lost its will to resist before its armed forces had been decisively defeated on the ground. War is, by definition, a battle for controlling land areas, and only conventional forces can achieve such an objective. On May 27, 1957, Mr. Sikes said that "air power gutted Germany—literally destroying it—but the Germans didn't stop fighting until their territory was overrun by the allied armies." It is true that the United States was hampered by the timidity of its allies in Korea, yet we learned the same lesson. Mr. Sikes said: "In Korea we had unquestioned air and naval superiority. Within territorial limits we bombed at will. What happened? We got kicked all over the lot until we had enough troops and weapons on the ground to stop the enemy." Hungary was given as an illustration of the primacy of conventional ground forces. So was Suez. The overwhelming air and naval superiority of France and Britain did not frighten Nasser into submission; France and Britain, Mr. Sikes concluded, "allowed themselves to be talked out of a successful land, air, and water campaign by another timid ally; this time the United States." The Israelis were more successful; they "kicked the living daylights out of the Egyptians on the ground with troops and armor."[22]

Representative Sikes wants, however, "to be sure that American fighting forces have a chance to defend themselves if trouble comes." He is not one who would like tactical A-bombs not to be used in localized wars. In other words, his position on the matter is most revealing. In spite of his verbal excesses, the Representative reveals nothing less than almost complete agreement, in principle, with the strategy he criticizes, and this at the very moment when the administration and its responsible critics seemed to be the farthest apart. All agree that it would be an error of the first magnitude for the United States to become committed to a strategy that is designed to destroy life and industry in the enemy's homeland while leaving his troops and other combat forces relatively intact. There is equal agreement that thermonuclear war is unthinkable and that tactical atomic weapons are an entirely different consideration. In other words, there is agreement that mere atomic devastation and mere conventional warfare would both lead (in the event of a major Communist invasion) to a lengthy, sprawling, and indecisive conflict. This finding completely shatters the conventionalist argument. There is simply no issue at all.

A war could be limited either because the belligerents pursue limited objectives or because they limit the use of force in the prosecution of the war. This assertion does preclude the conventionalist notion of limited warfare. On January 18, 1954, General Ridgway declared that "the sole criterion by which to judge the value of an army is its ability to achieve victory in battle."[23] In a letter to Secretary Wilson, the former Army Chief of Staff said that "Soviet satellite aggressions should be treated as limited or local wars until the aggressor is defeated or the United States and its allies are prepared for general war."

Such a doctrine may appear to be an astonishing reversal on the part of the conventionalists, for they have constantly stressed the recklessness of atomic weapons and have repeatedly accused the administration of seeking unconditional surrenders everywhere. Now they speak of victory as the objective of the "Queen of Battle" and espouse General MacArthur's much decried philosophy that "war's very object is victory." Let it be understood, however, that if the conventionalists did not demand victory, they would have no case at all. Atomic weapons are admirably suited to the conduct of a limited war for limited objectives, a war that would combine limited conventional operations with punishing air-atomic blows. It would be of no avail for the conventionalists to pretend, as Senator Douglas did on January 22, 1954, that "the great advantage of ground forces is that they can check local acts of aggression without expanding such acts of aggression into a world war."[24]

Now that the Communists are equipped with the means of massive retaliation, is it so certain that local acts of aggression can be checked with ground forces alone? This is a question which the conventionalists vainly try to avoid. Let us assume, for the sake of example, that the Soviet Union orders overwhelming Communist conventional power thrown into a local act of aggression and that the Soviets threaten the free nations of the world with massive retaliation if the United States uses atomic weapons to counter that aggression. Who could say that "ground forces" would be adequate for what the situation might require? In contradistinction, if the United States were to make determined and discriminate use of tactical atomic weapons in order to inflict unacceptable damage upon the aggressor, who could say that the Soviet Union would gladly unleash a thermonuclear holocaust from which no victor could possibly emerge?

An important principle must be stated at this point of the debate. If atomic weapons are to be used at all, they should be used quickly and decisively. There can be no doubt that if aggression breaks out, the policy of deterrence has failed, but only to a point, for the need to prevent aggression from becoming more and more violent remains. This means that the use of atomic weapons should be coupled with a clear declaration of purpose concerning the objectives we would pursue in case of war. If we should ever combine atomic bombing with political and diplomatic indecision, we would invite disaster because our determination to deter the enemy from expanding aggression might become uncertain.

In this respect, it cannot be denied that the administration could have been more explicit about the techniques of warfare limitations. In some instances, decisive retaliatory action can be combined with a declaration of limited objectives, and maximum deterrence be achieved. The China crisis of 1958 offered an ideal situation for a public statement on limitation. The administration could have made it clear that nuclear strikes on well-chosen targets were the only thing needed to deter Communist China. The United States' peripheral position in the Formosa Strait precluded a sprawling venture on the mainland, but it would have made possible a strictly conventional strategy of defense that could have been combined with punishing retaliatory blows.[25]

In other instances, it would be impossible to deny an area to the enemy if he were to attack in force. Any war situation that arises in such an area can be limited only if we refuse to limit it. President Eisenhower said on March 11, 1959, that the United States would not fight a ground war in Europe. He then said that we had the forces necessary for limited-war situations. If these forces were not sufficient, we must think, he said, "in much, much bigger terms." The Communists cannot deliberately start a war in Europe that would go beyond the limits of what U.S. forces can handle, for the alternative is nuclear retaliation. It is not in their interest to create, at a great risk to themselves, war situations that cannot lead to any real advance.

It is revealing, of course, that this reasoning has been inverted by the administration's critics, who claim that our forces-in-being are inadequate because we cannot wage a ground war in Europe. As usual, the fallacy is of the crudest type. We cannot wage a ground war in Europe because our forces-in-being are inadequate *for that purpose.* The forces required for a successful ground war with the Soviet Union would demand total mobilization. A country which occupies a defensive position like that of the United States cannot remain mobilized indefinitely. It makes no sense, either, to mobilize even partially for meeting a crisis engineered by the enemy for the purpose of increasing our difficulties. We cannot wage a ground war; we should not do it. As President Eisenhower said on March 11, 1959, "we just don't want to be fighting battles where we are always at a disadvantage. . . . That's all." The forces that we possess are adequate for what we intend to do.[26]

The Berlin crisis delivered a fatal blow to the notion that massive retaliation is not credible with respect to "minor objectives." It was believed that the Soviet Union might be tempted to embark on a series of "nibbles," none of which would justify the risk of nuclear warfare. These "nibbles" are the fabrication of scholars writing research papers in an environment that is void of experience and common sense. There is no such thing as a "nibble"— except for those who think that a "limited" defeat is preferable to nuclear war. Many of the administration's critics and many, many scholars long used Berlin as the classic example of prospective Soviet nibbling. With the exception of Quemoy, no situation appeared more limited or less tempting for the Communists than this Western outpost in East Germany; yet the Berlin crisis proved that nibbles require risky maneuvers and a good deal of biting. We can conclude that the issue is never likely to be what the enemy tries to nibble away but who is nibbling and whether we will let ourselves be bitten.

The evidence points to the fact that the Eisenhower administration has made a clear-cut and necessary decision as regards the measured employment of nuclear weapons to counter local aggression. If we have to commit our forces, Mr. Quarles declared on September 26, 1956, "it must be expected that we will bring to bear those weapons that will be most effective in the task of repelling aggression." The United States would not be automatically triggered into atomic retaliation in case of local aggression; furthermore, the weapons would be carefully chosen and their application would cease as soon as the aggressive forces appeared unwilling to continue. Mr. Quarles also said that he shared "the fear that limited war might graduate into total war." This is why we should exert every effort to prevent war and why, if limited war is thrust upon us, we should use our most effective weapons in a determined effort to end such aggression quickly. Atomic retaliation has no other purpose. It would be fatuous to say more.

Strange as it may seem, the conventionalists are guilty of the very error which they tried so hard to attribute to the administration. In their efforts to prove that atomic weapons cannot be integrated into a strategy based on limitations, they have thought of atomic weapons as superconventional armaments that are to be integrated into a conventional strategy. But the strategy of massive retaliation is as new as the weapons it employs; there is no longer such a thing as conventional strategy.

In view of the reactions that could be expected from a decisive use of tactical atomic weapons at the very outset of a local war, the decision to use them will be difficult to make. On November 30, 1950, President Truman declared in a press conference that the United States would take "whatever steps" were necessary to meet the situation created by Red Chinese intervention in Korea; the United States would do so "with every weapon" it had, he said. Mr. Truman did not actually threaten to use atomic bombs in Korea; he merely wanted to say that there had always been "active consideration" of their use. His statement created an anti-American furor. British Prime Minister Attlee flew to Washington on December 4, and a state of confusion resulted in the Korean situation. The Eisenhower administration allegedly shrank from using the atomic bomb during the Dien Bien Phu crisis. The best way to avoid such difficulties in the future is to warn the aggressor before the shooting starts and to call for public support of the administration's warnings. This can be done at no cost at all.

It is conceivable that under the umbrella of massive retaliation, limited wars could be fought in the future with strictly conventional means, even if this would require that the United States put forth some "heroic exertions" to rebuild more conventional strength. We obviously have the capacity of doing so. Atomic weapons demand a large infrastructure of conventional weapons systems which possess a dual capacity for both atomic and conventional warfare. It would be feasible to divert existing means from other missions temporarily. In contradistinction, the Anglo-French invasion of Egypt in 1956 revealed that even a limited action waged with conventional armaments against a virtually powerless enemy necessitates a deployment of force so considerable that the exact meaning of localized warfare is not clear for countries which do not possess a full measure of atomic power.[27]

The June, 1958, issue of the *Army Information Digest* said that "the first element of doctrine for limited war is that limited war is possible."[28] It is important that we not use this "first element of doctrine" in a self-accusing manner. The reasoning behind the administration's decision to maintain the forces we now have is simple and precise: it wants to be able to cope with limited aggression.

The critics of massive retaliation have confused the role of atomic weapons as a deterrent with their use in local warfare. If it could be proved that such weapons would never be used, they would not be a deterrent, but there is no reason why they should not be used. As far as their actual use is concerned, the question is not—as many believe—whether the atomic bomb will stop the aggressor in his tracks but whether it has a real military usefulness. Will it increase the firepower of our forces? Will it help to stop the aggressor? Will it make a valuable contribution? Now to put the question in this way is to answer it. In the actual fighting of a local war, tactical atomic weapons will be important; nobody has said that they will completely replace men and armor.

The conventionalists warn that the U.S. Army needs more armor, more flame throwers, more water purification systems, more communication equipment. They claim that the Lebanon operation displayed the weakness of our airlift and that our alleged inability to move decisively to stop local aggression could well prove to be the Achilles' heel of our present defenses. They add that the Strategic Army Corps is a paper grouping that has no real combat readiness.

Why not say that the United States moved into Lebanon with a speed and an efficiency that were as great as the situation required? Why not say that fifteen thousand American soldiers in the Middle East made up a force that was as overwhelming on the spot as it was small in relation to our total manpower resources? Why not say that six hundred aircraft could have been used, if necessary, for airlift operations? Why not say that even if we had thousands of aircraft, we could not use them as an airlift in most places where local aggression might break out because there are no sources of fuel, no airfields for the planes to land on?

Balanced security will demand some duplication of effort; it will be expensive, very expensive in terms of human and economic resources. One cannot demand victory and extol Truman's forebearance in Korea at one and the same time.[29] There is no inexpensive, mechanical solution to the danger of local aggression; there is no way of escaping from an effort long sustained. In every crisis there will be a need for clear and cool heads and for the type of courage which made and preserved the United States. So will it be. Who has claimed that it would be otherwise?[30]

CHAPTER VI

"A Bigger Bang for a Buck"

THE DOCTRINE OF MASSIVE RETALIATION has been attacked on a new count. It has been asserted that the Eisenhower administration has tried to achieve "a bigger bang for a buck," or what Adlai Stevenson called on March 6, 1954, "national security in the large economy size." From the beginning, the real purpose of the administration has allegedly been to balance the budget, as it promised to do in 1952. The administration has been unwilling to demand from the American people the sacrifices necessary for the security of America. It has thus displayed a lack of leadership at home, just as it has deceived the world at large with Mr. Dulles' bluff and bluster.

No responsible citizen is interested in balancing the budget if national defense and security are in jeopardy. The economy argument against massive retaliation raises an accusation that is precise because of its gravity and because of the base motives attributed to the administration by its critics. Unfortunately, it is an accusation that is easy to formulate but difficult to support. It has been even more difficult to conduct the argument in a manner that is consistent with the general line of reasoning followed in the debate as a whole. As Representative Price put it on March 29, 1954, nobody criticized the Republicans "for what they are proposing or doing, but for what they are not doing."[1] Adlai Stevenson spoke in the same way on March 6, 1954, when he claimed that the administration had been caught in a set of conflicting promises—to

cut the budget and to strengthen American security. It decided for
the former, he said, "because the one thing that could not be cut,
the *sine qua non* of our security was the new weapons and air
power." Since this one thing had been previously described as a
mad race leading to annihilation, the inconsistency of the argument has been self-evident from the start.

In a phrase typical of liberal intellectualism, Dean Acheson
wrote in the *New York Times Magazine* of April 15, 1956, that we
were "relaxing our efforts, very greatly relaxing them. The figures
leave no doubt of it. How great a gamble is being made of us, we
private citizens cannot know; factors are involved too secret and
complicated for useful public debate."[2] Appropriation figures are
not secret. They are established by Congress, which has the Constitutional power to levy taxes and to provide for the common defense of the United States. Now during all except four of the last
twenty-seven years, the Democratic party has been in control of
Congress, and if "a gamble is being made of us," the Democratic
party surely has its share of responsibility. In addition, appropriation figures are not as conclusive as Mr. Acheson seemed to claim.
The administration requests the new obligational authority which
it deems necessary in view of a well-established program of military procurement and expenditures. Enormous sums are carried
over from one fiscal year to the next. In past years, unexpended
funds have exceeded thirty billion dollars per year. The money
thus available for expenditure is always far in excess of appropriations.

The problem of large budget carry-overs has often been confusing. It must be borne in mind, however, that modern weapons are
so complicated that specifications require much time to prepare.
They demand protracted negotiations with defense contractors,
and technological difficulties or technological progress also complicate procurement. It takes several years, for instance, to build
a large warship. Although the full cost of the vessel is appropriated
in a given year, only the cost of the hull might be incurred before
the end of that particular fiscal year; propulsion equipment, armaments, electronics, and other items might not be contracted for

until much later. The result is that both obligated and unobligated funds are carried over from one fiscal year to the next.

Congress does not determine the level of actual expenditures, and this might be the best starting point for anyone who wants to prove that our security has been endangered for the sake of economy. Expenditures are made by the administration from available funds, but they have not been characterized during the past few years by sharp reductions; on the contrary, they have been marked by stability. The level of defense spending in the past six years proves that any argument based on sheer budget figures is a complete fallacy. As a matter of fact, the whole notion of a budget cut is meaningless, for it is essentially relative to other budget figures.

It is true that within a framework of relatively stable expenditures the United States has been forced to shift to new weapons systems which have become increasingly expensive and which have consequently squeezed available funds from conventional armaments. The heavy bomber we used near the end of World War II cost $600,000; the B-52 costs $8,000,000 and requires expensive tankers for refueling. The Nike-Ajax missile costs three times as much per battalion as the anti-aircraft gun it is replacing, and the Nike-Hercules costs three times more. A nuclear submarine is nine times more expensive than the conventional craft used during the last war. One submarine loaded with sixteen Polaris missiles will cost about $120,000,000. Modern weapons are so expensive that only the naïve can speak of "a bigger bang for a buck."

The crushing monetary weight of modern weaponry is no excuse for not achieving balanced security, but it is a reason for being increasingly alert to the damage that could result from extravagance and the rigidity of concepts. The critics are guilty of both. Their reasoning has led them in two mutually exclusive directions: it has tended to oppose change and it has leaned toward the development of new weapons on deadlines shorter than is both wise and necessary.

The critics seem to be particularly disturbed about cuts in military personnel and conventional forces. But at the outbreak of the

Korean War, the United States had approximately 1,500,000 men under arms, ten Army divisions, 243 combat ships, and a naval aviation force of 1,200 fighting planes; the Marine Corps had dropped to 74,000 men, and the Air Force was composed of 48 groups and 8,600 aircraft. Any criticism of the "New Look" refers to the goals reportedly established by the National Security Council on October 1, 1951, namely, 21 Army divisions, 409 combatant ships, three divisions and three wings for the Marine Corps, and 143 wings for the Air Force by June 30, 1954.

It would be untrue to say that the administration has dramatically departed from this program, except with respect to total military manpower, which was brought from a peak of 3,700,000 men in the last quarter of fiscal year 1952 to its present level of approximately 2,500,000 men. But in view of budget limitations, not to cut manpower might have been an intolerable waste. As the President said on August 9, 1956, one man can now fire a machine gun at the rate of 700 rounds per minute. In flintlock days, he said, 1,400 men were needed to get off that many shots, and yet no one would claim that because only one man is shooting—instead of 1,400—there has been any reduction of firepower. He declared on October 5, 1956, that since 1953 the administration had pointed out time and again that "new machines, new capabilities of a mechanical sort make it possible to do occasionally with fewer men." And the President concluded that "if we can do it with fewer men, of course, we will do it."

Personnel cuts do not always amount to combat personnel cuts. On June 20, 1955, Senator Saltonstall claimed that at the end of fiscal year 1953, the Army had about two non-combat personnel for each man in the combat units; by the end of fiscal year 1956, the ratio was to be one to one. To put it in another way, the Army declined in total numbers by 506,000 men from 1953 to 1956, but fully 87 per cent of the total reduction was made in the non-combat category. Any effort to hold expenditures to a given figure while costs are rising would lead to retrenchments in some categories; any retrenchment would leave military chiefs "all equally dissatisfied," said Secretary Wilson. But figures are relative to other figures. It is not enough to say that we have 14 Army divisions instead of 21 or 105 air wings instead of 137 or 143; still less does it suffice to say that the subject is too complicated for useful public debate. Once made, the accusation must be proved and alternative proposals made in due course.

The critics did not have the answers, and they have repeatedly said so. In the fall of 1956, Mr. Stevenson wanted to eliminate the "monetary and human waste" of the draft. On September 29, 1956, he made it clear that he wanted, of course, stronger defenses and added that the Democrats had fought "hard to prevent the administration from putting dollars ahead of defense." But his point was that "conditions change, and no conditions have changed more in our time than the conditions of warfare. Nothing is more hazardous in military policy than rigid adherence to obsolete ideas." He also told the convention of the American Legion that "many military thinkers believe that the armies of the future—a future now upon us—will employ mobile technically trained and highly professional units, equipped with tactical atomic weapons." Since Mr. Stevenson's conversion to massive retaliation had never been announced, it was startling to hear him talk about the "future now upon us." It was to avoid this "rigid adherence to obsolete ideas" that the administration had attempted to adjust our defenses to the realities of the atomic age, and it was this very adjustment that Mr. Stevenson had called "national security in the large economy size."

Thus in every crisis, public opinion will protest against the inescapable reality now upon us. The same outcry will be heard again and again: We are not ready; the divisions of the Strategic Army Corps exist on paper only; our divisions in Korea have been filled, to a considerable extent, with Korean personnel; NATO should raise fifty divisions; we should mobilize and send more troops to Germany.

"What would you do with more ground forces in Europe?" President Eisenhower asked on March 11, 1959; does anyone have any idea? How many divisions would be needed to win a ground war in that region? Is it truthful to pretend that an army of 870,000 men is a small army? What would we do with more troops in Korea? It is easier not to answer such questions and to assert that the administration wants us, as Representative Flood said on February 18, 1959, "to applaud the emperor's new clothes."[3] And if the President says that the budget is adequate, Walter Lippmann writes that "nobody is prepared to believe that by a wonderfully lucky coincidence" the money needed for our defense is just the amount that "we can afford to spend if the budget is to be balanced without raising taxes."[4] The defense of the budget has been mistaken for the defense of the United States. The President claims that Lenin has said that we will spend ourselves into bankruptcy—" a wholly unverifiable quotation." The whole Communist ideology is based upon the assumed economic instability of the capitalist system, but Joseph Alsop writes in the *New York Herald Tribune* of March 13, 1959, that it is "a transparent, glaring and rather ridiculous fraud" and that there arises the question of why a President of the United States should be "parroting such nonsense."[5]

The partisan rebellion against defense retrenchments is a classic example of political double talk. It now seems to be a well-established practice for the administration to freeze extra-defense funds, appropriated by Congress against its will, and for Congress to grant, in the form of supplemental appropriations, whatever money it refused to grant to the administration during the preceding session. Furthermore, the opposition challenged the administration to present what Representative Mahon called on May 9, 1956, "a more imaginative answer than just money and more money."[6] Senator Douglas said on July 1, 1957, that there were twenty million Americans who had served in the armed forces; every one of these men knows, he said, that great economies could be affected "without the slightest damage" to security. "The military have a built-in bias against economizing," the Senator continued. "It goes so far that frequently they will sacrifice military muscle in order to maintain or increase administrative fat. . . . Let those who may be tempted to raise the cry of national security . . . ask themselves whether it is not they who are reducing our military security in order to protect unneeded paper-pushers, overweight chairborne generals, useless plush and luxury, and a multitude of free riders."[7]

A stronger defense is not necessarily a more expensive defense. If thirty-three billion dollars will not give us a strong national defense, neither will thirty-four billion dollars. And while cutting appropriations, the opposition described Soviet power as overwhelming! In this manner, the administration was purposely crucified on the two arguments of growing Soviet power, the gradually whittling away of relative American power, and the cry for more imaginative answers to the problem of security than money and more money.[8]

We therefore conclude that partisanship has failed to prove that the defense program achieved by the Eisenhower administration within the limits of a balanced budget has jeopardized national security because too much emphasis has been placed on air-atomic power at the expense of conventional armaments. As a matter of fact, the debate on this particular point was so vague that it preferred to turn to irrelevant issues.

The Republicans have contended that the United States is fortunate enough to have its defense in the hands of an experienced military leader. Senator Knowland said on June 2, 1956, that it seemed sensible to think that President Eisenhower would not knowingly recommend to Congress a program "which would adversely affect the security of the American people for our survival as part of the free world of free men."[9] But partisanship retorted that the administration wanted to make of this debate what Adlai Stevenson called on October 23, 1954, "a public exercise of a personality cult." The Democrats turned it into a debate on policies and principles; this forced the great issues into what they called "the broad daylight of free discussion." There is no place in a democracy for the concept that the President cannot do wrong. The great issues and the principles remained as confusing as ever —if they were discussed at all, in broad daylight or otherwise— and in their effort to rid themselves of the personality cult, the critics of the administration extolled the valor and authority of other Army generals, all of them great leaders whose knowledge of military affairs was unquestioned. They closed ranks behind General Matthew B. Ridgway.

Representative Flood claimed on May 10, 1956, that the former Army Chief of Staff "was fired for telling us the truth."[10] Now this particular truth was not very interesting nor very important. The State of the Union Message of January 7, 1954, mentioned that the appropriations figures submitted to Congress for fiscal year 1955 were based "on a new military program unanimously recommended by the Joint Chiefs of Staff."[11] This program first comprised the development of a stable, long-range military policy, a concept which General Ridgway heartily endorsed as far as could be ascertained. It also included budgetary and manpower limitations which were reluctantly accepted by the Joint Chiefs—subject, of course, to reservations with respect to world conditions in 1957. These reservations included a stable settlement in Korea and Indochina and the rearmament of West Germany and Japan. Since the administration immediately proceeded to apply the program in terms of manpower reductions and since the stated assumptions on which the agreement was reached were not fully realized, General Ridgway felt entitled to make strong criticisms of the national policy. In a series of articles published in 1956, the General declared that "as a combat soldier" he had been "shot at from ambush and bombed by planes" which he thought were friendly but that he had never before experienced "a greater sense of surprise and shock" than he felt when he read the text of the State of the Union Message of January 7, 1954. He spoke of the military budget as a "directed verdict" and referred to pressures brought upon him in order to make his "military judgment conform to the views of higher authority" as pressures that were "sometimes subtly, sometimes crudely applied."[12]

In his press conference of February 2, 1955, President Eisenhower stated that the responsibility of determining manpower strengths was his. "General Ridgway was questioned in the Congress as to his personal convictions and, naturally, he had to express them," the President said. "His responsibility for national defense is . . . a special one, or, in a sense, parochial. He does not have the over-all responsibility that is borne by the Commander in Chief, and by him alone, when it comes down to making the recommendations to the Congress." Since it was not possible to invoke General Ridgway's personal authority without questioning his own good faith, the President said on January 20, 1956, that if he had ever made "a military decision out of deference to internal politics," he had been guilty of violating his "best determinations."

Other military men have resigned because they could not stay in the service "in good conscience." As the story goes, any proponent of bold new ideas first risks his career by being frank with Congress and then feels that it is more important for him to present his views publicly and dramatically than to remain ineffective in the service. The political prophets of doom will shove him into the arena of partisan politics and "egg him on," said Representative Scrivner on January 23, 1958, to a point where he is in open conflict over a decision made by his military superiors.[13] This practice helps no one. As President Eisenhower said on May 23, 1956, "the day that discipline disappears from our forces, we will have no forces."

The personality of former Secretary of Defense Charles E. Wilson was another distracting issue. General Gavin called him "the most uninformed man and the most determined to remain so." Representative Flood said on May 9, 1956, that Secretary Wilson had "a special and peculiar genius for saying the wrong thing at the wrong time." His chronic "foot-in-the-mouth" disease was illustrated by a long catalog of famous sayings. He spoke at will of draft-dodgers, kennel-fed dogs, and professional fearmongers. In January, 1955, he described the Formosa crisis as a mere ripple in the international situation. Congress restored fifteen thousand men to the Marine Corps in fiscal year 1956, and Mr. Wilson called this "a pretty snappy decision." He refused to comply. Asked whether he had not, in effect, vetoed an act of Congress, he answered that he had. He had no consultations with the President on the matter. Since the problem of legislative prerogative is delicate, the Attorney General might have been consulted, but the Secretary did not think it necessary.[14] Mr. Wilson described as "phony" Congressional efforts to increase funds for B-52's. This prompted Senator Chavez to say on June 22, 1956, that "the difficulty of the Secretary of Defense is that he forgets he is not running General Motors but is working for the public. He cannot get over the idea that notwithstanding his success with General Motors, as a public servant he is behaving as a child."[15] For that reason, perhaps, Mr. Wilson's political frolics did not cause any bitterness and even came to be regretted in Washington.

Since 1955, startling revelations concerning Soviet technological progress have been made, and this has given the administration's critics a badly needed chance to substantiate their charge that security has been sacrificed to budget economy. The pace at which the Soviets succeeded in building air power was the first tangible indication of the Soviet Union's real capacities. It was thought that the Soviets could not duplicate the B-29 in less than six years; they did it in two years. It was believed that the Russians could reproduce the British jet engine that came into their possession; in less than one year, they had produced a better version. As a defense against our B-36, they designed the MIG-15 and built fifteen thousand of these between 1948 and 1952. Moreover, they were quick to display supersonic aircraft. To say the least, American opinion was particularly distressed by Russian long-range bombers. On May Day in 1955, the Soviets showed more than forty new medium jet bombers—already displayed in quantity the year before. On the same occasion, they also displayed ten or more heavy, long-range, all-jet bombers—Bisons—although they had shown only one such plane the year before.

Astonishing Soviet progress was not the only disturbing factor in our defense. On May 2, 1956, General LeMay declared before a Senate committee that fifty-seven B-52's had been produced by January 1, 1956—sixteen of which had been rejected by the Air Force. After January 1, 1956, twenty-one aircraft were built, but only six were accepted. As one recalls, this mass rejection was brought about by the serious failure of one of the components in the B-52's electrical system, a fault which had caused one plane to crash in the winter of 1955. An intelligence report had placed Soviet production of Bisons at one hundred in May, 1956. On this basis it was considered plausible that the Soviets were working toward a peak production of twenty-five bombers per month and that they would possess a fleet of eight hundred heavy bombers by January, 1958. In contradistinction, our production of B-52's had not exceeded four or five a month. In spite of the speed-up ordered by the Air Force in 1955, some months passed without any delivery at all.

The critics suddenly became the apologists of super-massive retaliation. If America is attacked, it will be by Russia; if Russia attacks, it will be by air. Every other military asset possessed by the United States was nullified, together with the 200 divisions, 2,500 ships, and 32,000 aircraft of our allies. If the attack comes by air, asked Representative Cannon on May 29, 1957, how could the Navy intercept bombers and missiles flying at tremendous speeds so far above that they would be neither heard nor seen? "I ask anyone here to answer," he said. "How could the Army protect Detroit, San Francisco, Cleveland or New York? . . . How could the Army, with all its divisions . . . prevent the bombing of a single city? Let anybody answer. The war will be lost or won in the air. Every capital ship of the Navy would be sunk in the first few hours. . . . Within six hours nothing would remain of the United States Navy but the submarines. If our Air Force lost control of the air, our armies would be panic-stricken mobs in full flight." The one thing that stands out like the "headlight on a locomotive on a moonless midnight," the Representative concluded, is that in case of war, there will be no time for the Army and the Navy to "nibble around the edges."[16]

Economy-minded politicians thus formed an unholy alliance with die-hard exponents of air supremacy. It is not without reason that Senator Humphrey compared one of his colleagues, Senator Symington, to Cato the Elder.[17] As long as the walls of Carthage were standing, Rome was not safe. Soviet power will continue to grow, and those who demand more of everything will feel safer. But how much will they demand? The air-power protagonists did not demand thousands of B-52's, nor do the conventionalists demand forty Army divisions; but the critics demand seventeen heavy bomber wings instead of eleven. "Asking a military man how much money he would like to have," Representative Mahon said quite rightly on June 29, 1956, "is like asking a farmer or a rancher how much land he would like to have. He will say, 'Oh, not much; just that land that adjoins me.' Asking a photographer if he wants another picture will always bring the reply, 'Just one more.' With the Department of Defense, it is just one more billion dollars."[18]

Partisan criticism is relative to numbers rather than to strategic requirements, and this is the one approach that makes no sense at all. More than five years have passed since the policy of massive retaliation was declared. The opposition claims that they were vital years which we lost because emphasis was placed upon economic strength instead of military strength—"the years that the locusts have eaten," said Senator Kennedy in his theatrical speech of August 14, 1958.[19] It would have been very foolish, however, to assume that the Soviets would use them to build up an offensive air force. As Representative Scrivner put it on May 9, 1956, the Russians "would be complete dolts if they had not improved."[20] It would be vain to discount Soviet accomplishments, but let us remember that massive retaliation as a strategy was predicated on the assumption that development of Soviet power was unavoidable and that it settled on the perspective that the U.S.S.R. would one day achieve parity with the United States in striking power.[21]

On May 9, 1956, President Eisenhower warned against what he called "the number racket." The United States wants to deter, not to defeat, and the destructiveness of modern weapons is such, he said, that "enough is certainly aplenty." "Should we attempt to stay ahead of the Soviets in the over-all size of our air force and in the numbers of aircraft to be produced," the House Appropriations Committee Report asked in 1956, "or should we attempt to maintain what is determined to be a sufficient air force equipped with the best modern aircraft to act as a deterrent to any possible aggression?"[22] Obviously, our present strategy is based upon the latter determination. "It is vital that we get what we believe we need," the President said on May 4, 1956, and "that does not necessarily mean more than somebody else."

To put the question more bluntly, can our bombers get through? The State of the Union Message of January 9, 1958, emphatically asserted that "even if we assume a surprise attack on our bases, with a marked reduction in our striking power, our bombers would immediately be on their way in sufficient strength," to accomplish their mission. The Message also said that "every informed government knows this. It is no secret."[23] This asssertion has not been challenged by the opposition.

One must also keep in mind the relativity of the concept of control of the air. President Eisenhower said on May 18, 1955, that "anybody with a certain amount of air force in action" can gain control "over a place where he chooses to concentrate" his air force for a given period of time, "even in the face of quite great general superiority on the other side." As of now, there is no great general superiority in bombers on the Communist side. On February 26, 1957, the Secretary of Defense announced that the previous intelligence estimate of the number of Bisons which the Soviets had in operation as of July 1, 1956, had been exaggerated. It was assumed in 1958 that they had only 250 instead of the 800 which the opposition asserted they would have at that time. On April 18, 1957, the administration announced a new production schedule which brought procurement down to the rate first established in 1955. The partisan assertion that the Communists were ahead of the United States in the quantity of long-range bombers proved to be as unfounded in fact as it was in principle.[24]

The B-52 controversy paled into insignificance with the advent of the Soviet long-range missiles. For an extended period after World War II, the United States had no ballistic missile program worth mentioning. President Eisenhower said on October 9, 1957, that "until there were very great developments in the atomic bomb, it did not look profitable and economical to pursue that course very much and our people did not go into it very earnestly until somewhere along about 1953." Soviet testing of ballistic missiles had been detected ever since 1955; late in 1956, the testing rate became steady, and in August, 1957, the Soviet Union announced that its first intercontinental ballistic missile had been successfully fired. The Russian announcement was not very definite and "more notable," said President Eisenhower, "for what it didn't say than for what it did say." Yet on October 5, 1957, the Russians announced that the first earth satellite had been hurled into space the day before. The first sputnik was followed by others, and new spectacular achievements were predicted.

These facts were not easy to evaluate. The State of the Union Message of January 9, 1958, said that there was, at the time, "a consensus of opinion," that we were "probably somewhat behind the Soviets in some areas of long-range ballistic missile development."[25] It is difficult to imagine that the administration would deliberately misinform the American people on a matter of such importance. As our own missile program continued to progress, the only tangible fact about the Soviet lead seemed to be that the Soviets were producing a single-chamber rocket engine with a thrust great enough to propel large missiles for great distances. It was known that the Soviets fired several intercontinental missiles at full range from 1957 to 1958.[26] The launching of earth satellites proved, of course, that the Russians had designed the system of sensitive controls necessary to put a satellite into orbit. It should be kept in mind, however, that the guidance system needed to fire weapons for a useful purpose is much more demanding, and "until you know something about their accuracy," the President said on October 9, 1957, "you know nothing at all about their usefulness in warfare."

The race might thus be much closer than exaggerated reports appear to indicate. There is as yet no real evidence of any overwhelming superiority on the Russian side. As was the case in the B-52 controversy, the critics projected the problem into the future by referring to the "years of the gap." Among other doubtful news stories, Senator Symington peddled figures showing our position vis-à-vis that of the Communists in future years. He claimed that in 1960, the United States would have 30 ICBM's to the U.S.S.R.'s

100; in 1964, America would have 130 to Russia's 2,000. In their efforts to prove the foolishness of U.S. policy in the matter, the critics claimed that intercontinental ballistic missiles could easily be mass-produced and that both our Atlas and Titan would prove to be effective and could be ready if the administration would make the necessary effort to put them into production. While minimizing every American achievement in order to prove that we were in mortal danger, they used our very accomplishments to show that the problem was leadership, courage, and dollars.[27]

In testimony released on April 29, 1956, Major General B. A. Schriever said that the intercontinental ballistic missile could be produced just by applying "the state of the art." He added that there was "not an invention required to get the job done. It is a systems engineering job of great magnitude," and no more.[28] This double-edged phrase was reassuring to the extent that very great Russian achievements did not appear to be so formidable in the long run. But if the problem was just to apply "the state of the art," why did the United States allow itself to fall behind in such a critical field as missile development?

It would be unfair to make the present administration a scapegoat for problems that lie elsewhere and deeper. It is highly convenient to believe that if the administration had spent more money on missiles, everything would be all to the good in American education, science, defense, and national attitudes. No critics are more vocal than those who wanted to give Los Alamos back to the Indians in 1945 and who opposed the development of the hydrogen bomb. It is perfectly true that the American economy could support, without hurting itself, greater defense expenditures than the administration has recommended, but would the few billion dollars that it could thus support make so much difference?

There can be no doubt, in view of Communist economic expansion, that national solvency is an indispensable requirement for keeping our total security strong. As a matter of fact, our missile program was already so advanced in 1957 that it would not have been accelerated very much, if any, by the expenditure of more money; a certain amount of time is necessary in order to go from one test to the next in a profitable manner. The same answer applies to the demand, which came from every quarter after the launching of the first Soviet sputnik, for some kind of "crash" program that would have subordinated every other consideration to the singular purpose of firing an intercontinental missile. Such a program, under the authority of a "czar" endowed with stern instructions "to knock heads together" whenever necessary, might have been desirable years ago, but in the present state of affairs, it would retard progress. This does not mean, of course, that an acceleration of the ICBM program was impossible. The program was speeded up. The administration reduced what is called "lead time" when it decided to proceed with the construction of the facilities and the infrastructure that will be necessary for the use of these missiles once they are perfected. This could be done for the most advanced weapons, but not for those we use in the transition. Now the very people who complained that a lack of a sense of urgency dominated our missile program were the first to complicate problems of technical evaluation with political pressures. Any attempt by the administration to eliminate duplication of effort brought about the leakage of secret discussions and produced immediate reactions in Congress. Defense reorganization, for example, was opposed on the ground that the past showed that power cannot be concentrated in a man or a group without producing a Hitler or a Stalin.[29]

As in every instance, partisanship nurtures hysteria without committing itself to accomplishment. It demands the "blunt" truth, and if the truth is not blunt, it is no truth at all. The situation is always as "serious as it is" because the American people have not been given "the facts." Paul M. Butler said on November 8, 1957, that the Soviet missile threat cannot be "tossed out with quips and slogans, with tranquilizing phrases and golf-course decisions." Senator Fulbright declared on February 8, 1958, that "a bland diet of sugar-coated half-truths"[30] could have carried us into extinction—but for himself—in the naïve belief that Communism was defeating itself. President Eisenhower repeats every day that our prestige was never higher; John Foster Dulles pretends that the Soviet Union is a lopsided society. Those "comfortable illusions" were shattered, James Reston wrote on March 2, 1958. "Much of the political debate in this country, as all viewers of television know," he said, "sounds like the droning of two old bagpipes."[31]

There should be a crusade for truth. American policy belongs to the people because it is the people who will have "to do the dying by the millions," said Senator Morse on August 14, 1958, "if American policy is not properly administered."[32] Truth has a better chance of emerging in the free market place of thought. "There has never been a free government which was secret," Senator Symington declared on February 10, 1956, "and there has never been a secret government which was free."[33] Only the most strenuous exertions by those who grasp how information is vital to freedom can preserve democratic government against those who think that secrecy is vital to security. President Eisenhower "has drifted apart from the intellectual community," James Reston wrote in the *New York Times* of December 8, 1957; he has filled up "his social hours with bantering lockerroom cronies, and denied himself the mental stimulus that is always available to any President." If military men are enjoined to refrain from making public statements, public opinion professes to be angry; if they disclose information, they are praised. The senseless walls of super-secrecy must be broken down; they are keeping nothing from the Soviets, but they are preventing a democratic cross-fertilization of ideas.

President Eisenhower has frequently professed to be astonished at the amount of information that others get and he does not—a device that is just as good as any other to get rid of an annoying inquisitor. The President "ought to know that we do read the papers," Senator Mansfield said on February 10, 1956, "and that we get what is public information. We put the pieces together and come up with a fairly complete story."[34] The people are entitled to the truth, and they do not find it in rosy State of the Union Messages; Congressmen never divulge any classified information because all of what they say is in the newspapers. But if everything is public, is it secret?

President Truman wrote in his memoirs that for the price of a good clipping service, the enemies of the United States could easily acquire much information that foreign governments normally obtain through more expensive processes. And President Eisenhower remarked on May 4, 1956, that "most of the secrecy" in the thermonuclear and atomic areas is "in conformity with the law that is written by the Congress." Although there is some truth in the notion of security through achievement rather than secrecy, is secrecy a real problem in a country whose people know how many B-52's are produced every month, when the Atlas will be operational, and how successful the firing of a Thor was?[35]

The myth of secrecy illustrates how partisanship finds it advantageous to distract public opinion with false problems and to sanction attitudes against which it would be infinitely better for the American people to react. The same remark should be made about the assertion that the Russian sputnik was a shattering blow to American leadership. "By a single spectacular scientific achievement," Mr. Stevenson said on December 9, 1957, we have been brought face to face with the fact that not only are Russian children better educated than our own but "perhaps most serious of all—that Russia stands today in the eyes of the majority of the members of the world's population as more skillful, more powerful, yes, and ironically, more peaceful than we are."

Mr. Stevenson's revealing proposition assumes that American prestige was formerly based upon a superior power and technology—the very reason that is always given in partisan debates for the jealousy and the misgivings of world opinion toward America. It also assumes that the free world has no stake in American power and that the allegedly humiliating reversal the United States has suffered was nothing but a most exhilarating experience.[36] If Mr. Stevenson meant what he said, he would believe that the nation which demonstrates its technological superiority is bound to win the battle of the minds. This is what is said now that the United States appears to lag behind. In better times, however, a pretended infatuation with weapons and technological superiority was denounced as the ominous expression of our materialistic outlook, and to compound the confusion, the same alleged materialism is now being described as anti-intellectualism and complacency.[37]

Let us conclude, however, that it is not Mr. Eisenhower's smugness or the boastfulness of our Secretary of State that has been shattered by the sputniks, nor is it the naïve self-admiration attributed to the American people by their liberal critics. The sputnik has indeed awakened us to the need of silencing the old bagpipes of a decadent liberalism; it has awakened our friends to the dangers of anti-Americanism. This the sputnik has done, and for that reason it may go down in history as Mr. Dulles said on January 16, 1958, as "Mr. Khrushchev's boomerang."

The intercontinental ballistic missile has often been described as the ultimate weapon. It has been said that the ICBM could completely upset the balance of power between East and West. This is not true, of course. The missile perfects still further a balance of terror already existing; it is a means of delivery. The ultimate weapon is still the hydrogen bomb. Yet it cannot be denied that Soviet future capabilities make it urgent for us to re-examine once more the validity of our present strategic concepts. The line followed by partisanship in this necessary self-evaluation is exceedingly simple. "The Communists respect only power," Senator Symington said on August 23, 1958, "that is my premise."[38] In this life-and-death struggle with international Communism, it is plain, brute, military strength that counts, and we have been soft-soaped into a position of outright inferiority. The time has come to foster a dynamic foreign policy, not foster Dulles. What is this dynamic new policy? The only feature of this mysterious policy that has been stated is that it will not be massive retaliation.

Senator Kennedy said on August 14, 1958, that "our past reliance upon massive retaliation has stultified the development of new policy." The power foundation that stood behind our strategy is now lost; the Soviets are in the driver's seat; the prop is gone, and the alternative seems, to many, to be inaction and the fatalistic acceptance of the inevitability of defeat. "Up until now," Senator Jackson said in his Paul Revere speech of February 1, 1956, "the

Soviets have been put on notice that all-out Red aggression would be answered by our superior air-atomic strength."[39] And on May 9, 1956, Representative Mahon complained that in the past, Mr. Dulles "talked glibly about massive retaliation"; well, now, the Soviet Union has developed the same massive retaliation capability; and the "bleak fact is," he concluded, "that massive retaliation is rapidly becoming a two-way street."[40]

If Senator Kennedy quotes Mr. Kissinger about our alleged "Maginot-line reliance upon massive retaliation," it is because, with Kissinger, he identifies massive retaliation with overwhelming air-atomic superiority, a misconception for which there is no excuse whatsoever. As long as the United States truly possesses the ability to inflict upon the Soviet Union the kind of damage that she could never accept, massive retaliation will remain the only strategy that can preserve the peace. The greater Russia's capability, the more it will need to be deterred and the greater our reliance upon the strategy of massive retaliation. As the President said in his speech of November 13, 1957, "the Soviets must be convinced that any attack on us and our allies would result, regardless of damage to us, in their own national destruction." This is nothing new, indeed, but it is a truth that must be repeated as many times as it is overlooked.

Senator Lyndon Johnson said on March 9, 1959, that he wanted "to get the truth with the bark off." The truth is that the United States can destroy the Soviet Union, as Admiral Arleigh Burke said in his address of February 20, 1959, "in several ways, and several times over." There is no reason at all to assume that what Senator Kennedy so profoundly called "our exercises in brink-of-war diplomacy"[41] should become less obligatory or less effective than in the past. An inflated estimate of Soviet capabilities weakens our will, but a consciousness of our power does not eliminate the demands made upon us. An erratic public opinion can prove to be the true Achilles' heel of our security. Senator Kefauver said on March 12, 1959, that it was "dangerous to talk of balancing our budget with death and destruction waiting around the corner." A serious situation calls for serious debate. The defense debate has been noisy and hysterical. It has shown how the most serious issues can be debated without seriousness. Instead of working, too many people lectured about "inhibited thinking" in the government, about the "incredible ineptness" with which the administration has managed scientific resources, or just about salaries. As Senator Capehart noted on August 14, 1958, many "great" speeches are delivered in the United States Senate, speeches dealing in trite generalities and "praising this Senator, that Senator, and some other Senator, as in a mutual admiration society; referring to other Senators as being great Senators," and while selling the United States short, these speeches fail to offer any concrete solution to any problem.[42]

As President Eisenhower said on January 28, 1959, some people seem very prone "to give 100 per cent credence" to Soviet statements if they happen to touch upon their "anxieties." They dismiss as lies the assurances which they receive from their own leaders. The strange dialectics of partisanship thus reconcile what the President called the "hangdog attitude of humiliation" with the self-assured arrogance of querulous criticism. The remedy is a measure of national pride. In our "cold evaluation of brute facts," we must not succumb to Soviet bluff by taking Soviet boasts as facts. Never should we affirm as fact what is at best an opinion. If we should live up to the underdog strategy—as the opposition requests us to do—let us, without deceiving ourselves, affirm as mere opinion what could be fact. This would be a salutary discipline.[43]

On the other hand, public opinion is entitled to receive repeated and unqualified reassurances concerning our military capabilities. To provide for the ominous power of massive retaliation is the one responsibility now entrusted to the United States. It will not be an easy task. The work that lies ahead is Herculean, and it is quite conceivable that we may fail to meet it with an aggressiveness that is commensurate with the requirements of the situation. It must be prayerfully hoped that both the administration and the people will fully understand it.[44]

"Any orderly balance sheet of military strength must be in two parts," declared the State of the Union Message of January 9, 1958. "The first is the position as of today. The second is the position in the period ahead." No weapon in the development stage is an effective deterrent for the present, but unless we act now, we may lose our capacity in the future. On the other hand, we have made our own plans. "We want to keep adequate forces and we want to keep as strong in our hearts and our heads as we do in our military," President Eisenhower said on March 11, 1959, "and then carry forward our policies." It would be ruinous, he said, to be "pushed off" these plans "time and again by something suddenly described as a crisis." Every time one of these incidents occurs, "whether it is sputniks or it's Quemoy . . . or whatever it is," everybody seems to have "a new answer." As the President warned, "what we have to do is to stand steady . . . to be alert, to watch what we are doing, and to make certain that we know how and where we would have to produce action, if action became necessary." The "years of the gap" is a notion that can draw us, through fear, into making an all-out effort for being ready for a particular period of time at the expense of both current readiness and the development of future weapons. It is not possible to maintain a proper balance between expenditures for our forces-in-being and expenditures for future strength unless we are willing to maintain adequate retaliatory power and limited conventional forces while developing future weapons, and that is massive retaliation.[45]

On February 8, 1956, President Eisenhower asked his reporter audience the following question: "Can you picture a war that would be waged with atomic missiles, well knowing that atomic missiles can be of little value unless they have . . . a tremendously powerful explosive head on them?" The intercontinental missiles will not be as accurate as shooting a gun or dropping a bomb from a plane; whole salvos might have to be used on a single target. "Consequently," said the President, "you must visualize these things in such numbers and using the kind of ammunition that means just complete destruction." Such a war would not be "a contest," the President concluded, but simply "race suicide and nothing else." We have no need for what have been called "overkill" capabilities, nor does the answer to our predicament lie, as the President noted on November 13, 1957, in a "misguided attempt to eliminate conventional forces and rely solely upon retaliation." The defenses of the free world must be flexible enough to permit graduated retaliation. And while further cuts in our present conventional strength still appear feasible through better management and increased firepower, it seems certain that we are now approaching a limit below which it is not possible to reduce manpower still further. Even in the missile age there will always be a need for a sizable contingent of ground forces, for a navy of increasing strength, and for manned aircraft. Missiles impose such exacting requirements as the precise location of targets. They cannot be expected to become a total substitute for a general-purpose weapon like the airplane, which can be used against either fixed or moving targets and armed with either conventional or atomic weapons in both total and limited war.[46]

It seems astonishing that the administration has been placed on the defensive on this particular issue. General Gavin, for instance, wrote in *Life* magazine on August 11, 1958, that the Soviets had led us to believe that they were building a great long-range bomber force "when in fact they were investing heavily in ballistic missiles. They merely built and displayed before Western observers enough long-range manned bombers to cause apprehension." Since we "fell for it," much time and money was "wasted" in the B-52 program; we were "investing heavily in a weapons system that the Soviets themselves knew to be obsolescent."

Soviet missile capabilities do not necessitate our building up overwhelming conventional defenses on the assumption that the U.S.S.R. has now stalemated the West's atomic arsenal and could safely embark in local aggression of a conventional type.[47] In contradistinction, our own conventional strength must be adequate for dealing quickly and effectively with limited aggression. It needs not be superior to Communist conventional power, which remains, as in the past, checkmated by our capacity for massive retaliation. In other words, nothing should be changed with regard to the administration's doctrine on local aggression.

We can therefore conclude that our defense policy is as sound in 1959 as it was in 1954. It bears the stamp of brilliant statesmanship. God grant that we may one day say the same of the policies of the present administration's critics if they are ever entrusted with power and responsibility! More important to us than a missile gap is the frozen rigidity of our public opinion, its contradictions, its insincerity. After having been panicked into unwarranted fear, we were told that science will not save us, that "our missile program is the swan song of a dying civilization." We were told that security does not depend on weapons, that we do not need better missiles to destroy one another, "that the ones we have now will do the job adequately."[48] Along with Mr. Khrushchev, the liberals say that we are concerned with bigger television screens and bigger cars but not with the big ideas on which freedom depends. How could any new American missile be an answer to the Soviet mechta? If we were to develop a weapon more terrible than anything the Russians have, it would be a Pyrrhic victory. Yet Senator Lyndon Johnson accuses the administration of believing that the budget "can be balanced if we turn our back on opportunities and resign ourselves to the status of a second-class nation—weak, but thrifty."[49]

"Unpopular as it is in a time of fear," said Senator Morse on February 9, 1959, it should be said that the Soviet Union and the United States are "in violation of the moral law." When a nation violates the moral law, "it writes its own destruction. One cannot proceed with the immorality of a nuclear armament race if he believes in a God, and expect his civilization to survive."[50] In a public letter published in the *New York Times* of December 9, 1957, James Warburg expressed the "shame and anger" he felt at the spectacular failure of the satellite launching of December 6. The lesson he drew was that "the nuclear arms race is suicidal madness," no matter who is temporarily behind or ahead. "The arms race cannot be won; that leads to war." There should be, he wrote, a willingness to negotiate "which does not now exist in Washington." The administration is disarming, the Democratic Advisory Council declared on January 20, 1959, "not by negotiation, a solution that it apparently rejects, but by unilateral action." The United States should lead and be superior, but the arms race is madness. And yet, as usual, the reality of the situation is really quite simple. As long as it is necessary, the arms race is the most elementary form of political wisdom. There is no inconsistency between a policy of relative strength and negotiating in the hope of achieving some limited gains for peace.

CHAPTER VII

Massive Retaliation and World Opinion

IN HIS SPEECH OF MARCH 6, 1954, Adlai Stevenson expressed doubts about our allies' willingness to go along with massive retaliation as a strategy. It was true, in spite of assertions to the contrary, that the new strategy represented, at that time, a sharp break with past policies and that it had to meet the fate of all assertions of American leadership. First approached in an antagonistic spirit, massive retaliation was debated over the years without there ever being brought forth a formal recognition of its intrinsic validity.

This is not to say that our allies did not have any legitimate misgivings about the new strategy when it was first formulated, but the questions which arose at the time resulted from misunderstandings that could have been redressed by explanations supplied by the administration. Since the free world now has no strategy other than massive retaliation, it is not necessary to repeat here the various objections to American policy that were originally put forth by foreign statesmen. On the other hand, it cannot be denied that massive retaliation became the catalyst of anti-Americanism, for it was not possible to raise doubts about such a central point of our policy without putting in question American leadership in general. Our inquiry is thus forced to move from questions of military strategy to the overriding problem of the United States' position at the head of the anti-Communist coalition.

According to the administration's liberal opposition, America has all but lost the battle for the minds of the peoples of Asia and the Middle East. Justice William O. Douglas said on January 26, 1957, that the United States had "propped up decrepit war lords, financed medieval kingdoms and been the close ally, not of liberal leaders, but of the reactionary influences in Asian life." In an equally typical editorial published in the *Washington Post* of January 29, 1956, H. J. Morgenthau claimed that Dulles' statement that Goa was a Portuguese province had "exploded like a bomb among our friends, spreading consternation, derision and regret." In the same breath he said that "little needs to be said about Thailand, a traditionally misgoverned state with a traditionally quiescent population whom the revolution of Asia has bypassed." He described Pakistan as a "monstrosity of a state in whose viability, let alone defensibility, even few Pakistanis believe." The Chinese soldiers captured in Korea who refused to return to Communist China were described by Morgenthau as people "whom the Chinese Communists wanted to get rid of as liabilities." The 800,-000 refugees who left North Vietnam in 1954 were, in the majority, Roman Catholics who left "in a body under the leadership of their priests," and they certainly did not represent the true Asia either.

No one was spared, not even the late Prime Minister Nuri al-Said of Iraq or King Hussein of Jordan—a problem for American policy rather than an asset. The South Korean administration got the same treatment. On May 10, 1956, Senator Morse asked if the United States were not betraying its own heritage, as well as the people of Korea, "by rendering any support to totalitarian governments." The Rhee government was, according to the administration's critics, utterly reactionary. "If the chips were down," asked the Senator, "what sort of support could be expected from non-democratic governments which we are supporting in the name of the rationalization that they are a buffer against Communism?"[1] Little needs to be said, of course, about Chiang Kai-shek. On February 10, 1958, Senator Morse spoke of Spain and of Saudi Arabia. The administration is "pouring out, by way of gifts to that completely totalitarian state," he said, "millions of dollars of the American taxpayers' money to maintain the military forces of a dictatorship." What a degrading spectacle to see President Eisenhower bowing and scraping before a slave-trading tyrant! And Senator Morse added that "we ought to have our heads examined. It is pure fantasy. It does not make common horsesense. I have a mare that knows how to open farm gates. She has more sense than this policy reflects."[2]

This is a dismal picture indeed. Our allies in Asia and the Middle East are people who have lost the confidence of their countries; they consider their association with America to be the entering wedge into the U.S. Treasury. The democratic countries of Asia—the real and revolutionary Asia—have turned away from us. In Europe, the situation is no better. American policy is at best ineffective; at worst, the damage it does is completely out of proportion to its relative merits. According to Chester Bowles, "NATO has come to represent to most people jets, tanks, taxes, and American influence—the price that must be paid for military security against the Red Army."[3] Under the threat of the cold war, European nations have supported the North Atlantic Alliance, but always with little enthusiasm. Soviet tactics have now changed. It has become less certain than ever that American influence means security, and, consequently, American dictation has become increasingly irritating. The more people "think" about it, wrote James Warburg in the *Reporter* of June 14, 1956, the more irrelevant appears the American idea to build a shield of strength against Communist aggression in Europe. At any rate, France, the Continental bulwark of NATO, has withdrawn her divisions; the United Kingdom will "soon" do likewise; and German rearmament has given the U.S.R.R. "good" reason to believe that NATO could becomes an offensive alliance. Moreover, western Europe is not the main Soviet target; it is in the Middle East that the decisive battle for Europe will take place. In other words, NATO is obsolete.

The picture of the global failure of American policy drawn by American public opinion is astonishing in view of the fact that the universal value of Americanism is also asserted in no uncertain terms. On July 13, 1957, Senator Lyndon Johnson said that America should "not be fearful about the effects of Communist tactics" but should, "instead, proceed on the assumption that American ideals are so much stronger than anything the Soviets have to offer that the result of any clash will be a foregone conclusion."[4]

It is also asserted that none of the true objectives of American policy conflicts with neutralism, nationalism, or economic expansion in Asia and the Near East. Nasser represents honesty in government, devotion to the people's welfare, the dream of Arab unity. Nehru is the standard-bearer of democracy in Asia. The paradox is that any progress towards the objectives pursued by these great leaders is progress in the achievement of our own objectives. If the nationalists have come to see us as major foes, it must be because of our own ineptitude. How many more lessons must we learn—if time is given to us—to understand this?

The people who say these things speak with equal force about the fullness of the American spirit and the ideological emptiness of American policy. The bankruptcy of our leadership is unnecessary; it has no cause other than the doctrinaire, foolhardy attitude of our present policy-makers—people who have lost sight of the power of ideas in an era of total revolution. Our approach is barren because of our established illusions about the world. Among the crude stereotypes that paralyze creative thinking in government is the idea that states have been established for all time by a law of nature and have come to represent something like divine will. If there is a revolution, we should attempt to restore legitimate rulers and normalcy. We identify justice with the *status quo*, but there is simply nothing we can do to stop the revolution. Louis J. Halle wrote in the *New Republic* of August 18, 1958, that when rocks begin to fall from a mountainside, "the prudent mountaineer does not rush forward to catch them and stop them and put them back." He takes cover and waits. But Mr. Dulles has a penchant for obstinately getting hold of the wrong end of the stick and refusing to let the damn thing go. As was the case in regard to Lebanon, he concentrates on what William H. Stringer called in the *Christian Science Monitor* of July 26, 1958, "unimaginative rearguard actions."

None of the illusions we have is more deadly than what Mr. Halle called "the devil theory," a primitive, vulgar habit which imitates Communist thinking and attributes every trouble in the world to some Communist conspiracy that has been masterminded in the Kremlin. Mr. Dulles' bipolar world of good and evil, of cowboys and Indians, does not exist, of course. "As long as we are simply anti-Russian," Senator Morse said on March 2, 1957, "we are doomed to a sterile, negative policy of reacting to Russian initiative."[5] America is so obsessed with Communism that it must approach every issue in terms of anti-Communism. Its present leaders seem to forget that if Karl Marx had never been born and if the Soviet Union did not exist, the "same" problems would still bedevil the world. Millions would still be starving in India, the Arabs would fight Israel with the same hatred, and Governor Faubus of Arkansas would enforce the same segregationist policies.

Public opinion professes that this truth is particularly relevant to Asia. One of the most widely accepted slogans in American intellectual quarters is that Communism as an ideology is irrelevant in Asia. And while they also pretend that the Marxist philosophy contains some hard-core elements without which its "persistent intellectual attraction"[6] could not be explained, they constantly repeat that any opposition between Communism and anti-Communism does not make sense to the Asian masses. What the masses understand is the difference between reaction and revolution. In China, for instance, the "revolution" was an upsurge against years of social injustice and foreign dictation. On this point, the American liberals and the most rabid Asian neutralists are in perfect agreement. They all speak with great pathos about this tidal upheaval of hungry people struggling for food and freedom in Asia, Africa, and the Middle East. Communism—which again is irrelevant as an ideology—is described as "a great social movement" which the starving masses understandably identify with freedom, self-realization, and justice. How could the people of the Near East fear the loss of liberty? How could they lose something that they have never had?

So it is neither Russia nor Nasser who is responsible for the Arab revolution; it is history and the people. This is what Dulles has never understood, for he has given himself to the idolatry of

155

anti-Communism. This is why America has been turned from a land of hope into a land of reaction. This is why the blind negativism of American policy translated itself into threats and militarism.

Mr. Stevenson said on April 11, 1955, that "if the best hope for today's world is a kind of atomic balance, the decisive battle in the struggle against aggression may be fought not on the battlefields, but in the minds of men." And yet, he added, "too often of late we have turned to the world a face of stern military power . . . the rattling of the saber." The situation demands "more statesmanship than challenging enemies." The United States is the strongest of the free nations, and it is our task to find a way to provide "positive" leadership and to fill the world's moral vacuum with human values. Most of recent American aid has gone for the unproductive purpose of building armies—too weak to fight—in countries whose economies are unable to support them. India is forced against her will to take part in an arms race that she cannot afford because the United States is arming Pakistan. Money that does not go for military establishments is used to support totalitarian dictatorships; it is futile and wasteful. "A team of efficiency experts and public accountants," H. J. Morgenthau wrote in the *New Republic* of March 26, 1956, "might well have improved the operations of the Al Capone gang."

While we think more in terms of dollars and guns than in terms of people, the Soviet Union nurtures dreams of human development. Mr. Stevenson said on February 4, 1956, that "when we brag of massive retaliation and atomic intimidation, Russia talks of peace, of trade, of friendship, of economic development and the things that the sensitive, suspicious and hungry Asians want to hear." On April 21, 1956, he asserted that "we, whose position is fundamentally decent and honorable, we must now try to prove that we love peace as much as the Russians and are as much concerned with the problems of economic development and national independence as they are. It is fantastic, but true."

Once the militarism inherent is U.S. policy had been so denounced, it remained to brand military alliances as a threat to the peace. This has been done. Senator Kefauver declared in Los Angeles on April 20, 1956, that the administration's lack of concern for human values led to "the inescapable conclusion that the administration in Washington has no faith in peace and no hope of achieving it in its time." He added that the United States has deliberately sought to involve the new nations of Asia and the Middle East in military associations, although these countries well know, he said, that "they can exist and create better conditions of life for their people only in an atmosphere of peace." And it need not be said, he concluded, that such associations are not much stronger "in a military sense than the paper on which they are written." It would be naïve, of course, not to concede that in the interest of security, the United States can legitimately form alliances with countries with which it does not see eye to eye, but when expediency becomes the overriding impulse and is allowed to obscure all other considerations, a fatal process sets in. Because "we have persisted in construing the Communist threat to the underdeveloped world as essentially military," Mr. Stevenson said on April 21, 1956, "much of the world has come to think of us as militaristic and even a menace to peace."

It would be plain self-delusion not to recognize that the Soviet Union has interests in Asia and the Middle East. Walter Lippmann wrote in the *Washington Post* of July 29, 1958, that in his view, the paramount issue was not oil, "which the Arabs must sell to the West," nor Israel, "which is on the sidelines in the present crisis. It is not the revolutionary force of Nasserism." The real issue is Soviet determination "not to have the United States military power stationed on her southern flank," a new reason for blaming U.S. military involvement. How would we react if the U.S.S.R. stationed troops in Mexico and grouped the republics of Central America into an anti-American coalition?

Whatever the administration's obstinacy not to recognize legitimate Soviet interests and not to reach a settlement with Moscow, it remains that the great masses in Asia and the Near East are in full revolt against any form of political control from the West. In their desperate efforts to control intolerable misery, they are attracted to Communism as a way to resolve their problems. Soviet ideas are "less complicated"; they are "flexible," "untried," "exciting." All Asia is now convinced that any country which does not rapidly industrialize its economy is doomed to degeneracy. Some are watching the Indian experiment, for India is the country of revolution by consent. They are watching to see which pays off better, democracy or Communism. Most are already convinced that the great example of Soviet accomplishments promises them more rapid success. But the administration does not seem to understand that much of the future is staked on the success of Indian democracy, nor does it understand how great is the admiration for the "vigor" with which the U.S.S.R. and Red China have attacked the "real" problems of illiteracy, starvation, and the lack of industrial facilities.

It goes without saying that if the administration would attempt to counter the fascination allegedly exercised on the masses of Asia and the Middle East by Communist technological progress and stress the blessings of the American way of life, the idealists of both America and Asia would reject as loathing and repulsive materialism any suggestion that the patient Orient ever attempt to achieve the type of unspiritual mastery of man over his physical environment illustrated by Hollywood motion pictures. We are reminded that we cannot win friendship with dollars and machines. The decisive power lies with ideas and with people. Senator Fulbright said on February 8, 1958, that "fat, rich nations— like fat, rich old men, are prone to overestimate their powers." They believe that they are entitled to respect because of their money or at least, he said, they believe "that money will purchase the subservience of less fortunate people."[7] And yet when sputnik began to circle the globe, it was again said that the prestige which America enjoyed in Asia and Africa derived from our past technological achievements and not from our ideology.

All of this is replete with hopeless contradictions. There is not a single idea which deserves to retain the attention of a self-respecting individual. The wonder is that so many intelligent persons can assert, in dead earnest, that the American cowboy is as idolized in Asia and in Africa as Mr. Dulles is loathed. The prodigy is that the lurid images of anti-Americanism, instead of eliciting a just wrath from the American people, appear as enormous stumbling blocks that doom our foreign policy to failure and call for a drastic readjustment of approach. The contemptible union of criticism and self-criticism creates a truly formidable pressure against American policy. Public opinion dreams about the allies that we do not have, and it drags into the mud all those who seek American protection. It identifies itself with every lie and then claims that the important thing is not whether it is true that the United States wants war but that Mr. Krishna Menon says so. It is fantastic but true.

The most revealing feature of this self-indictment is its universality. What is said of Asia and the Near East is also said of Latin America and Europe. It is claimed that NATO is people and that the military functions of the Atlantic Alliance are barren and destructive. The European nations consider economic development to be more important than military gear. Rifles, missiles, and atomic bombs cannot win the battle of minds in Europe any more than in Asia. As Mr. Stevenson said on October 9, 1954, ever since Mr. Eisenhower became President, "all around the world" our "good name and the respect of both friend and foe has suffered, and any pretense to the contrary is misleading and dangerous."

The idea that NATO is people fits admirably with the vague idealism of our intelligentsia and is consistent with the general pattern of national defeatism which characterizes public opinion in this country. It leads once again to a self-contradictory reasoning: the Soviet threat is unchanged, more ominous than ever, but the power of the Atlantic Alliance is allegedly in a crumbling stage; the whole concept of a military shield against Soviet aggression in Europe is out of date; when it praises NATO's achievements the administration is accused of being complacent, but when it asks our allies not to lose sight of what is still to be done, it is inflexible. And to make matters worse, our allies talk about transforming NATO into a "community," and they do so because they just want to relax; relaxation makes them more dependent upon American power, yet they want to de-Americanize the Alliance; they speak of increased interdependence in order to achieve more independence.[8]

These movements of opinion paralyze American policy and tend to make both political co-operation and an increased military effort more difficult to attain. Yet it seems evident that if NATO would fail as a military alliance, it would be vain to expect that other forms of Allied co-operation could be successfully devised.

As a military organization, NATO is worth what massive retaliation is worth. American opinion still has doubts about the fact that our strategy has been fully accepted by our allies. This should be dismissed as a projection of its own attitudes on the matter. It is not a little amusing that the British White Paper on defense, issued on April 4, 1957, was greeted by many American critics of massive retaliation as a courageous and original statement, although the British statement did little more than repeat the strategic concepts adopted by the administration since 1953 in a form more striking than any single American document but in many instances with the very words used by American statesman for many years.[9]

The White Paper recognized that the time had come to revise "not merely the size, but the whole character" of Britain's military defense. It accepted as basic postulates the long-haul concept, the reliance on new weapons, and the principle that the British economy had to be maintained in form despite stable and flexible military procurement. It also stated, with great clarity, that there can be no real defense against modern weapons and that the "overriding consideration" had to be "to prevent war rather than to prepare for it." It also repeated the well-known doctrine that "the only existing safeguard against major aggression is the power to threaten retaliation with nuclear weapons."

In retrospect, the British policy is a complete vindication of American policy. The features that are specific to British defense indicate a reliance on atomic weapons and missiles that is more drastic than in American strategy—for instance sharp cuts in manpower and discontinuance in aircraft research at a certain date.

But despite such revolutionary changes in military planning, the White Paper made it clear that the defense of the United Kingdom was possible only as part of the free world's collective security. It claimed that the trend was "toward the creation of integrated allied forces." This implied that no country would seek to build military forces that would be "self-sufficient and balanced in every respect." The United Kingdom claimed to be the only European power capable of contributing nuclear weapons to the Western alliance. Having thus given herself the role of a nuclear power, Britain announced her intention to reduce her commitment to NATO.

To be frank, the United Kingdom insisted, in the name of economy, upon duplicating the expensive nuclear weapons system of the United States. She left to other countries the task of supplying the conventional ground shield necessary for the common defense. The basic wisdom of the decisions made by the British government seems to be beyond doubt. Armed with nuclear weapons, the United Kingdom will add more to Western strength than what she takes away through reductions of her conventional forces. However, it has always been NATO's policy to achieve total deterrence of Soviet aggression by maintaining both a capacity for massive retaliation and an adequate infrastructure of conventional power. The British government has often reaffirmed this principle, but at the same time it has reduced its manpower commitment to NATO, as we just said. In addition, the state of opinion in the United Kingdom showed a trend toward emancipation from American policy on the assumption that the United States had proved during the Suez crisis of 1956 that it could not always be trusted for support of British policy.

In its anti-American aspect, this policy would be, if deliberately pursued, both dangerous and unrealistic. Any reduction in British conventional power increases the need for American support, for it makes the United Kingdom less able to cope with local situations alone, the prototype of which situation is precisely what happened in the Middle East in 1956.[10] It would also increase British dependence upon Continental countries, West Germany in particular, and it presupposes a willingness to collaborate with the Continental powers that is much greater than Britain seems ready to accept at present.

The second important aspect of the new British policy was to free the United Kingdom (and, indirectly, NATO itself) from the American nuclear monopoly. This led to greater self-reliance and a closer association with the United States, an ostensible paradox compounded by two other factors: a relative disengagement of American policy from European politics and the need for making the contribution of the Continental countries in conventional armaments more and more complementary to the Anglo-American nuclear deterrent. For this reason, the Eisenhower-Macmillan talks of October, 1957, might prove to be of historical significance in that they outlined the new direction of NATO policy, a policy of increased interdependence and mutual disentanglement.

The principle of interdependence should have two main fields of application. Soviet successes in space control have served as a timely warning that the Atlantic powers should not carry on independent research programs which imply a duplication of effort and a corresponding waste of time, precious manpower resources, and money. The NATO Communiqué of December 19, 1957, declared that effectiveness of national efforts must be increased "through the pooling of scientific facilities and information and the sharing of tasks." It should also be possible to bring about closer co-ordination in organizing the forces of the Alliance. The Communiqué declared that the purpose of co-ordination is to insure that "each NATO member country makes its most effective contribution to the requirements established by the alliance." Common resources should be used more effectively "through as high a degree of standardization and integration as possible in all fields, particularly in certain aspects of air and naval defense, of logistic support and of the composition and equipment of forces." More use should be made of European industry for supplying weapons, and the concept of balanced national forces should be resolutely abandoned.[11]

This policy can be achieved at a cost that is economically and politically bearable. It is as vital as it is limited in scope. The interest of the United States is to build the deterrent strength of the Atlantic Alliance; the interest of the European countries is to be defended. In 1957, G. F. Kennan proposed a disengagement from Soviet power in Europe. His proposal was the exact caricature of NATO's new approach. Let our power in NATO be engaged vis-à-vis the Soviet Union. Let our influence be disengaged from internecine Allied rivalries. Let France acquire nuclear weapons, and let every country in Europe pursue, with increased vigor, a policy of self-realization.

We must therefore conclude that the North Atlantic Treaty Organization is alive and strong. There can be no true justification for the treacherous contradictions fabricated by partisan debates. The situation simply calls for intellectual honesty. If NATO's power of massive retaliation is considered a monster as terrifying to itself as it is to its enemies, it cannot be said that deterrence of Soviet aggression is an imperious necessity. If Mr. Dulles is accused of speaking of nothing but bombs and missiles, it is dishonest to assert, with equal authority, that our allies are falling away because they no longer feel protected by our superiority. Senator Neuberger warned on March 4, 1957, that the European countries have "no perpetual friends" but only "perpetual interests."[12] If this were true, others cannot say that our allies need no lesson from us. On February 1, 1956, Senator Jackson asserted that if the U.S.S.R. fired an intercontinental ballistic missile before the United States, our allies would be forced "into neutralism or even into tacit cooperation with Moscow."[13] But on March 28, 1957, he said that "our allies are not easily frightened" and predicted that ballistic blackmail would not work. He added that "if the Soviet Union attempts to intimidate any of our allies . . . we should make it clear that we, too, can deal decisively with atomic and hydrogen weapons in a way the Soviets will understand."[14] In other words, we described our allies, in order, as gallant and timid, venal and self-reliant, and as great idealists and sober realists. The idea that none of them can afford estrangement from the United States is hardly given any thought.

This lack of seriousness was revealed with even greater evidence in the debate on NATO's political problems. The formulation of a "common" policy as the sole basis for the Alliance's military establishments has long been considered its supreme test. Partisanship has claimed that unless NATO becomes a community of friends, it will have no inner strength. There is no liberty without equality of status, and if the United States continues to reserve for itself certain rights and secrets, it is no longer a leader but a master. We could, of course, coerce the free nations into submission, but then there would be no free world. Leadership cannot be imposed; it must be deserved.

It is a fact that the principle of Allied co-operation has become a divisive element in NATO. It must be denounced as one of the many mirages occupying public opinion everywhere. A "common" NATO policy is justified by the notion of the Alliance's "totality," which, in turn, is a revolt against the Alliance itself. President Gronchi of Italy told a joint session of Congress on February 29, 1956, that no one could consider "without anxiety and anguish the prospects of a world where peace is solely based on military strength or on limited political alinements." He described NATO as "an emergency measure" and warned that the time had come to advance it to the fullness of its meaning.[15] But NATO is a political alignment that cannot exist without excluding others; to do away with exclusion is to do away with the organization. It can therefore be concluded that this introspective reluctance to identify oneself with the true purpose of the Alliance is self-defeating.

The same can be said of less dangerous concepts, such as "organic cooperation," "diplomatic solidarity," or "political integration," among the NATO allies. For the Italians, *Neo-Atlantismo* means more active intervention by Italy in the Alliance's policies, more autonomy in the Mediterranean and the Near East. For the Dutch, it means that NATO should help the Netherlands to retain control of New Guinea. For the French, it means that the United States should support France in Algeria. No country speaks so scathingly about Atlantic solidarity than the one which does most to undermine it.

In contradistinction, American opinion uses the concept of NATO's totality in the manner of self-criticism. The Pentagon generals, the Republican Old Guard, the isolationists, and the reactionaries are solemnly warned by the liberals that Allied restiveness is to be taken in dead earnest. "There exists a shabby readiness" in America "to smear" its closest allies, wrote H. S. Commager in 1954, "because they do not always see eye to eye" with Dulles.[16] Adlai Stevenson said on September 15, 1953, that Americans have "many illusions about others, and one of them is that irritations, doubts, disagreements are symbols of ingratitude or anti-Americanism." On April 3, 1955, Governor Harriman asserted that "the whole world is a party at interest and it has been not only illogical but deadly dangerous" for this country to "arrogate" to itself "the sole responsibility for decisions which involve the future of many peoples."[17]

These statements epitomize our philosophy of leadership. The tendency is not to smear our allies but to lay faults on ourselves. Occasions when diplomatic pressure was actually exercised on our NATO partners by the present administration are too few and are inconclusive. The long delays by Italy and France in ratifying the European Defense Community Treaty brought forth Dulles' famous "agonizing reappraisal."[18] During the Indochinese crisis, Mr. Eisenhower said that if necessary, the United States might go ahead with Southeast Asian defense without Britain. During the Suez crisis, the United States voted for the withdrawal of Anglo-French troops from Egypt, and we apparently delayed emergency action on Europe's oil shortage until we obtained assurances on withdrawal. Such rebuttals may or may not produce wholesome results as far as U.S. policy is concerned. The interesting thing is the deep resentment expressed by American opinion, not about the Suez invasion or the lack of support for our policy on the part of our allies, but about the impertinence of the American administration to propose policies that its allies choose not to support.[19]

American opinion deliberately implicates our foreign policy in problems from which it would be wise to stay aloof because they are clearly the responsibility of someone besides ourselves. The

Cyprus situation was a striking example of the queer processes set in motion by partisanship in an instance of this sort. The people of Cyprus were first described, in vivid terms, as the innocent victims of bloodshed, curfews, martial law, searches, and the most repressive governmental methods to be found in the world. Then the situation was pictured as a deadly blow to Western solidarity and was linked to the fateful name of Dulles. The British government asserted that NATO was strong enough to resist the effects of the dispute and refused to consider the future of the island as a negotiable issue for the Alliance. But American opinion saw in Cyprus a dramatic proof of the failure of American leadership.

Still more striking was the situation which resulted from the Suez crisis. In both England and France, the opinion was that the United States had let them down in their hour of need. On November 27, 1956, Conservative members of the House of Commons signed a motion to the effect that the U.S. policy to work through the United Nations instead of NATO had "gravely endangered the Atlantic Alliance." The Suez invasion would not have occurred if Mr. Dulles had agreed earlier to support a more forceful policy toward Nasser. Parallelly, American opinion greatly exaggerated the effects of Suez on Allied solidarity. The crack in the Western front was described as fatal. Mr. Dulles offered a revolver to the Egyptian dictator; he let himself go to an orgy of self-righteousness; Nasser was through at the time, but we saved him. The least that could have been said about our allies' bold move was that it aimed at the right target. But Dulles was utterly indifferent, if not hostile, to the maintenance of British influence in the Near East. His policy was a policy of "desperate expediency," said Representative Hays on July 2, 1957, and the greatest contribution the Secretary could have made to our policy would have been to resign.

The Algerian problem is another illustration of the self-destructive dualism of American opinion. The United States should be more patient toward France and should also express sympathy for the nationalist movement. No hypocrisy; no half-measures; no anti-colonialism; no colonialism by association. Ambassador Lodge was criticized for having voted against France during the Suez crisis; he was criticized for voting in favor of France on the Algerian issue.

By failing to support France and Britain, the administration endangered the future of the Western coalition. By failing to commit itself to anti-colonialism, it antagonized all Asia. "We find ourselves ranged in the mind of Asia along with the colonial powers," said Senator Kefauver on April 20, 1955, "with all the Asian memories which they invoke." This was due, he said, to the administration's stubborn refusal "to stand up fair and square on the issue of colonialism." Senator Kennedy said on July 2, 1957, that the "most powerful single force in the world today is neither Communism nor capitalism, neither the H-bomb nor the guided missile" but "man's eternal desire to be free and independent." The great enemy of freedom today is what Senator Kennedy called "imperialism." Imperialism, of course, means Communist imperialism, but it also means "whether we like it or not, and though they are not to be equated, Western imperialism."[20]

This sottish oversimplification is nothing new in American politics. Senator McCarthy has been compared to Lavrenti Beria and General Franco with Stalin; the South American regimes—and many other friendly countries—have been called "totalitarian." The highly revealing fact is that Senator Kennedy's formula concerning "imperialism" is another attempt to deemphasize the anti-Communist direction of American policy. It is another way of saying that Communism is not the "real" problem in the world today; the "real" problem is Russian imperialism—or simply imperialism. What the liberals find irritating and troubling is the accusation that America is dominated by an anti-Communist hysteria, that Mr. Eisenhower speaks of a "crusade," and that Mr. Dulles wants to resurrect the Holy Alliance. They speak of the "totality of NATO"; they want the United States to stand "fair and square" on the issue of colonialism. These vague notions provide public opinion with an alibi. Along with the Asian neutralists, public opinion flogs the dead horse of colonialism. With the European critics of America, it flogs Dulles. In both cases, it flogs itself.

The real problem is whether American opinion will identify

itself with the primary task of American foreign policy, namely, to oppose Communism. Strange as it may seem, public opinion refuses to commit iself to an anti-Communist foreign policy. The task of opposing the growth of Communism is and will be performed, of course, but as far as public opinion is concerned, it is done reluctantly and with constant misgivings. Adlai Stevenson asked on September 15, 1953, whether the objective pursued by the administration was to plunge the world into atomic war or "to discover through negotiations ways to relax tensions." He asked whether our aim was "coexistence or is it the extermination of Communist power?"

Every American who writes and speaks asks the same question. So do Jawaharlal Nehru and Aneurin Bevan. So do President Gronchi of Italy and President Heuss of Germany. The main thing, they all say, is to disentangle diplomacy from slogans and ideologies. The Soviets have an ideology, "of course," and yet the critics of America also express a measure of admiration for the sober realism of Russia. The slogans, therefore, are Dulles'; the ideology is the American anti-Communist ideology. On December 1, 1957, G. F. Kennan said that military tension between East and West would increase if atomic weapons and ballistic missiles were supplied to our NATO allies. But the same had been said before of German rearmament. In other words, any move to strengthen Allied power would make a Russian withdrawal from eastern Europe less likely; it would induce her to arm Poland and China with atomic weapons; it would render peaceful accommodation more difficult.[21]

In November, 1958, the U.S.S.R. accused the Western Allies of having violated the Postdam agreements, which, according to the Soviet note of November 27, 1958, stand as the trunk of a tree "once mighty and fruit-bearing, but now mangled and with its core cut out." West Germany had been shoved onto the road of militarism and revanchism. In order to create a "normal" atmosphere for the solution of the German problem, the Soviet Union declared that it regarded as null and void the occupation agreements concluded by the wartime Allies. "At an appropriate moment," it would turn over to the German Democratic Republic the functions exercised by the Soviet authorities in Berlin in virtue of these agreements. Should the inhabitants of West Berlin desire to preserve their capitalistic way of life, it was "up to them to do so." West Berlin would then become a demilitarized free city whose status would be guaranteed. But the U.S.S.R. could no longer accept the existence of West Berlin as a "kind of state within the state." Although it would supply the free city with raw materials and foodstuffs, it would not contribute to the continued "cancerous growth" of its economy. Still less would it accept the continuation of subversive activities directed at East Germany and the Soviet Union, the war propaganda of the agents of the West in Berlin, the "slave traffic" conducted under the guise of refugee welfare, or the espionage activities of more than fifty agencies now operating in the German capital.

Western consent was not at all necessary for the implementation of the proposed measures concerning the future of Berlin. If the "constructive proposals" made by the Soviet Union were not acceptable to the United States, there was "no topic" left for talks on the Berlin question. However, the U.S.S.R. proposed to make no change in military traffic procedure for six months. If this period was not used for "reaching a relevant agreement," it would effect the planned measures by agreement with the German Democratic Republic; a separate peace treaty would be signed; no encroachment against the East German territory, in the center of which Berlin is situated, would be tolerated, either by land, water, or air, and such a measure would be considered as the beginning of war. "Immediate and appropriate retaliation" by the entire socialist camp would follow. The Soviet Union is not an Iran or a Jordan; any threat by the United States would not be "in accord with the real correlation of forces."

The United States long objected to the signature of a peace treaty with Germany by referring to the absence of a unified German state. It also prevented any *rapprochement* between the two German states. In order to do away with this anomaly, the

Soviet Union proposed the draft of a peace treaty on January 10, 1959. It would formally accept the existence of Germany as two separate German states, free from obligations contracted under the NATO and the Warsaw pacts and bound equally by the provisions of the new treaty. Germany would not become a party to any treaty which did not include all of the four principal anti-Hitlerite powers; the activities of subversive organizations—such as emigrant bodies conducting hostile activities against any of the Allied powers—would be forbidden. All foreign troops would be withdrawn from German territory and bases there would be closed forever; Germany would have the military forces necessary for her own defense, but no nuclear weapons, rockets, missiles, bombers, or submarines.

Moreover, the problem of German unification was separated from the Berlin question and the signature of a peace treaty. The Soviet Union emphatically declared that unification was a concern of the Germans themselves, that it should not be discussed by the Big Four on any account, and that the only "businesslike" formulation of the problem was to have unification come about through agreements and contacts between both German states. If a gradual *rapprochement* would thus lead to a confederation, the Soviet Union would see to it that the "social advances" made by East Germany would not be liquidated by capitalism through unification, for the German Democratic Republic was the home of the entire German working class.

Senator Mansfield said on February 12, 1959, that the West should never become "distracted or obsessed by the twists and turns of Soviet behavior." There was no point, he said, in trying "to interpret the charades" of Soviet conduct; whatever the Soviets might do, we should be certain that they act "to enhance the position of the Soviet Union and that of totalitarian Communism."[22] The Communist scheme concerning Berlin was a charade because of its elaborate and artful particulars. In its objective and its form, it expressed a threat of the crudest type, and its Machiavellian subtlety went to waste. The United States would not be driven from Berlin by force. It was not prepared to relinquish rights acquired through victory, nor would it negotiate under an ultimatum. It would reserve the right to uphold by all appropriate means its communications with West Berlin. As Mr. Dulles said on November 26, 1958, it would insist that there was "an explicit obligation, on the part of the Soviet Union, to assure to the United States . . . normal access to and egress from Berlin." Even if the East Germans were to act as the Soviet agents in checking military traffic, the U.S.S.R. would have to accept ultimate responsibility.

The idea of a neutralized, isolated Germany was rejected by the Western Allies as cruel and absurd. Mr. Dulles said on January 27, 1959, that the Soviet proposals for a peace treaty with Germany were "obviously designed not to bring about reunification but to perpetuate the division of Germany." He considered them, in other words, "as proposals for permanent partition." It had been agreed at Potsdam on August 2, 1945, that the four victorious powers were responsible for the rehabilitation of a unified Germany with a single government based on free elections. This principle was reaffirmed at Geneva in 1955. "The heart of the matter is reunification," Mr. Dulles added. "The method is less essential, as long as it is a method which achieves the result and assures that the result is obviously desired by the people."

It has been suggested that in case German reunification could be achieved, the NATO powers should not push their military positions into East Germany. The Secretary of State emphasized on January 13, 1959, that the United States did not expect reunification "under conditions which would involve, or seem to involve, the Soviet Union in increased risks or losses." Reunification would be coupled, he said, "with security provisions and limitations which would make sure that the Soviet Union would not, through the reunification, seem to have weakened its strategic or political position." Any comprehensive security arrangement for central Europe would provide, according to our note to Poland of May 4, 1958, "for limitations on both forces and armaments, measures for the prevention of surprise attack in the area, and assurances of reaction in the event of aggression." The Anglo-Russian communiqué of March 3, 1959, endorsed the usefulness of further study on this subject. It made no mention about reunification and for that reason legitimately angered England's allies. Mr. Khrushchev signed the declaration without reading it because, he said, "time is money."

The Berlin crisis has shed considerable light on the impact of Soviet diplomacy upon public opinion in democratic countries. It proved that the blunt enormity and suddenness of Communist actions generally create an equally violent and irrational revulsion against American policy. "Lacking a policy of our own for the unification of Germany," Walter Lippmann wrote in the *New York Herald Tribune* of November 25, 1958, "we have become hysterically attached to the status quo." We are not quite sure any more, he added, "of the distinction between hardening of the will and hardening of the arteries." We have made it a point to repeat our own formulas publicly and solemnly; now we are in a straitjacket; we cannot maneuver and negotiate. This might suit those, "some in very high places," who do not want to negotiate, but we must negotiate.[23] It is clear that Moscow is willing to negotiate; otherwise Mikoyan would not have come here and acted as he did. In this changing world, immobilization is a grave danger. We automatically reject every Soviet idea just because it is novel, but "flexibility in our foreign policy is a must," said Senator Church on February 12, 1959. "A steel blade bends. Pig iron breaks."[24] President Eisenhower said that we would not yield one inch. What about half an inch, asked James Reston, who, after this astonishing display of wit, blandly asserted that courage is not policy, but "a chip on Uncle Sam's shoulder."[25]

All this amounts to is that we have no policy because the policy we have demands courage. In one stroke, fourteen years of diplomacy were erased as if nothing had ever been discussed or agreed upon. Although the *status quo* was preferable to an insoluble crisis, any insistence on past agreements was denounced as legalism. Public opinion in democratic countries shares with the Communist ideology a strange fascination for revolutionary thoughts, for starting everything anew in defiance of past experience, reason, and duty. The burglar breaks the windows and the master of the house is overwhelmed by fresh air, feels ashamed of his confinement, and expresses envious admiration for the criminal's bold ideas! We should bombard the other camp with dynamic proposals! We should give careful consideration to the Rapacki Plan, to the Eden Plan! We should urge West Germany to discuss with East Germany the establishment of an all-Berlin government! We should withdraw our troops from the German capital and have them replaced by West German soldiers!

None of these ideas were new. All of them were ill timed and impracticable. As President Eisenhower said on February 18, 1959, "everybody seems to have ideas of many things, in particular, when they have no responsibility." Moreover, elementary wisdom required that we hide our hand and refuse to present any alternative to the Soviet ultimatum as long as this could be done. Nothing could have been more contrary to our idiosyncrasy. Representative Flood asserted on February 18, 1959, that the administration's exercises in "self-hypnosis" created in this country a "condition of torpor" which rendered us "toneless amid the clanging alarums. Like Mr. Micawber, the administration drifts along in the sublime hope that something good is bound to turn up."[26] Senator Humphrey returned from Moscow with the warning that the Soviet ultimatum had to be taken seriously. He said on February 19, 1959, that "unless we are statesmanlike and very careful, unless we can come up with a legitimate program of negotiation, we may have a shooting war over Berlin."[27] The hard way, the real statesmanship, was not to make hasty proposals. The Berlin crisis excluded neither the possibility of making some progress toward the settlement of the German problem nor the possibility of war. Being ready for better and for worse, we had to chart our own course without letting ourselves be alarmed by the Soviet threats or enticed into undesirable controversies by fraudulent diplomatic tricks. As Mr. Dulles said on February 8, 1959, firmness did not exclude being conciliatory, but "merely making concessions" for which there was no "counterpart." We have been in Berlin fourteen years. It was better to wait and to preserve the *status quo* rather than to submit to Soviet arrogance. Let us persevere with "the same tenacity," said Senator Dodd on February 26, 1959, "with which the Communists pursue their evil program for world domination; that long and then one day longer."[28]

The Senator remarked that we have made progress when we have been firm. "There is no peculiar virtue in the concept of flexibility," he said, but when it is applied to principles, flexibility "becomes a vice." This statement disturbed Senator Fulbright, who could not accept the fact that good and evil were the only things involved. Otherwise, declared the Senator, there would be "no hope whatever for any kind of adjustment or compromise, and therefore we must reconcile ourselves to inevitable war." He agreed, of course, that American society was "a superior society" and added that "we believe we are more right than the Russians are." But he would be reluctant to base his belief "on that basis because there is an absoluteness about it which admits of no compromise."[29] This Fulbright doctrine is most revealing. It equates principles, absoluteness, uncompromising rigidity, inevitable war. According to his arithmetic, we are "more right" or "less wrong" than the Russians, and that means that we are less right and more wrong than we think.

Whether Senator Fulbright liked it or not, the freedom of the people of West Berlin was a question of principle. Senator Dodd was quite right when he insisted that all this "mumbo-jumbo and mental mush about rigidity and inflexibility . . . will never help us" in solving the problem of Berlin. The most realistic policy is to stand by principle when there is a question of principle involved. The Berlin debate proved, however, that public opinion let itself be drawn away from duty by the mirage of "realism." It was asserted that the Soviet Union would never agree to the reunification of a free Germany. Was it realistic to have as the core of our German policy an objective so completely out of reach? Senator Mansfield said on February 12, 1959, that "a policy which merely clings to an unrealizable slogan of free all-German elections . . . is no policy at all. . . . It is an excuse for immobility. It may well lead down the blind alley of an unnecessary conflict or disastrous diplomatic retreat." It is not realistic to expect that a unified Germany would be permitted to stay in NATO. If we think coolly and realistically, why should we fear a withdrawal of Germany from NATO so much? The claim of Bonn, endorsed as it is by the entire West, to represent all of Germany and to ignore the existence of East Germany—a going concern as a state—is not realistic. In view of these "hard realities," we should allow the two German states to work out their own problems. There are "compelling reasons" why German unity should be effected without delay. Any "valid policy" on Germany, said Senator Mansfield in his celebrated speech, must be based upon "the premise that Germany, in one way or another, is going to unify soon." If there is to be "any possibility of peace," the United States must make concessions, he said; we might have to accept some form of disengagement or withdrawal, and "we would be the ones who would take a loss in position." But "we have to develop give and take," he concluded, "by starting from the bottom and working upward."

Starting from the bottom and working upward; to be bold in the future, to surrender with courage and imagination—this is the formula of Mr. Mansfield's realism. It is only our fears that enable the Russians to maintain their hold on world opinion by making reasonable-sounding proposals for a unified Germany. Instead of reacting to their initiative, why not "compel" them to react to ours? Why not take Mr. Khrushchev at his word and see whether he would permit the two German states to negotiate on equal terms? Instead of standing firm on Berlin, why not agree to the Soviet terms for a German confederation in the faith that democracy is so attractive, especially to people who have lived under Communism, that we are bound to win the allegiance of every German, whether Germany is demilitarized or not? Let us move from positions that have become untenable to new positions from which we will recover the initiative. If we let West Germany take over our role in West Berlin, we would operate the transfer under "ironclad guarantees for free communications with the West." Berlin would then become a sort of "microcosm" where patterns of peaceful unification would evolve spontaneously and be successfully tried out. No doubt would be cast on our determination to guarantee the right of West Germany in Berlin since West Germany is a member of NATO. She thus has the right to insist on our protection, and our courage would have been well proved by abject surrender to a Soviet ultimatum.

The liberal opposition was indeed very sore on this particular point. Painful and irritated sensitivity was displayed at the accusation of appeasement—an accusation that nobody had the courage to formulate. Senator Mansfield's speech of February 12, 1959, was literally the Magna Charta of surrender in Germany, but this appeaser raised his voice to denounce, with great pathos, the notion of appeasement as the "stamp of political chicanery." He said that some people "regard as appeasement not only talk, but even thought, which apparently is alien to them, on the serious problems of the Nation." He did not want any quibbling, but a serious discussion of "the life or death problem of peace or war." The suggestions he made, said Senator Lyndon Johnson, were "predicated upon the great philosophy of Isaiah's advice, 'Come now, let us reason together,'" and should be heard around the world.

They were. In his speech of March 16, 1959, Senator Fulbright quoted a prominent French editor as saying that French officials thought that we were about "to commit treason in a war that has already started."[30] The exaggerated, melodramatic tone of this quotation illustrates the insuperable dilemma of the administration's critics with respect to collective security. Our allies denounce the rigidity of our diplomacy and deprecate our lack of reliability. In our effort to prove that we are flexible, we call free German elections a slogan and past agreements a straitjacket. Policies which long seemed sacrosanct suddenly appear to be in a state of flux for no other reason than partisan criticism. The effect on Allied opinion is deplorable. When we realize it, we accuse our leaders. "Must we sit in paralyzed horror for two more years," asked the Advisory Council of the Democratic National Committee in March, 1959, "watching our strength, our influence, our position in the world and our alliances dissolve," just as our people had to watch, a hundred years ago, the Union dissolve "under the weak and palsied hand of Buchanan?" And to compound the problem, the appeasers request an immediate mobilization of NATO defense forces, both on land and in the air. The United States should not put its missile program on a crash basis. French and British divisions should return to Germany.

The Berlin debate has illustrated how twisted and distorted human reasonings can be when they depart from the evidence. Soviet insincerity was taken as a reason for yielding to their pressure for the purpose of being able to denounce this insincerity. It was said that it would be strange if we should go to war in order to keep the Russians in Berlin. Joseph Harsch wrote in the *Christian Science Monitor* of February 4, 1959, that it would be inconceivable to anyone "brought up on Mr. Dulles' bold projects for rolling back the Iron Curtain" that the United States would become a party to a policy "shoring up the shaky, sordid and shabby Ulbricht-Grotewhol regime in East Germany." The situation was serious, not because the Soviets were strong and confident, but because Soviet rule in East Germany was on the point of collapsing. The Russians feared a new Hungary; they well knew that we would not let Germany go down the drain as we did Hungary. But Mr. Dulles wanted them to stay and to occupy eastern Europe.

Strangely enough, the Berlin question was the prototype of a situation from which the United States should have deliberately disentangled itself. The diplomatic initiative should have been entrusted to France and Germany. It was their responsibility, in this instance, to define Allied policy. England and the United States should have limited themselves to the role of honest and interested partners. This is not, however, what we mean by "leadership."

In his book *Realities of American Foreign Policy*, Mr. Kennan spoke of the missing qualities of our leadership and of its unhappy tone. If these were what they should be, he said, they would automatically "radiate themselves to the world at large" and affect our enemies as well as our friends. As in Aesop's tale of the north wind, he said, the cloak in which the Soviet Union wraps itself is "that zone of inordinate power and influence . . . with which it has tried to shelter its inner sanctum." All of us recall, he concluded, that it was not "by the direct huffing and puffing of the North Wind, but by the gentle indirection of the sun that the stubborn traveler was at last induced to remove his cloak."[31] It is not by accident that this tale assigns to the United States the role of the sun. Infinitely distant from everything and everyone, sharing its beneficence upon the just and the unjust with proud indifference, the United States should be the fountainhead of all light and yet act only by gentle indirection.

The United States as the sun of the world is a notion that curiously combines the most unbearable of prides, an amusingly simple outlook on political realities, and a measure of aloofness which makes Senator Langer's isolationism pale into insignificance. In contradistinction, Mr. Dulles did not display very much imagination when he repeated again and again what he had said so many times before. On April 22, 1957, he claimed that Communism was not a great social movement but that it had proved to be "oppressive, reactionary, unimaginative. Its despotism, far from being revolutionary, is as old as history." He also said, on October 29, 1957, that "Soviet propaganda has never been characterized by consistency" and added that the Russian leaders "say one thing in one part of the world and something quite contradictory in another part of the world, and they can carry on what would appear to be contrary policies at one and the same time." Vice-President Nixon said similarly on June 8, 1956, that "in the cold light of history it seems fantastic that a nation with the Soviet record of terror and aggression could hope to make widespread gains by announcing a simple change of policy."

These are simple thoughts, intelligible thoughts, but they are not pleasant thoughts. Public opinion denounces them as platitudinous and annoying. But the Stockholm Peace Movement, the travels of the Soviet Comrades, their smiles and their threats (which would all appear to be clumsy blunders if people's minds were not already in a state of aberration) are seen as clever, bold, successful, always true, always novel. Mr. Kennan can rake together forlorn ideas and be praised for his originality. Under the cover of a reputation as brilliant free thinkers, many of our polit-

178

ical Hamlets choose to be borne along by the tide of opinion rather than to stand against it; they bend their minds to the demands made upon them. Acting, often against their expressed will, as hirelings and minions, they couch disturbing thoughts in sparkling phrases. They can always claim that a more careful reading of their doctrine would uncover qualifications and circumstances so ingenious and so cleverly expressed that their conclusions are, as a rule, formally true. They can always say that their proposals have not been understood as they intended them to be understood. With the authority of truth, let us denounce them as tellers of lies.

If we want to lead the free world, we should understand that Soviet propaganda is successful because it seems so clever. It is a tragedy, of course, that Arab nationalism has taken a militant, anti-American course. It is another tragedy that Indian neutralism has come to mean support of Soviet policy on disarmament, SEATO, and Hungary. But no tragedy is more heartbreaking than the free nations' disunity and the damage they so inflict upon themselves.

There is a legitimate desire on the part of our allies to be informed about those of our policies that may affect their own future. There is a need for co-ordinating Allied policy when it deals with matters of common concern. There should be procedures for the settlement of disputes between Allied countries. But we cannot allow ourselves, in the name of Allied solidarity, said Secretary Dulles on April 23, 1956, to "drift into some new and ill-defined relationship which could be provocative of future misunderstandings." President Eisenhower asserted on December 14, 1954, that "in certain areas and in certain fields, of course, our own right to act as we saw fit was unquestioned," and it should remain so.

None of our treaty commitments represents the totality of our policies. The special responsibilities assumed by the United States in the Middle East require independent judgment. We should not expect support for our Chinese policy. We should never give to others a veto over actions which we might deem indispensable for our national interest. As Mr. Dulles noted on September 27, 1958, the strength and the immunity of the free world from aggression "depend very largely upon what the Soviet leaders consider to be the will of the United States." If the United States should give in to any pressure, the consequences would be felt everywhere. The principles upon which NATO rests are indivisible. "If they are not valid and not sustained in Asia, it cannot be confidently assumed," the Secretary said, "that they are valid and will be sustained in Europe."

It would be a strange paradox if utter dependence upon American power should ever be considered as Allied interdependence. Political realism demands that we use Allied dependence upon us to control and lessen pressures upon American policy. It also demands that this dependence itself be alleviated by a true interdependence through division of labor, the assignment of specific sectors of responsibility in common defense, and greater equality in mutual independence.

The same realism should apply in the solution of the differences that have shaken Allied solidarity. The seriousness of intermember disputes should be used to press for their solution but not to destroy the Alliance. If the NATO Council could have settled the Cyprus dispute, it would greatly have served the cause of Western unity. Such disagreements as the Cyprus issue cannot be allowed to obscure the true objective of the Alliance. It is easy to understand why the United Kingdom would not support our Chinese policy, but it is beyond the pale of reason to use the notion of Allied solidarity for ruining American authority in the Far East.

Finally, realism requires greater public support for policies that are more difficult to enforce. It is true that American policy has to contain the erratic actions of nationalist revolutionaries, and for that reason, it appears to be opposed to nationalism and change. The United States must cope with the divisive forces released by a resurgence of nationalism, and when we do so, we seem to be self-interested. The administration must emphasize the continuing military threat posed by growing Communist power, and if and when it does, it is accused of being military minded. We denounce the Communist ideology, and this cannot be done without upholding the ideology of freedom. In relation to the evil trends of public opinion, American policy is reactionary. It is unrealistic to help King Hussein and Chiang Kai-shek because they cannot subsist without our help. It is contrary to American ideals to align ourselves with colonial powers who must receive our assistance in spite of their colonialism. All of these are reasons given for not upholding American policy; in reality, they are reasons why support is most necessary. With this finding, we finally penetrate into the heart of our problem. The time has now come to expose the processes of partisanship in America.

PART THREE

Partisanship in America

CHAPTER VIII

The Techniques of Debate

MANY ANALYSTS HAVE NOTED that American political debates often suffer from a lack of issues. There exists in this country a measure of political harmony that has never been attained in any other country. But it has not always been understood that although it reflects political maturity, this situation is not devoid of grave dangers.

It is a fact that if some influential minority would profess ideas that are abhorrent to the great majority of Americans, public opinion would be forced to consider clear-cut alternatives and public debates would be conclusive one way or the other. This is not the case, however. American opinion does not feel the influence of a catalytic factor such as the one exercised in certain Western countries by a Communist minority. Our debates are thus characterized by patriotic self-righteousness. Since there exists virtual agreement on the issues, it seems just to assume an equal devotion to the common good, equal insight, equal wisdom on the part of all. The question is never one of dedication to one's country; it is purely a question of judgment and methods. There should be no personal attacks, no McCarthyism; the democratic process cannot be foreclosed. Anyone—from the high school student and the disk jockey to the Presidential candidate—can and does debate on the Soviet sputnik, Arab nationalism, and Mr. Nehru. All views should be heard; everyone can cloak himself in the garb of an assumed virtue; never could the moral integrity of the dissenter be impugned, for dissent is virtue.

This philosophy of democracy is completely devoid of rational contents; from a practical standpoint, it is the doctrine of a decadent society. The dilemma of American politics is that when the administration's policy happens to be consistent and valid, partisan criticism must destroy this consistency by deliberately creating confusion. Unless some real issue can be found (and this happens only rarely), there is no real choice between acceptable and unacceptable policies; rather, the choice is between a consistent policy and the absence of such a policy.

Partisan criticism is thus bound by a law of nature to do, in most instances, purely negative and destructive work. More serious than the destruction is the will to destroy; graver still than passing confusion are the reasons why confusion becomes an habitual state of the mind, an objective unconsciously sought and always achieved because of its mysterious magnetism. The mortal dangers threatening American democracy are that we identify ourselves with our own evils, that all the processes of partisanship constantly make deeper inroads and seem always more inevitable, and that all the lies which occupy our attention appear more truthful each time we accept them as valid evidences. The most critical danger is that the more we recede from the evidence of knowable truth, the greater becomes the fascination of despair. In other words, the evil is within ourselves, and for that very reason, we can overcome our own sloth and set ourselves free from the nemesis of self-destruction. The first step toward true liberty is the will to be free; the second is mental clarity.

Partisanship flourishes in confusion, just as it withers away under logical analysis. The test of our sincerity is therefore whether we accept notions that are incompatible with the light of reason, whether we are willing to look the problem in the face, whether we agree to meet the issue. The existence of a problem—like Nasserism or Quemoy—is no issue at all, but its evaluation can be. If we criticize the administration's policy, we must first state the administration's analysis of the problem; we must define, with implacable honesty, any other analysis that can be proposed. A policy can always be an issue, but here again, it is necessary to state which parts of the policy are considered to be controversial and why. On the other hand, policy often gropes for a solution when many factors in the situation are unknown. The unknown factor can never be a point at issue, yet partisan criticism often has no other basis than the risk that must be assumed in the face of an unknown future.

If public opinion would submit to the discipline of mental honesty, most of the destructive negativism which characterizes partisanship in America would be eliminated. Besides the test of rationality, there are other tests that can be applied, with complete certainty, to determine the sincerity of our political judgments. If a reasoning process is erroneous, so is the conclusion that it reaches. If a critic refuses to commit himself to a clear-cut and single conclusion, his argument must be discarded as a whole. If an assertion is unproved, it has no validity at all.

Taking massive retaliation as a vantage point, we have already treated many of the issues of American foreign policy. We can now turn to a study of the debating techniques and processes which are employed in American politics and without which partisanship could hardly sustain itself. These are typically few, easily recognized and unchangeable. Whenever they are used, the reasoning goes wrong; if we accept untruth, we are guilty. Since we are the willing victims of insincerity, to know our own debating processes is to know ourselves.

Of all the techniques used in political debates, outright *assertion* is the simplest. It consists of dogmatic statements which attribute to the government a certain policy that is patently wrong or which formulate what is asserted as a valid substitute for the mistaken policy attributed to the administration by the critic himself. The latter is illustrated by the following statement, which was made by Senator Lehman on April 28, 1955:

In my opinion—it has always been my opinion—Quemoy and Matsu are positions of weakness from which we should withdraw as rapidly as possible. The purpose of the withdrawal would be to strengthen our position vis-à-vis Communist China and vis-à-vis our allies. A withdrawal from Quemoy and Matsu would greatly add to our strength—would greatly increase our prestige among our allies and among the uncommitted peoples of Asia. It would be a move to strengthen our security and not to weaken it. I am sure that the Chinese Communists as well as the rest of the free world [*sic*] would recognize it as such. I think this truth is almost self-evident. Yet it is widely overlooked.[1]

Attributing a policy to the administration by way of an assertion is exemplified by the following editorial published by James Reston in the *New York Times* of January 17, 1954:

The President and the Secretary of State did not say, as President Truman had said in the Truman doctrine, that the United States must be prepared to oppose Communist aggression wherever it occurred. They went beyond that. They said that the United States must be free to retaliate instantly, not necessarily against the Communist troops in the field, but anywhere we chose with any weapons we chose.

In other words, they told Moscow and Peiping, as clearly as governments ever say these things, that, in event of another proxy or brushfire in Korea, Indochina, Iran, or anywhere else, the United States might retaliate instantly with atomic weapons against the U.S.S.R. or Red China.

This was not, like the Truman doctrine, a mere paragraph out of a speech. It was a decision by the President and the National Security Council.

The very point the critic must attempt to prove is thus stated as "self-evident." A fantastic oversimplification of massive retaliation is asserted under the authority of the President and the National Security Council. Whatever unclarity there is in the critic's interpretation is rationalized by the notion of diplomatic comity: it is as clear as governments can make it. There is no attempt to reason or to argue; the point is asserted forcefully. It is the assertion, and not the substance of the argument, which is missing, that carries what little weight there is.

As a matter of fact, most partisan assertions do not even bother to raise an issue that could be usefully discussed. How many times were we told that unless the "whole" approach of our foreign policy were "quickly and drastically" changed, American prestige would drop to an "all-time" low? "I was in Europe last summer," said Senator Lehman on January 27, 1954; "the fund of goodwill for America is running lower and lower."[2] After so many years of bluff and bluster, slogans and saber-rattling, contradictions and confusion, our situation has never been so precarious. The United States is criticized, and criticism does not prove, as Mr. Dulles claimed on April 13, 1956, that our allies are not afraid of criticizing us. "What criticism reflects," said Mr. Stevenson on April 21, 1956, "is the infinitely sterner, more ominous fact that we have lost the moral initiative and the rest of the world knows it."

This kind of assertion is, of course, without meaning. Who can establish with certainty that the United States is "losing the initiative" or that the voice of America has sunk to a whisper and its influence to a shadow of its former stature? The fact is, however, that such things are said back and forth with great seriousness. It is also said that the only steady feature of our policy in the Middle East is the refusal to have one, and Mr. Acheson asserted on September 6, 1958, that we seemed to be drifting, "either dazed or indifferent," toward war with China. Apparently, he said, Eisenhower and Dulles, "with or without military advice, will make all the decisions for us, surrounded by secrecy designed to keep everyone guessing." The law of partisan assertions, therefore, is that they must draw their seeming validity from their very weakness. There is no internal evidence. It goes without saying that if realities were so self-evident, objective evidence would certainly be offered and the issue would be hardly debatable, but there is no such evidence, and the assertion is as forceful as the case at hand is unclear.

As a debating technique, assertion is likely to be used when a policy statement is couched in carefully chosen words and duly qualified, as in the Dulles' speech of January 1954, or when a policy deliberately includes an area of vagueness, as did the Formosa Resolution of 1955, or simply when facts are undecisive and cannot be established one way or the other. The dissenter pushes aside all qualifications; he does not respect any unknown;

he is all the more assertive when the issue is more complex.

A last remark must be made about assertions. When a complex policy is attacked by means of oversimplifying statements, it can be expected that the administration will supply explanations and prove the assertion to be erroneous. Neither Mr. Reston nor anybody else would ever apologize to readers for having misled them on purpose; quite the contrary, official explanations are made to appear as readjustments of policy and concessions that the dissenter had forced the administration to accept. The habits of American political society do not demand redress from self-appointed leaders of public opinion when circumstances prove them to be wrong. As we know, the doctrine of American democracy is that the electorate is always kept in the dark; policy is often decided behind closed doors by appointed, rather than elected, officials; the administration suppresses unwelcome opinion as "sabotage." But political leaders in a democracy must respect public opinion; why, otherwise, do we have elections? The verdict of public opinion in a general election, however, does not always impress the dissenter. The results of the last Presidential election, for instance, were interpreted by many as the "triumph of conformity." Mr. Stevenson said on November 7, 1956, that "apparently all you have to do to win elections is to make fatal mistakes in foreign policy." The last "endorsement of disaster" revealed just how much dissent and democracy are endangered in America.[3] For this reason, partisan debates never end; for good or for evil, arguments linger indefinitely, and they continue to create a choking atmosphere of doubt and uncertainty long after the debate itself has ended.

On October 9, 1954, Mr. Stevenson referred to the "long procession of ringing slogans that lie forlorn but not forgotten, unhappily, along the winding path" of Dulles' diplomacy. He meant the slogans that the Democratic opposition attributed to the administration—"liberation," the "New Look," the "unleashing of Chiang," the "brink of war," and many more.

A *slogan* is a special variety of assertion. It generally has the nature of a humorous gag, such as the comment once made by Senator Russell of Georgia, who said that "if cutting the Air Force $5 billion made it stronger, why not cut it $10 billion and make the Air Force twice as strong?"[4] But a slogan can be dismal, too, like the famous "public's right to know." When candidates claim that truth is "sold rather than told" to the people, they appeal to a deeply rooted attitude of doubt and individualism, and this explains the success of the slogan.

Slogans are not always expressed in a terse formula. On February 10, 1956, Senator Humphrey said that the United States was signing more and more treaties all over the world; according to the administration, he said, each time a document is signed, the security of mankind becomes "absolutely perfect." We dismiss another division of troops; this means that the administration is "burdened with a kind of legal mentality."[5] The administration's "legal mentality" is a slogan, of course, but it is not possible to convey its meaning in a single, vigorous phrase nor is it a challenging formula.

The various features of political slogans are easy to define. Like all assertions, slogans are characterized by the absence of internal evidence. It is easy to assert that "our China policy is molded by pressures," but who can prove it? Slogans possess a self-sufficiency that is not normally present in plain assertions. Slogans must be pungent, and precious, and they can be passed around like coins. The Middle East burns while Dulles fiddles; the administration claims that massive retaliation is a calculated risk, but the policy is more risk than calculation. Mr. Stevenson spoke on February 16, 1957, of Dulles' rock-and-roll diplomacy. All of these formulas are stimulating; they are dispensed from critical evaluation; they soon become independent from the problem to which they pertain; their literary value is such that they deserve preservation in the national scrapbooks.

Because they are self-sufficient, slogans are always dangerous and deceitful; misrepresentation is the distinctive feature of all of them. In addition, slogans have a durability that their worth does not explain, and because it is durable, a slogan gives the impression of general acceptance. Now the formula is versatile and useful; it can serve in multiple capacities. With each use, further credibility is obtained at the expense of truth, and the formula's lease on life is prolonged. So it was, for instance, in the story of Dulles' salesmanship. This slogan was launched when massive retaliation was declared to be little more than a phrase designed to hide the administration's failure to develop real policies. The formula was also used on the theme of the public's right to know. Mr. Dulles travels too much. He spends much time outside the country trying to sell his diplomatic wares. Off-again Dulles! Let him cease to be a salesman and start, at long last, to act like a statesman and stop slighting Mr. Herter and the State Department. He described de-Stalinization in Russia as a victory for the West; this Madison Avenue stunt was credited to his salesmanship, and on August 13, 1956, Governor Clement exclaimed: "How long, O America, will you permit a State Department under a wandering minstrel to tell you from a magazine newsstand that you were brought three times to the brink of war?"

Slogans are used so much that they eventually wear out. Like a joke too often repeated, a slogan must sooner or later fall victim to its own sting. It gains recognition because of its piquancy; it loses the public's favor for the same reason. Slogans are doomed to destruction, but this is little consolation, for by the time they finally decay, they have accomplished their destructive course. When it was new, the formula had a capacity to hurt; the damage and confusion it has wrought cannot be undone. Moreover, slogans follow one another in quick succession; the newer slogan takes public opinion by as much surprise as the one it replaces; its novelty is increased by the fact that the old stunt was in bad need of replacement. Finally, the sloganeers insist that their own devices are the handiwork of their political enemies. Rare indeed are the speeches of Adlai Stevenson where some new slogan cannot be found coupled with the declaration that the American people want the truth and no slogans. In his great indictment of massive retaliation on March 6, 1954, Mr. Stevenson claimed that the new strategy had been marketed as "a program of more for our money, 'a bigger bang for a buck,' national security in the large economy size." Having thus fabricated a whole series of slogans, he concluded that "issues of life and death should be clarified and not clouded, for security in our age cannot be bought by slogans and gimmicks."

Instead of taking the positive form of slogans, assertions can also be stated in the form of *accusations*. President Truman, for instance, accused the Eisenhower administration on February 4, 1956, of "playing politics with national defense." He said that the Republicans were "putting economy ahead of national security." Accusations of this sort are honest and forthright, even if untrue. But most partisan accusations are only implied and are loathsome. "There has been plenty of massive verbal retaliation," said Mr. Stevenson on April 11, 1955; "these extravagant words" alarmed our friends, he added, because they assumed that "the great United States meant what it said." G. F. Kennan wrote in *Realities of American Foreign Policy* that the Soviet leaders have long considered that a general war was now too risky. "The Soviet leaders are not like many of us," he said, "they do not suppose that military victory solves all problems; they know that it is only a beginning and not an end."[6] On September 26, 1956, Dean Acheson said that the United States "seemed to be playing Russian Roulette with an atomic pistol."[7] In a memorandum circulated by the Democratic National Committee in early 1955, B. V. Cohen declared that "most of our friends and allies want to have peace, not war, in the Straits of Formosa."[8]

Our distinction between outright and implied accusations does more than refer to the manner in which these accusations are formulated. Public opinion has developed a marked aversion for clear-cut accusations; it cherishes tolerance and dislikes clear ideas. Vice-President Nixon has been branded for having spoken, among other things, about Dean Acheson's color blindness—a sort of "pinkeye," he said, toward Communist infiltration. The late Senator McCarthy spoke of the twenty years of treason under Democratic leadership. The "fifth column" in the State Department is a standard accusation in that category. These slogans owe their reputation to the scandal to which they give rise. It has become equally scandalous to refer to the "loss" of China or to say, as Mr. Nixon did on March 13, 1954, that "in the seven years of Truman-Acheson policies, 600 million people had been lost to the

Communists—and not a single Russian soldier had been lost in combat." Such talk has given Mr. Nixon the reputation of a man "whose trademark is slander."

The fact is, therefore, that public opinion reacts violently to the type of accusation now associated with the tactics of Truman, Nixon, and McCarthy, but it swallows with relish the poisonous indictment of national policy concocted by the systematic, intellectualist doubter. The important aspect of accusation as a debating technique is thus whether it insidiously attempts to sap national self-confidence. The prototype of such accusations is the condemnation, made on January 26, 1955, of the Formosa Resolution by Senator Flanders. "Put in plain English," he said, "this is preventive war."[9] Or it is the assertion made by Senator Kefauver on March 30 of the same year when he said that it would be unthinkable to plunge the United States into war for the sake of Quemoy. "Yet," he added, "there are those in high places in the present administration itself who are plotting and planning to bring such a war about."[10]

All partisan assertions follow the same pattern: they are always self-accusations. It is highly revealing that none of the leaders of American opinion has ever noted that the whole world criticizes, at will, everything American and that America accuses no one but herself. Everything that sounds anti-American around the world is carefully collected by American travelers and American reporters, dumped on the domestic scene, and scrutinized with morbid accuracy and a lack of national dignity that the foreign observer himself frequently finds shocking. And, as usual, those who practice self-incrimination combine reckless accusations with grandiloquent exhortations to greatness. "Let us stop slandering ourselves," said Adlai Stevenson on April 11, 1955, "and appear before the world once more as we really are—as friends, not as masters; as apostles of principle, not of power; in humility, not arrogance; as champions of peace, not as harbingers of war."

Another assertive process that is constantly used in our political debates consists in forcing a situation into the framework of *false alternatives*. In his speech of March 6, 1954, Adlai Stevenson said that if it meant anything, massive retaliation implied the "grim choice of inaction or a thermonuclear holocaust." Either the United States must be ready to unleash total nuclear war or it must be ready to concede defeat. Thus did former President Truman express himself on August 17, 1956. "With atomic war on the one hand, and retreat on the other," he said, "as our only alternatives, the defenses of the free world will crumble before the piecemeal assaults of the Communist enemy."

During the Indochinese crisis, Senator Kefauver asserted that the administration had nothing to offer but a set of ugly alternatives. "We have been told," he said on April 10, 1954, "that we can appease—which we will not; fight—which we hope will not be necessary; or abandon the area to Communism—which is unthinkable." The Middle East situation was similarly defined in terms of ugly choices. We can defy Khrushchev and deal sternly with Nasser—and we should do it to save the area from Communism— and yet we cannot defy Arab nationalism, risk war, or defy the whole world for the sake of oil interests. If our policy was right in 1956 when we backed Cairo against London, it was not correct in 1958; if it was proper to land troops in Lebanon, our policy was wrong two years ago. If we should withdraw from Quemoy and Matsu under fire, said Mr. Stevenson on April 11, 1955, "we again act the 'paper tiger'; if we join in their defense, we are at war, without major allies and with most of the public opinion in Asia and Europe against us." Either the islands are "essential" to our defense or they are not; either we have a "legal" claim to hold them or we do not. And so it is in every crisis of some magnitude.

Two features of false alternatives as a debating technique are of special significance in a study of partisanship. First, the use of alternatives is generally very coarse, for the real alternative is never considered. Massive retaliation is defined in terms of suicide or surrender, but why not mention the possibility, at least, of successfully deterring Communist aggression? Mr. Stevenson seemed to believe that the eventuality that the Communists would not attack Quemoy for fear of American retaliation was not even worthy of some consideration, and yet of all possible alternatives, it was the most likely and the most important.

Secondly, false alternatives are characterized by a nihilistic trend of reasoning. Whatever the United States does or does not do, it is always wrong and too late. Every alternative is utterly unacceptable. The situation is described as one of the most calamitous episodes in the history of American diplomacy. Our policy in the Middle East was based on "such wrong assumptions" that it was bound to lead into a dead end; no matter which way we move, we are blocked; no matter what we do, we are caught in some insoluble dilemma. The landings in Lebanon were inept, said Walter Lippmann. "We find ourselves, therefore, in a dead-end street." In his speech of April 11, 1955, Mr. Stevenson revealed the same negativism in a striking way. He refused to enlarge upon the injury our Chinese policy had done us and the confusion it has wrought. "We now face," he said, "the bitter consequences" of our government's policy—"either another damaging retreat, or else the hazard of modern war." And he concluded that "at this late hour, there may be no wholly satisfactory way of resolving the dilemma we have stumbled into over the offshore islands. But we can learn something from the experience if we realize at last that we have been pursuing a dead-end policy in Asia."

False alternatives are, in other words, like a Procrustean bed. The situation is forcibly pushed into an incomplete and misleading description of it and is thus distorted at the will of the critic. A choice must allegedly be made between peaceful co-existence or mutual destruction; either the recognition of Red China or the reconquest of the mainland by force; the Soviets want war or they desire genuine peace; liberation is an armed crusade or it means nothing at all; France's policy in Algeria must be formally branded as imperialism or it must be officially supported; we have committed our prestige totally in Lebanon and we must follow through; if we cannot right the situation in Iraq and overthrow the revolutionary government, Lebanon and Jordan will fall, but in order to right it, we must take a gamble as serious as death.

This process is indeed common to all the techniques of assertion that we studied thus far: a little frame is superimposed on a complex whole. The technique used—be it a simple assertion, false alternatives, or accusations—is forceful enough to focus all of our attention at a single point, on one particular risk, but we are not allowed to look right or left. There seems to be nothing beyond, no other evidence. Let us, however, remove the frame; the situation presents itself in its totality, and the partisan argument immediately flounders.

As a matter of fact, the phony logic of this process is a prison that traps the critic who is beguiled by his own words. He cannot free himself from his reasoning and it is for that reason—and no other—that he speaks of dead ends and points of no return; he clamors for bold new programs, but it is of no avail: he cannot escape without losing face. Partisan assertions thus imprison their authors, and for this reason, they often reveal political immaturity. Diplomatic situations that can be described in terms of "either-or" are unusual indeed, but we cannot be sincere and yet lie to ourselves. It is either truth or it is deceit.[11]

The processes we have analyzed so far are employed to spread the tawdry brilliance of a faked logic on political issues; conclusions are dazzling; public opinion is confused because it is surprised by an excess of light. Partisanship can employ other techniques that are diametrically opposed to the techniques of assertion. The argument is left unfinished. The line of reasoning is not drawn all the way to a single conclusion. Instead of defying the government's policy in an outspoken way, partisan criticism chokes it to death. It drags the issue into a swamp of contradictory evidence, where it can be left to its own fate. Processes of this sort obscure the public's perception of an issue. Left in the dim light of an inconclusive debate, public opinion is bewildered and intimidated; looking for a culprit, it finally puts the blame on the administration, and partisanship thereby achieves its purpose.

The simplest way to suffocate a problem is to discuss it so loosely that no single conclusion is permissible or that contradictory conclusions even impose themselves. This process is so intellectually dissolute that it can be described best as sheer *drifting*. The argument passes from one theme to another; it is impossible to determine where it starts and when it stops. The whole reasoning is informally bundled together by conjunctive phrases, and yet there is no rational unity of any kind.

Drifting as a debating technique is illustrated by the following statement which was made in the Senate by Hubert Humphrey on April 28, 1955:

Again I say that Americans must be prepared to negotiate any time, any place, with anyone who wishes to negotiate; and I think it is an expression of weakness on the part of any citizen of the United States to say that we will "be taken," that we will lose out. *That means* that we could lose out and could be fooled and could "be taken" if we are not prepared to go to such a negotiation with a strong program and a strong policy and if we do not know what we want. We have had *one example* of that situation. We went to Geneva, last year. The Geneva Conference will go down as one of the greatest and most colossal diplomatic failures in American history. . . . Our representatives went there. The United States invited the Red Chinese to send representatives to Geneva. After our representatives went to the conference, the Secretary of State decided—because of a little political heat, back home—that he should go home; and he decided to leave his assistants in charge at Geneva. *Mr. President,* one does not win football games by having the captain go home, particularly when the team is playing Notre Dame or the University of Minnesota; and one does not win diplomatic conferences, when Mr. Molotov and his kind are there, and when there is present Chou En-lai, an able and astute man, as opposition. Mr. President, I say that once our country has invited the Red Chinese to come to Geneva, our best representatives should have been there, to see that the Red Chinese did not run off with . . . half of Indochina. . . . *In my opinion,* Chou En-lai, the Red Chinese Foreign Minister and Premier, wants to negotiate because he, too, would like to have a little time—time in which to see whether Southeast Asia may simply fall into his lap. *I say that because* we Americans have whipped ourselves into a frenzy of thinking that the whole world rises and falls on Formosa.[12]

In this instance, the reasoning has drifted from the notion that the United States should negotiate at any time with anybody to the assertion that Chou En-lai wants to negotiate because he knows that he could gain from negotiations. It is an expression of weakness to say that the United States could be taken and the Communists run off with half of Indochina. Americans have whipped themselves into a frenzy about Formosa, but Chou knows that Southeast Asia might simply fall in his lap one day.

It goes without saying that the Geneva Conference—one of the greatest and most colossal failures of our diplomacy—hardly proves the usefulness of negotiations. Rather, the fact that the Communists want to grab Southeast Asia should justify a firm stand on Formosa. Perhaps with a little care, the Senator could have avoided formal contradictions. Most of the time, however, drifting results in hopeless contradictions. Obviously, great labor is necessary to unravel these entangled reasonings, a labor of which opinion is not always capable. On the other hand, such reasonings are so poor, intellectually speaking, that they do not warrant such an effort. If that is the case, public opinion should decide for a whole rejection of the argument. This it does not do. Nor does it labor its way through confusion. Drifting reasonings are read and heard, never refuted nor denounced; their contribution to the general fund of political confusion is unmeasured, but it is considerable.

A particular form of drifting consists of *alarmist litanies*, with which electoral campaigns have made us familiar. The Korean armistice is not a peace. War can break out in Indochina, which has also been partitioned. There is trouble in Malaya. "Italy has voted itself a Communist form of government," Representative Teague said on February 12, 1954, and France "is gripped by internal paralysis. Japan is weak and . . . Communist gains are noted in the Arab States. . . . Europe as a whole is apathetic to the threat of Communism, and anxious to trade with the Reds. Asia is all but lost."[13] Much more can be said, of course.

Nothing is easier than drawing a list like this. All of the vicissitudes of the world, when catalogued on one side of a page, will always present a discouraging case. The device is too crude to deserve further consideration. It must be understood, however, that completely heterogeneous issues are lumped together for the purpose of establishing a background of failure and frustration on the basis of which the administration can be indicted en bloc, that is, without any reasoning at all. The process carefully avoids any definite conclusion; it is replete with fantastic exaggerations. No single point would prove that the administration has truly blundered, but the critic gets away with the simple idea that American policy has been a failure everywhere.

One of the most successful ways of creating a choking atmosphere of doubt and confusion around an issue consists in discussing two themes simultaneously without ever bringing them together because they logically lead to opposite conclusions. We call this process *insulation,* for the trick is to keep separate two lines of reasoning that would destroy each other if the reasoning would ever be brought to a single and consistent conclusion. So defined, insulation is one of the commonest reasoning processes in America.

Governor Harriman said on August 3, 1955, that the "sincere" statements made by President Eisenhower at Geneva "undid much of the damage" done in recent years by the Republicans' "warlike and irresponsible" statements, such as Dulles' massive retaliation. The President's sincerity has "re-established among our friends and allies that we are a peaceful nation." But the Governor also attacked the spirit of Geneva as utter naïveness. He said on June 22, 1956, that the President had credited the Kremlin leaders "with a desire for peace no less earnest than our own." This was responsible, he added, for "a psychological disarmament among free people." The breakup of NATO is the Kremlin's principal objective, "and here is the President of the United States playing right into their hands."

On January 26, 1956, Representative Melvin Price quoted an editorial by Drew Pearson on Dulles' brink of war. Pearson said that the brink-of-war debate did not amount to "a hill of beans." He claimed that Dulles had not been bold but vacillating and unsure. On that basis, Mr. Price concluded that the Secretary's "bungling" had lost Indochina, "destroyed the confidence of our allies," and given the Soviets "the initiative in the cold war." And yet the Representative immediately added that Mr. Dulles had not given credit "where credit was due—to Congressional leaders." It was the Congress that opposed American intervention in Indochina and rescued the administration when it was about "to go over the brink." Mr. Price asserted that "Dulles would have gone over the brink and into war if Congressional leaders had not applied the brakes." Indochina was lost, wrote Pearson, because "the Chinese Reds, knowing how confused we were, kept right on advancing." Dulles was saved from intervention, said Price, on the authority of Pearson, because Congress applied the brakes.[14]

This shows how opinion can be torn apart by two arguments pulling in opposite directions. Heroic Hungary is a mute witness to the hollowness of Dulles' liberation policy, but it is also said that we missed our great chance and Hungary was crushed in blood. The United States should stand clear of colonialism, yet "let us not be too quick in judging others," the critics stress. "Had there been some tough talks mingled with the hearts and flowers at the Summit Conference in Geneva," said Adlai Stevenson on November 2, 1956, the Russians would have thought "a long time" before supplying arms to Egypt. In its rush to frustrate British policy in the Near East, the administration joined hands with the Soviets, and the cohesion of NATO was ruined. For decades, Britain kept Russia from applying its imperialist ambitions in that area—a necessary and successful policy as long as it was in British hands. Now the United States finds itself backing the Chamouns, the Sauds, the Husseins against the tide of Arab renaissance; we distribute arms, and they serve to assassinate our best friends. The time for quibbling has past: there should be a new meeting at the Summit. Public opinion demands it, our strategic position requires it, and when the parley convenes, it will consecrate Moscow's right to speak for the entire Middle East!

No illustration of this process is clearer than the position taken by the Democratic party on the Middle East Resolution. The opposition claimed that the President was originally asking for powers he already had. If the President ever felt that the national interest is at stake, Senator Kennedy said on March 1, 1957, "he could take the United States into war without consent of the Congress"[15] and later come to it for approval. It was high time, in other words, to reverse the unfortunate precedent established by the Formosa Resolution in 1955; otherwise the Presidency would be fatally weakened and future Presidents—of a tougher composition—unnecessarily embarrassed. Senator Mansfield said on February 21, 1957, that "if the President comes to us now for permission to order the Armed Forces to fire if necessary in the Middle East, how long will it be before other Presidents will feel impelled to come to Congress for permission to move the Armed Forces to the firing line?"[16] Senator Morse said on March 1, 1957, that American boys are "too precious to be sent to the Middle East to die there without the representatives of the people knowing the purpose for which the President is sending them there."[17] The President made a commitment to President Chamoun of Lebanon and landed U.S. troops; Senator Morse asserted on August 5, 1958, that the President had "no authority under the Constitution of the United States for any such purpose without the approval of the Congress of the United States."[18] Naked executive power cannot be allowed to rule our most fateful interests. If the administration were to have its way, every member of Congress would be hogtied and the United States would start down the road to a police state.

This example is particularly striking because the two lines of reasoning taken by the critics were so exaggerated that they became irreconcilable, although in its intent, their argument was correct. As it stands, the reasoning leads to contradictory conclusions; formal inconsistency is avoided by the critics' failure to draw the line to a single, well-defined proposition. Public opinion lost sight of the problem, but the resulting confusion was unnecessary. In its original phraseology, the Middle East Resolution would have authorized the President to use force in that area. As Senator Mansfield rightly said on February 21, 1957, this authorization might have brought about a subtle change in our system of government that would lead in the direction of reducing the President "to a mere agent of Congress." It would have also been an imperceptible step away from our system of checks and balances.

As Senator Mansfield said, Congress would have assumed "responsibility for actions which have not yet taken place and whose nature we cannot anticipate." Could it be contended, asked the Senator, "that the original language of the Resolution could not have worked both ways, that it could not have provided precedence both for a parliamentary system of government and arbitrary Executive power?"[19]

The answer to Senator Mansfield's question undoubtedly is that the Resolution could have worked both ways in the sense that it could have limited at one and the same time the authority of both the President and the Congress. But the latter could reserve its Constitutional right of independent criticism and correction while reasserting Presidential prerogatives. In actual practice, Congressional dissenters invoke the principle of separation of powers in order not to commit themselves to executive actions and in order to denounce them as executive tyranny. This is parliamentary government at its worst.[20]

It might be necessary to recognize at this point that our Constitutional system furthers political irresponsibility, or rather that it requires a measure of political responsibility generally lacking and always flimsy when achieved temporarily. There is no remedy for this basic failure of the system except to understand that every diplomatic situation is characterized by complexity. When it isolates the various aspects of a situation by means of incorrect reasoning, partisan criticism can always destroy national policy. This is illustrated in the following example.

On January 22, 1954, Senator Douglas criticized the administration's decision to withdraw two divisions from Korea because it might result, he said, "in the withdrawal of Chinese divisions from Korea and their transfer to Indo-China."[21] On the other hand, the Democratic opposition demanded, and soon obtained, executive assurances that the forces we withdrew from Korea would not be transferred by the administration to the Indochinese theater.

The Douglas criticism is consistent with the argument of deterrence by use of conventional power at the point of danger—an approach that would have justified commitment of American forces in Southeast Asia. On the other hand, withdrawals from Korea evidently released pressure on Red China in that area. The administration's move was justified, as we said earlier, by the need for disengaging our forces and allowing them to regain the flexibility that might be necessary in order to bring our power to bear in Indochina if it were needed. But the administration was forced by Congress to allay fears about military involvement in Southeast Asia. In this way, the Chinese Communists gained twice: we withdrew from Korea and promised not to intervene in Southeast Asia, which was the reverse of policy.

All of the various techniques defined so far have the effect of misrepresenting the evidence, and for that reason they all are techniques of distortion. We can, however, push the analysis to a deeper level at which the processes of partisan misrepresentation can be more explicitly comprehended. Most of the time, misrepresentation stems from *false assumptions,* which are neither proved nor even clearly stated. It was assumed, for instance, that massive retaliation was predicated upon offsetting Communist superiority in manpower and conventional weapons with American "superiority" in air power and nuclear armaments. Our policy allegedly was to cancel out Communist superiority in conventional power with our "trump card of technological supremacy."[22] Soviet progress in air power and missiles was therefore a reason for hysteria, for it seemed to destroy the very foundation of our security. But the notion of superiority, understood as technological supremacy, was not at the basis of our policy, as was assumed, and the argument missed the point.

It was assumed that the Atomic Energy Commission deliberately withheld information concerning fallout, and Admiral Strauss was consequently branded as a traitor to humanity. It was assumed that the U.S.S.R. was sincere when it discontinued atomic tests, and the critics wrung their hands about the propaganda disaster thus inflicted on American leadership. It was assumed that Chiang Kai-shek planned to use the offshore islands as jumping-off places for an invasion of the Chinese mainland, and for that reason, Communist maneuvers were justified as self-defense against an open provocation of Red China. Adlai Stevenson said on April 11, 1955, that we have "to face the fact that General Chiang's army cannot invade the mainland unless we are prepared to accept enormous burdens and risks—alone." We should abandon this "go-it-alonism," he added, and the world will respect us if we recognize our "mistakes" and if we intend to correct them.[23]

We should cease "to deceive ourselves over the hard realities of power in the Formosa situation," said Mr. Stevenson. This statement implied that American mistakes were the sole obstacle to a peaceful settlement. It assumed further that the United States should never act alone. If our allies fail to support us, something must be wrong with American policy. It was finally assumed that our Chinese policy was nothing more than a bid for military reconquest of the mainland by the Chinese Nationalists—an astonishing oversimplification directly contradicted by the terms of our treaty with Chiang.

Public opinion can protect itself from being confused by such arguments only if it makes a point of formulating the premises from which criticism is inferred and examining their validity in the light of the evidence. This is a simple remedy; a deduction cannot be worth more than its logical antecedents.

Exaggeration is another elementary process of partisan misrepresentation. When the British and the French refused to back up the administration's plan for united action in Indochina, this reverse was described by the *Washington Evening Post* of April 29, 1954, as "the most serious setback in generations—probably the worst since we started to play in the international big league." We have already noted that the Geneva Conference of 1954 was considered by Senator Humphrey to be "one of the greatest and most colossal diplomatic failures" in the history of American diplomacy. The second conference at Geneva opened a still darker era. As Walter Lippmann put it in the *Washington Post* of February 21, 1956, the spirit of Geneva was responsible for "the biggest and most serious setback" we have suffered "since the Communist victory in China." And there were simply no words left to describe

205

the havoc caused by the Soviet sputnik, the revolution in Iraq and the Berlin crisis.

When a diplomatic reverse is compared with the loss of China or pictured as the most colossal ever, the power of exaggeration instantly exhausts itself. It is typical in our partisan debates for the argument to reach this ultimate height all at once. There seem to be no degrees, no limited risks, no temporary setbacks. It is all or nothing, and the reasoning instantly passes to the limit. If Dien Bien Phu is allowed to fall, all of Southeast Asia is lost. If we intervene in Indochina, the Chinese will step in; the Russians will follow suit. This is war, all-out war, national suicide. If we fail at one point, everything has failed; all of our policy was wrong; a new approach must be devised immediately. If we are rebuked, we have no friends. In other words, *exaggeration is a fatal jump into desperation.*

There can be no doubt that this finding is of paramount importance for two main reasons. First, exaggeration possesses the power to alter our outlook to such an extent that we suddenly find ourselves in a strange world of contradictions, insoluble problems, and unmeasurable risks. This power is mysterious, for the critic uses words which he does not take quite seriously, and yet the result is inevitable. The floodgates are opened, and every valid evidence is submerged in the deluge. From that moment on, the exaggerated notion which made us stumble into confusion ceases to be relevant. What counts then is the infinite multiplicity of pessimistic ideas which again become attractive because they correspond to the state of our mind. What counts then is the inept, stubborn recanting of a well-known litany of evils which has occupied our attention many, many times before and seems truthful for no other reason than that we have sanctioned its validity that many times.

On the other hand, exaggeration is a process likely to be used in time of crisis. Now when peace is threatened, the administration must make declarations to awaken public opinion to the dangers of inaction. Such declarations generally consist, as we know, in stating that the crisis must be checked before it leads to war.

We are told that the national interest is involved and that the real stakes go much beyond Dien Bien Phu or Quemoy. A climate of resistance to Communist pressure must be created. The reasons why we should act are stated, and the administration deliberately enlarges the immediate outlook and rightly shows what the consequences of surrender would ultimately be if we were to yield now.

Any valid policy has a logic. It transcends the limited issue, which tends to set bounds to our courage. But when public opinion reacts to the administration's declarations by exaggerating, it uses that very logic to destroy policy. *It transforms the reasons why we should act into reasons why we should fear.* Although it refuses to commit itself to policy because the peril is too great, public opinion takes as accomplished fact and an actually existing calamity that which is still the aggressor's bluff and from which danger our policy ought to guard us. The Suez crisis endangered Western solidarity, and public opinion claimed that NATO had been "shattered" and that the breach could never be healed. Was there any other way to make real the very difficulty to set right? Our Chinese policy was described as loaded with disproportionate risks. What else could be said to insure the success of Communist pressures?

Public opinion's refusal to support national policy compounds its own problems, for it forces the administration to emphasize anew the need for action. The more the administration does so, the more opinion finds reasons to fear. The case finally comes to be grossly overstated on both sides. Nothing could serve the aggressor better. The Communists are experts at creating diplomatic situations out of nothing. A reckless charge is made; a plane is shot down; American nationals are indicted as spies. "A few shells" are fired around Quemoy, said a Red Chinese communiqué of October 6, 1958, "just to call your attention." Threats and *intransigeance* can always be followed by some conciliatory move. The wicked well know that in the state of tension they purposefully create, at no cost to themselves, a smile on their part calls for an expression of gratitude from their intended victim and, more likely than not, for the solid rewards of diplomatic concessions.[24]

A willingness to turn realities upside down is to be found lurking in every one of the techniques of debate we have analyzed. It was encountered at every phase of the massive retaliation debate. We were told again and again that nobody was to blame but ourselves if we were at the brink of war. Anyone who threatens to go to war in the atomic age is either mad or bluffing, and who could anyone be but our Secretary of State? The Eisenhower administration has never wanted disarmament, and Mr. Dulles makes it certain that all peace proposals come to nothing. Defensive policies were depicted as aggressive policies; deterrence was turned into bellicosity; serious bargaining in negotiations appeared to be insincerity; realism seemed to be callous indifference to public opinion.

The most striking feature of this process of *inversion* is that it strikes directly at fundamentals. The *New York Times* of February 3, 1955, published the letter of one Professor Bodde on the Formosa crisis. "By what conceivable right," this professor asked, do we presume to tell the Red Chinese government, "Communist though it be, what it may or may not do about areas which we ourselves have declared to be a part of China?" Once started, the reasoning had to continue relentlessly to the bitter end. "By what right," he asked, "do we threaten military action if the Communists even move against islands like Quemoy, only three miles from their coast?" Americans have traditionally placed their faith in moral principle rather than in political expediency. "Today is a time when we should reaffirm that faith," said Professor Bodde. The accused is not the Communist aggressor; it is the United States. A policy solemnly affirmed by the President and endorsed by virtually unanimous Congressional majorities is branded as sheer expediency and contrary to moral principle. The administration's position was that the use of force to accomplish political objectives could not be condoned. But if it was wrong to use force to take over territory that rightfully belongs to another, it must have been equally wrong to use force to hold territory that belongs to another. Chiang, with our backing, was doing just that.

Such loathsome charges were not enough, however, to consume entirely the power of inversion. On March 26, 1955, a dispatch

208

published in the press reported that certain high policy advisers had suggested an operation "smash China" against the mainland in case of hostilities. All-out war was allegedly planned by the administration, with a complete destruction of the Chinese industrial potential if necessary. This report raised a storm of anger throughout the country. In an open letter to the President, fourteen religious leaders wrote the following:

Why then shall we start allout war against the Chinese mainland? . . . We think that to risk world-wide atomic war for the prestige of Chiang Kai-shek would not be a folly, but a crime of the first magnitude. The arguments in favor of waging preventive war are flimsy and faulty. . . . Mr. President, we implore you to stop this drift toward atomic war. . . . As Christians, we cannot be silent at this critical juncture of United States history. Our conscience compels us to oppose an aggressive allout war policy.[25]

With this statement, inversion is complete. It can go no further. On the basis of a doubtful report, it accuses the United States of preventive war, an aggressive, all-out war policy, and folly, a crime of the first magnitude.

It is important to realize that inversion is a process that cannot be controlled once it has been unleashed. Pushing the dissenter farther and farther away from truth and decency, it cannot stop until his hand has struck at the very heart of our position in the world. Once the right to discipline Communist aggression in the Far East had been opened to question, the logic of inversion did the rest.

The ugliness of this process is often more clearly revealed by the critic's coarse impertinence than by the seriousness of his accusations. When the Soviet Union crushed the Hungarian revolution, prominent Americans asked whether the United States had ever acted differently in Central America. When Mr. Dulles warned against indirect aggression in the Middle East, all accused him of hypocrisy. Was his celebrated "liberation" policy less subversive than Nasserism? Does the Voice of America do anything less than Radio Cairo? On October 25, 1958, Communist China ordered its troops not to shell Quemoy on alternate days. This partial cease-fire was particularly absurd and revulsive, but anyone familiar with American politics could have predicted that sooner or later our newspapers would put in print some letter or editorial asking: Are the Chinese Communists, "with their alternate shellings and truces," not simply reacting "to the mind of Secretary of State Dulles on even days or odd days?"[26] The Eisenhower administration denounced the Soviet proposals on Berlin as a Trojan horse. Is West Berlin anything but the Trojan horse of freedom, planted by the West in totalitarian East Germany?

The vulgarity of feeling displayed by an inversion of this sort permits us to discern the final hardening of partisanship, a conscious acceptance of untruth, and a refusal to listen and to debate the issue seriously. The dissenter limits himself to an absolute, unqualified indictment of American policy and then buries his head in the sand. No inverted reasoning ever dares face up to the consequences to which it leads. It is pure negation. And yet inversion is the ultima ratio of partisanship. Let us therefore assume that if our reasoning processes are irrational, something must be wrong with ourselves. There can no longer be any doubt that the source of the evil is within us.

CHAPTER IX

The Deterioration of Rational Evidence

OUR ANALYSIS NOW TURNS to the sources of political conduct in the United States. As in every other field of human behavior, we encounter in politics certain kinds of forces. First of all, there are irrational forces which determine the political decisions of a nation and the conduct of political debates, even though the people are not always conscious of their influence. We call these forces *political dynamisms*. For example, allegiances and opinions are influenced by nationalism, a force born of ignorance of other countries and blindness to one's own shortcomings. Another potent dynamism is party politics. A political party is an institution that naturally tends to place its own good above the objectives which it is designed to serve. Interservice rivalry is another. As long as our armed services are not unified under a single command, this dynamism will have to be taken into consideration. Budget-makers will always struggle with defense planners; governments will always suffer from a lack of revenue and complain about the "programs" that have to be sacrificed to budget "austerity."

The dynamism of partisanship, understood in the most general sense, is the only one with which we shall concern ourselves here. Partisanship is a dynamism characterized by continuity. It is a built-in force that carries in its stream both the old and the new: slogans and partially valid arguments; McCarthyism and Knowlandism; Harry Dexter White and Colonel Nasser. Any new issue furnishes fuel for the same kind of debate: one must criticize and criticize continuously.

The continuity of partisanship is the counter-image of policy continuity. It is obvious that the process of policy-making cannot be broken; successes must be diligently exploited by the policy-makers and reverse turned to good use. Now partisanship imitates policy in reverse. It puts confusion in the place of consistency. It refuses to acknowledge victories, and it exaggerates defeats. It is as continuous in destruction as policy must be continuous in creation.

Like all dynamisms, partisanship is an irrational force. It drives political action in a direction that, as citizens, we do not freely control. Mr. Stevenson said on October 5, 1956, that "the political party can never be considered an end in itself. It is an agency for a larger purpose." *We do not have to succumb to partisanship, but a free, conscious, personal act is necessary in order to emancipate ourselves from its ever present influence.* This is to say that no one can free himself from the irrationality of the dynamism simply by denouncing it in noble and general terms. It is only at the very moment when partisanship actually exercises its blinding influence upon us that a true emancipation can occur. Opinion first yields to partisanship and then attempts to justify itself as well as it can. The readiness to succumb to partisan reasonings and to find good reasons for being wrong is thus an important part of the power of partisanship as a political dynamism.

Political behavior is also determined by the attitudes, or moral predispositions, of society. These are the prevailing standards of value, or *mores,* in terms of which we are inclined to assess the validity of a policy. Like dynamisms, the mores exercise and all-pervading influence on the conduct of political debates. They differ from dynamisms, however, in that they are rational: what is considered to be a value is formally praised; what is explicitly condemned should have no part in what is called the "true picture of America."

It goes without saying that in the course of a debate, one can adopt various attitudes in turn and pass from one to the other according to the exigencies of the moment. It is also well to remember that some of our mores concern the objectives that our policy should pursue, while others are relevant only to means and methods of implementation. The dilemma of peace and "brinkmanship" illustrates this point quite clearly.

Political values are defined as rational standards only in the sense that they are so recognized by our society. We cannot assume, of course, that because they received a conscious sanction, the values that guide our political behavior are in conformity with moral principles, nor can it be assumed that they serve the national interest. On the other hand, attitudes that are branded as contrary to our mores do conform to both the national interest and the universal principles of morality. In other words, there is no such thing as spontaneous goodness in politics, and still less is there some form of national goodness that would express itself in the form of a creed that is sociologically accepted by an entire nation. No principle, perhaps, can appear more contrary to the philosophy of democracy; the fundamental dogma of Americanism is that democracy purifies itself like running water. This is not true.

The massive retaliation debate has shown that the simplest of notions can be misunderstood. It has revealed how easily certitudes deteriorate, how the most elementary evidence can be inverted, and how doubt can creep in everywhere. It has proved, in other words, that public opinion constantly drifts from knowable evidence into confusion and smugness. Obviously, the trend is not toward an increasingly rational perception of problems but, rather, toward irrationality and a slow deterioration of all certitudes. This contention of basic irrationality in the political behavior of a "free" society will be explained in two stages. We shall first show how public opinion tends to react in various situations, and then we shall define various forms of irrationality.

There are situations which are so self-evident that an extreme measure of political bad faith would be necessary for one not to understand their essential features. For instance, the mental picture American society has formed of Communist imperialism is clear and unambiguous. No politician would openly profess that compromises could be made with the Communist ideology. It could be expected, therefore, that such a comprehension of Communist objectives would also produce a clear understanding of Communist tactics, yet the massive retaliation debate proved that *the concepts which have less bearing on political behavior are precisely those which are the most evident.* The simpler a proposition is, the easier it is to take it for granted, that is, to divorce it from the reality of our political conduct. Such propositions tend to be placed above the level of useful discussion—as if they were too valid to be considered and too important to exercise any influence on our public debates.

In his speech of April 21, 1956, Mr. Stevenson made this ringing declaration:

This is a time of change in world affairs. The peoples sense it, even if the statesmen don't, for the peoples are, in a deep sense, forcing change. No one knows just where these changes will lead. The administration has been slow to respond to this new mood. The Russians, on the other hand, have exploited it diligently. Their objectives, we are told almost every day, have not changed. Of course, they haven't. No one said they had. The Soviet rulers frankly state that their goal is a Communist world. But they have changed their approach and we have not changed ours.

The Eisenhower administration has clung, Mr. Stevenson added, to "its military emphasis in pacts, foreign aid, trade and international exchanges of all kinds." As an alternative to these rigid, stubborn policies, he proposed a unilateral H-bomb testing moratorium; he wanted economic aid to be increasingly handled through the United Nations. In this way, he said, the Russians would be involved in what he called "responsible international cooperation all over the world." It is true that the Soviets have rejected a similar arrangement in the past, but "this was," he concluded, "Joseph Stalin—of now dishonored memory."

Mr. Stevenson's reasoning is a Frankenstein monster. Twice the argument has slipped. Change was first described as a deep reality that the people force statesmen to accept. This romantic declamation served to indict the administration's refusal to change, and it also served to imply that Soviet de-Stalinization was perhaps a fundamental change. But change was also referred to as a new mood; and, of course, the U.S.S.R. has not changed. This very truth—which should have guided the reasoning—is sidetracked as a boring proposition that Republican leaders repeat every day. Mr. Stevenson proposed that the United States change its "approach," but the changes he suggested were not changes of approach but of policy.

In his lighter manner, Senator Humphrey declared on April 28, 1955, that Russia "turns off the faucet one day, and on the next day. She is sweetness and light one month, then a vicious dragon the next." He claimed that "we should not be deluded by Communist strategy. We know its objective." And yet he immediately added:

I am one who does not want war either. I think a defense based on nuclear or atomic weapons is just planned suicide. . . . Therefore our policy must be dedicated to peace. It must be a policy which is based on strength and knowing what we want, and there must be a consistency of policy. Let us not talk about hydrogen bombs.[1]

To talk about hydrogen weapons scares away the friends of America. There should be, said the Senator, more "talk and more emphasis upon our real resources and the real strength of our country, namely our faith; our economics; our political system; our land system; our programs of health, education and welfare; and our love and understanding of people."

This statement illustrates the nature of the dynamism now under consideration. Instead of resolving a problem in the light of knowable truth—which the dissenter asserts as such—the reverse is done. The Soviet Union is described as a vicious dragon; American policy should be a policy that is based on strength; there should be a consistency of policy. But Mr. Humphrey "does not want war either." Therefore, American policy should be based not upon massive retaliation but upon our love and understanding of people.

This crude reasoning also shows how the self-evidence of a situation is used to make simple truths appear tedious and politically inert. Nobody is deluded by Communist tactics, but few understand massive retaliation. One is not debatable; the second is a controversial issue. There is a contest between a boring truth and a challenging problem. Since provoking thoughts would vanish if we were merely truthful, we prefer to remain in the glamor of defiance.[2]

In other instances, the main features of a situation are equally clear. A policy is proposed by the administration in terms that can be understood by all, yet public opinion pretends to see nothing but confusion and mystery. It claims that the President, Mr. Nixon, Secretary Dulles, Admiral Radford, and Mr. Stassen speak out of turn, apologize, and contradict one another. The policy is a Machiavellian maneuver executed by the administration in order to appease the Republican Right Wing. It is a bluff. It is anything but what it really is.

In 1950, Mr. Dulles wrote that in the past, the United States never thought of peace in terms of a settlement which might allow this country to go on existing "as an oasis in a totalitarian desert." The issue was not a question of saving one's neck but how to save freedom. How, Mr. Dulles asked, could it be different now? "It is time," he said, "to think in terms of taking the offensive in the world struggle for freedom and of rolling back the engulfing tide of despotism. It is time to think less of fission bombs and more of establishing justice and ending terrorism in the world."[3]

In due time, this doctrine became national policy. During the 1952 campaign, Mr. Eisenhower declared that the American conscience would never know peace until the enslaved peoples of the world were again restored as masters of their own fate. In his message to Congress on February 2, 1953, the President said that he would ask the Congress to promulgate this liberation policy by joining him in a declaration making it clear that the United States would "never acquiesce in the enslavement of any people in order to purchase fancied gain" for itself.

Since a declaration of this sort could have been made without formally repudiating past agreements and since the two houses of

Congress have often passed resolutions on the liberation of the Communist satellites, it is beyond comprehension that the liberation policy ever became the prototype of Mr. Dulles' improvisations. The Eisenhower administration never meant to encourage open rebellion by unarmed people against superior force. The President emphasized on December 2, 1956, that liberation would have to be brought about "as an evolutionary process." On October 27, 1956, Mr. Dulles had tried to make it clear that the United States merely wanted the satellites to be free and that we had never looked upon these nations "as potential military allies." He added, on December 18, 1956, that we had "no desire to surround the Soviet Union with a band of hostile states, and to revive what used to be called the Cordon Sanitaire." We were "very open-minded," he said, to any solution of the satellite problem that the U.S.S.R. might consider, "whether neutralization or otherwise."

Public opinion refused to understand this point. It insisted that if liberation did not mean a war of liberation—or direct armed intervention in case of a spontaneous rebellion—the policy was a policy of containment or that it meant nothing at all. The difference between containment and liberation is self-evident. As Mr. Eisenhower said on December 2, 1956, the United States "doesn't now, and never has, advocated open rebellion by an undefended populace against force over which they could not possibly prevail." It would be "the most terrible mistake for the free world ever to accept the enslavement of the Eastern European tier of nations as part of a future world." To contain an aggressor, as in Korea, Berlin or the Middle East, at the moment when he plans further advances is a dynamic, valid policy. To contain an aggressor when he is engaged in assimilating past conquests is the reverse of such a policy. The principle which demands that the United States oppose an aggressor in the act of committing aggression also demands that we refuse to acquiesce to conquests which we were not in a position to prevent. In that sense, liberation is the exact opposite of containment. It makes as little sense to contain Russia in eastern Europe as it would to liberate Iran or Vietnam.

In contradistinction, containment demands that the United

States accept as fact the Communist domination of enslaved countries. Indeed, it has been said that there is a "finality, for better or worse," in what happened in eastern Europe. It has been said that whether we like it or not, time is the agent of legitimacy.[4] But the Hungarian revolution proved that there is no such finality at all. Rather, it proved that even competent observers like G. F. Kennan have been dramatically mistaken in their past evaluations of the satellite situation. To accept the enslavement of captive peoples as a matter of policy would reveal an astonishing lack of political realism, for the trend toward freedom is what Mr. Dulles called on July 2, 1957, "a basic truth." After many years of ruthless domination, the Communist rulers have failed to gain free allegiance, even of those they fondle, the workers and youth. It is more than evident that they never will.

No other foundation is necessary for a valid policy of liberation. Unlike containment, liberation formally refuses to recognize enslavement as final. Together with the architects of the containment policy, it asserts the failure of the Communist ideology. Neither containment nor liberation postulates a belief that the U.S.S.R. or Red China would soon collapse from within. Mr. Stevenson attributed this notion to the Eisenhower administration. He said on October 18, 1958, that "it is wishful thinking at its worst, and most dangerous, to think, let alone to pretend, that the Soviet system is about to collapse. It isn't. It is here to stay. And we may as well face it." He proved his point by stressing the resources, the economy, the will of the Soviet Union to overtake us.

It is true, of course, that the Soviet economy, even if utterly mismanaged, would never collapse; to expect such an event would be like expecting all of Russia's atomic bombs to detonate themselves. But it is sheer dogmatism to pretend that the Communist empire will never break down. Unlikely as this eventuality appears, it cannot be excluded. If ever there was an ideology unbearable to the human mind, it is the Communist ideology. If ever there was a system of government designed to foster popular discontent, it is the Soviet constitution. The Czechs are reported to bear Communism in patience out of hatred for the Germans, and they say that

Communism will not last but that Germany is here to stay. The prospects for the liberation of the captive peoples are not bright. Equally certain is the fact that the Communist system cannot go on without undergoing fundamental changes. As Mr. Dulles said on October 28, 1958, "it is going to collapse through the fact that in the long run people are not going to allow themselves being exploited." Whether this evolution will require decades or centuries is totally irrelevant. The principle of liberation must be asserted, and that suffices.[5]

Since liberation is founded on principle, no responsible statesman can say that it is an unacceptable policy. It strikes at the most sensitive weakness of the Communist system, and it is therefore a realistic policy. Yet public opinion continually asserts that this is not true. Public opinion sees darkness instead of light and stubbornly refuses to accept any explanation. Liberation seems to be nothing but a "campaign gimmick." The people of Budapest curse Mr. Dulles, and the security police continues its activities. But if liberation is a gimmick, the United States has no liberation policy; we are not conscious of the injustice Hungary has suffered; we have no hope, no faith in the future. To be against the policy of liberation is, in other words, no solution at all.

The brink-of-war debate is another example of how an erratic public opinion stumbles on a problem that is its own handiwork. A well-known article quoted Mr. Dulles as having said this:

You have to take chances for peace, just as you must take chances in war. Some say that we were brought to the verge of war. Of course, we were brought to the verge of war. The ability to get to the verge without getting into the war is the necessary art. If you cannot master it, you inevitably get into war. If you try to run away from it, if you are scared to go to the brink, you are lost.

The substance of this doctrine is as clear as daylight. As the Secretary of State explained on January 17, 1956, "it was important to make clear the fact that we were going to stand firm, even though that might involve a war." And yet public opinion succeeded in deceiving itself by forcing into the phrase the notion that Dulles advocated "brinkmanship" as a new diplomatic approach. "At long last," wrote the *New Republic* of January 23, 1956, "the Eisenhower administration has officially conceded that on three successive occasions during the last three years it has as a matter of deliberate policy brought the United States and the world to the verge of nuclear war." It is true that *if* the Secretary had described himself in the role of an artist juggling threats of atomic war, it would have been quite shocking. It is also true that *if* he believed the natural route of American diplomacy to be the edge of the precipice, our present policy would be a reckless gamble camouflaged as statesmanship. And one would have to agree with Adlai Stevenson, who said on January 17, 1956, that "instead of torturing history, demeaning our friends, hurling threats and brandishing weapons," the administration would better serve the cause of peace by exerting what he called "moral force with positive determination to end the hydrogen race and to rid the world of this ghastly menace." Unfortunately for Mr. Stevenson, however, none of this was true. Mr. Dulles had not meant brinkmanship.

Whatever damage was done to America's good name by the brink-of-war debate came from partisan misrepresentation. More serious than the ruin accomplished in a moment of passing folly was the fact that massive retaliation had been identified with brinkmanship. "Most of us thought," Senator Humphrey said on January 12, 1956, "that the doctrine of massive retaliation had been so thoroughly discussed, analyzed, and exploded that it had gone into a well-deserved and massive sleep." According to the Senator, Mr. Dulles' pride of authorship had forced him "to this fraudulent reassertion" of a doctrine that was considered by all as an "artless phrase tossed upon the winds of public opinion."[6] If this were true, what strategy would the United States have for its defense and the defense of the free world?

The offshore islands of Quemoy and Matsu sparked a debate that clearly illustrated the processes of self-deception. In his press conference of February 2, 1955, President Eisenhower said that the purpose of the Formosa Resolution was "to make certain that no conflict occurs through mistaken calculations on the other

side. . . . The purpose is honestly and hopefully to prevent war."
This country had been "as exact as it seems possible," he added,
and we "certainly tried to avoid being truculent." As Mr. Dulles
explained on March 8, 1955, the United States had to deal with
"two distinct matters, first the political decision as to what to defend, and then the decision as to how to defend." It had been
decided to defend Formosa and the Pescadores, but the Resolution permitted a flexible defense which the President would determine, said Mr. Dulles, "in the light of his judgment as to the over-
all value of certain coastal positions to the defense of Formosa
and the cost of holding these positions." The President himself
had announced on January 27, 1955—as we said earlier—that he
alone would make the decision regarding American action toward
the offshore islands, "the responsibility for which he has not delegated."

It is difficult to see in what manner the administration's policy
lacked candor or clarity, but public opinion could not be satisfied.
Instead of accepting the administration's contention that circumstances offered the occasion to stand firm and do so at little cost,
it worked itself into a frenzy. The administration's deliberately
vague approach carried with it a terrible risk. The Chinese Communists, well knowing that the United States would back down
in the end, would not hesitate to attack. The offshore islands
would eventually be given to the Reds anyway. This was undoubtedly the best way out of a bad business, yet the consequences were
bound to be appallingly unpleasant.

The Reds demanded on January 29, 1955, that the United Nations do something about American aggression. Why, indeed, not
to submit the whole issue to the UN? The Reds were invited to do
so by the Security Council on January 31, but on February 3, they
contemptuously turned down the invitation. Every American
newspaper was on the alert for confusing information, and jitters
were carefully exploited. On February 10, the Chinese Nationalist
foreign minister asserted that the United States was committed to
the defense of the offshore islands, but the administration denied
that there was any such commitment, either explicit or implicit.

On March 9, the administration was forced to deny a press report from Tokyo asserting that the United States thought that war was imminent and that preparations were being made to that effect. In a week-end scare story, Admiral Carney was reported as having said that the Reds would attack by April 15. But the Admiral was talking in terms of the enemy's capabilities, he said on April 5, and not about the enemy's intentions. New clarifications on every aspect of the situation were constantly required, and as soon as they were supplied, public opinion claimed again and again that the United States had maneuvered itself into a dead end.

It was so little of a dead end that a relaxation of tension soon came. In the last hours of the Bandung Conference, Chou En-lai proposed direct negotiations between the Reds and the United States. Mr. Hoover, then Acting Secretary of State, issued a statement asking that the Communists first show their sincerity with a cease-fire, by releasing American prisoners, or by making any other move to prove their good will. The demanding tone of this statement irritated American public opinion. Returning after the week-end, Mr. Dulles announced on April 26 that he would try to determine the sincerity of Communist intentions. The debate came to a stop as suddenly as it had started.

Public opinion did not look back and reflect upon the extreme ugliness of the situation which it had created. A simple check on dates would have sufficed to make Communist maneuvers manifest. Artillery fire against Quemoy was resumed on September 3, 1954—exactly three days before the opening of the Manila Conference. On the very day the United States initialed our security pact with the Formosan government, the condemnation of eleven American fliers was announced in Peiping. The Secretary of the UN went to Peiping to discuss their release with the Communists. On the day these talks were concluded, four hundred Communist aircraft raided the Tachens. The critics of the administration did not consider how ridiculous was the idea that Red China would risk a war with the United States and send troops in junks to liberate Formosa. What they wanted was an official announcement that the United States would not defend the offshore islands if they were attacked or surrender them to the Communists, who did not demand that concession at all.

Having thus assumed a Communist victory, partisanship spoke about the administration's pattern of big, bold talk followed by surrender. After such a mismanagement, why should Peiping worry after all, no matter what America says? This was what A. M. Schlesinger described as "alternations of bluff and back-down, the fantastic 'massive retaliation' phrase, the vacillation before Dien Bien Phu, the administration's blank check on Formosa, the march-up-the-hill march-down-again on Quemoy and the Matsus, the week-end reversal over negotiation with Communist China."[7]

The 1955 China debate hinged on the administration's refusal to declare that the coastal islands would not be defended if attacked. In 1958, there was no issue other than appeasement. From August 1, 1955, until December 12, 1957, bilateral negotiations between the United States and Red China continued. Our diplomatic effort failed to bring about a renunciation of force that would apply to the Formosa area without depriving anyone of the right of self-defense. The *de facto* cease-fire which prevailed during that period came to an end when the Communists resumed intensive shelling of Quemoy and other positions on August 23, 1958. A violent propaganda offensive was launched simultaneously. The Communists asserted, as usual, that they would liberate Taiwan; a landing on Quemoy was supposedly imminent; Quemoy had to give up or face complete destruction. The administration displayed more firmness than it did in 1955, and the Communists were brought around almost at once. Mr. Dulles declared on September 4 that the United States had recognized that the coastal islands had become increasingly related to the defense of Formosa, and he also said that this country still intended to arrive at a renunciation of force through negotiations. On September 6, Chou En-lai agreed to a resumption of ambassadorial talks with the United States. The talks were actually resumed—without much hope for an agreement on either side—on September 15, 1958.

The Communists failed to carry any of their threats to execution. The effectiveness of the Sidewinder missile was reported as having come as a shock to them; heavy shelling, supplemented by sea attacks on Nationalist convoys, could not blockade the coastal islands. The obvious hazards of a sea invasion—a military balance temporarily tipping in favor of the Nationalists and the presence of the Seventh Fleet—made it more than clear that the islands could not be taken with anything less than a full-scale attempt which would be doomed to almost certain defeat.[8]

Not only were the facts clearer in 1958 than in 1955 as far as the military situation was concerned, but the diplomatic situation was also much more favorable to American policy. Criticism from abroad was more restrained; Prime Minister Macmillan took a calm view of the situation, which was a sharp contrast to Sir Anthony Eden's introverted feebleness. The Communist attacks came at a time when Burma, Thailand, and Indonesia were meeting the Reds' pressure with increased resistance.

Communist propaganda blundered repeatedly. The crisis was deliberately created immediately after the Middle East situation had quieted down and at a time when Congress was not in session. The accusations and threats hurled at the United States were so contradictory that they could not be taken seriously. Chiang Kai-shek was treated as a hated shadow of the past and the betrayer of his people, but after Dulles referred to his foolishness, Communist propaganda appealed to its friends of the Kuomintang to return to the embrace of the motherland after having been betrayed by America. Khrushchev accused the United States of throwing its fleets around and threatening the peace by dispatching formidable navies armed with nuclear weapons, and yet he also said that nowadays, fleets are fit for nothing, in fact, but courtesy visits and gun salutes. They are merely targets for rockets of all kinds. The U.S.S.R. loudly proclaimed that an attack on Red China would be an attack on the Soviet Union, but nothing could be more erroneous, they said, than to try to read a threat into this warning. Nothing would have been more contrary to the Soviet policy of peace than intervention in the Chinese Civil War. The United States was the aggressor, of course, and America should go home—or be thrown out. How ridiculous it was of Dulles to demand a cease-fire when not a single shot had been exchanged between Americans and Red Chinese! On September 4, 1958, Red China extended its territorial waters to twelve miles. On September 19, Mr. Khrushchev sent an abusive letter to President Eisenhower, who immediately returned it. Three successive cease-fires were ordered. These crude maneuvers revealed growing inconsistency in the Communist position.

As was the case in 1955, public opinion lost control of itself at the moment when the Communist offensive had already been broken.[9] The administration was driven, by public pressure, not to the brink of war, but to the brink of appeasement. Our policy in the Far East finally emerged basically unchanged by the crisis, but it suffered wounds inflicted by public opinion. Nothing was more revealing than the pleasure which public opinion derived from its own contradictions. Secretary Dulles claimed that Quemoy was, like Berlin, an island surrounded by Communist power, but Walter Lippmann said that the comparison made no sense at all. "Quemoy is not like Berlin," he wrote in the *New York Herald Tribune* of October 7, 1958, "any more than it is like London, Paris or Washington."[10] President Eisenhower warned against a new Munich, and G. F. Kennan proved that such analogies have no meaning whatsoever. They ignore, he said, "the very significant differences in political personality and method as between the Nazis and the Communists." We cannot allow ourselves to confuse "a highly complex situation with extremely simple ones." Whatever the international implications of the Quemoy crisis might be, the whole problem is very much, he added, "an internal Chinese problem." Czechoslovakia had an immense strategic value; Quemoy has none. But in the offshore islands, he concluded, "we and Chiang have manufactured our own Czechoslovakia."[11]

There can be no doubt that the Generalissimo is holding the offshore islands for the invasion he dreams of making on the Chinese mainland, but the islands could never be used for such a purpose. Could it be that a matter of principle is involved? The administration claims that one of the basic principles of peace is that armed force should not be used for aggression. James Reston wrote on

September 10, 1958, that this doctrine is really "something to think about." The Monroe Doctrine, the Truman Doctrine, the Eisenhower Doctrine—all were limited in one way or another but there are no such limitations in the Dulles Doctrine—the most sweeping, the most absolute, the most incredible on record.[12] The administration also claims that the Communists never indulge in understatements; when a threat does not work, it is no problem at all for them to desist from the course they have threatened. However, the liberals insisted that Krishna Menon was wringing his hands in the United Nations, for we had assumed that the Red Chinese were bluffing when they threatened to enter the Korean War and Menon had told us that they were not. The Secretary of State said that strength was not merely material and that the allies of the United States have to be supported. Public opinion could not accept such an unheard-of doctrine, for the world knows that we have fought three big wars and that our courage does not need to be proved any more. Thomas K. Finletter's position was simply that the United States had "no business being in Formosa."[13] Senator Green wrote President Eisenhower that our Chinese policy could result "in military involvement at the wrong time, in the wrong place, and on issues not of vital concern to our own security, and all this without allies either in fact or in heart." And Senator Morse simply asserted on September 26, 1958, that "if Eisenhower and Dulles persist in their present policy based upon warlike action over the Quemoys and Matsus they should be impeached."

In contradistinction, the liberal opposition wildly greeted the concessions which the administration saw fit to make (as part of the diplomatic process) as major retreats, radical changes of policy, and proof that the United States had finally come out of its dreamworld. A tiny crack had appeared on the surface, and it would soon change the entire structure. But why did these alleged concessions come so late and under such obvious Communist pressure? It is well for Secretary Dulles—the expert on the zig and the zag—to say that it was foolish for Chiang to put so many troops on Quemoy, but this belated concession does not eliminate the public's "just" complaint that the United States stood idle when the Chinese Nationalists took that fateful step. And has Mr. Dulles recanted his incredible pledge to meet force with force everywhere? Under the administration's prodding, we were clenching our fists against a possible invasion of Quemoy, but the Chinese Reds never intended to invade the island. How naïve it was for us to speak of no retreat in an invasion that would never come! The fact is that the bombardment of Quemoy means nothing to Dulles. He accepts it; he does not want Chiang to destroy the mainland guns, which the Communists turn on and off at will. In this way, the administration's notion of a cease-fire gave Peiping the initiative. Never, indeed, was American policy so self-defeating, so blind, so deadlocked!

It is very true, of course, that Quemoy is an apple of discord, but the quarrel is voluntary. The issue is complex but not complicated. If the Communist challenge was real, would it not have been better to meet it at once and directly? There are reasons to think that the challenge was not real. The coastal islands could be shelled, but they could not be taken by bombardment alone. They could be supplied, despite a partially successful blockade. They could be defended. If the fundamental military facts of the situation permit defense at a bearable cost, fear is not justified. The islands could be surrendered, but no responsible critic of the administration ever proposed that they be surrendered at the point of a gun. This means that we should yield to force. If we decide not to yield to force, we must stand firm. So far, there is not a single issue that is truly debatable.

What about the offshore islands' future? First of all, there should be a dependable cease-fire. Nobody in the United States objects to the idea of a cease-fire. "If there were anything like a dependable cease-fire in the area," Mr. Dulles said on October 14, 1958, considerable changes in the situation would come about "automatically, almost as a matter of cold logic." The offshore islands would no longer be a source of provocation. Would Chiang agree to the idea of a reciprocal cease-fire? He has. Would he remove his troops from Quemoy? This should depend on the nature of the cease-fire, but we cannot force him to do something against his own better judgment. Neither is it so certain that a demilitarization of Quemoy would truly serve the cause of peace. In addition, who among the administration's critics believes that we can treat our allies like lackeys and force them to do things to which they are opposed?

What about Chiang's future? Since the United States would not be a party to an aggressive war in the area, Chiang will not return to the mainland by using force. On the other hand, if there were some major uprising on the mainland, it would probably be under local leadership. Yet as Mr. Dulles said on September 30, 1958, "the presence of a free China with considerable power a few miles away could be a very important element in the situation." Does U.S. policy postulate a Chinese revolution? It does not. Neither does it exclude the possibility of internal difficulties for the Chinese Communists. Now what is the usefulness of Chiang if there is no uprising in China? Chiang exists; he has power; he is not an *émigré*; he is not a Kerenski; he exists as a trustee of Chinese culture and Chinese freedom. Could the Chinese Communists tolerate his continued existence? Would Communist power not continue to grow?

It is not Chiang that the Communists cannot accept; it is freedom. Communist power will continue to grow, and the more it grows, the more it will have to be restrained. Is this an inflexible policy? As Mr. Dulles said on September 30, 1958, "if the situation we have to meet changes, our policies change with it." Nothing could be easier, and for this reason alone, the merit we can acquire by not changing our policies will be greater than if we change them. But is the risk we assume out of proportion with the gain? The risk has been fully controlled up to now, and the gain has been far from negligible. If these simple principles are unclear to American public opinion, their significance has at least not been lost to the Communist rulers.[14]

In most cases, the problems confronting U.S. policy are dialectical. They make conflicting demands upon us. Our defense effort must be adequate, but economic stability must also be safeguarded.

Instant atomic retaliation might be necessary, and our allies must be consulted; the Constitutional process must be respected. The free nations must be ready to go to the brink of war, but their will for peace must be beyond doubt. In all of these situations, contrary principles must be upheld simultaneously because they all present valid aspects.

So defined, a dialectical problem cannot be coped with or defined in a single formula; it requires diversity in approach. This can sometimes be achieved by a division of labor within the administration. During the various crises of his administration Mr. Eisenhower has played the role of a restraining influence, a role that is entirely in conformity with his personal character and the dignity of his office. To others was left the less rewarding task of stirring up trouble. It happened repeatedly that an important statement was made by Secretary Dulles one day and repeated by the President the next, but with a difference in tone. On March 15, 1955, for instance, Mr. Dulles warned Red China about tactical atomic weapons. On the following day, Mr. Eisenhower stressed that these weapons were very precise and that they could be humanely used in warfare. On September 30, 1958, Chiang Kai-shek was rebuked by Secretary Dulles, and on October 1, Mr. Eisenhower made appeasing remarks on the same topics. On May 14, 1956, the Soviet government announced that a manpower cut would be made in Soviet armed forces before the end of the year. On the day following the Russian statement, Mr. Dulles said that the move might not be motivated by a love for peace and added that the cut might very well result, "not in a weakening, but in a strengthening of the Soviet military capacity." The Secretary of Defense described the Russian announcement as "a step in the right direction." Harold E. Stassen said that it was "an initiative we wanted them to take," and Admiral Radford declared that he would not trust the Russians in this any more than in anything else.

A variety of official comment is always considered by public opinion to be a painful illustration of official confusion. The Soviet announcement should have been handled "adroitly." The Voice of America must convince the world that America seeks peace.

We should not have been placed in an embarrassing position by Secretary Dulles and Admiral Radford. Such contradictions are unbearable. If the President says that foreign policy issues should be kept out of campaign debates, why does Mr. Nixon insist that they should be discussed?

It should be pointed out, however, that contradiction is more apparent than real. Consciously or unconsciously, the administration dilutes the official position on a problem in order to cover its various aspects. The problem of contradiction is never so important that a diversity of opinion should become an object for scandal. Above all else, the problem is dialectical. It would have been a great misfortune if Mr. Dulles had not been so outspoken on the Soviet manpower cut. If Mr. Stassen had not been the pious mouthpiece of political expediency, Admiral Radford's blunt statement might have caused some damage. On the other hand, public opinion clamors for a univocal description of an issue that cannot be so described.

The administration does create confusion. The Soviet cut could not have been described simply as an empty promise, nor was it an unmixed blessing. The Dulles declaration on tactical atomic weapons was, at the time, a salutory threat, but if the President had not spoken of tactical atomic weapons as a means to humanize nuclear warfare, the threat might have been overstated. In other words, the national interest is best served by a measure of apparent confusion, for there exists no other way of avoiding the difficulties that would result from a candid statement of the case. Conversely, the dynamism that drives public opinion to demand logical consistency serves no useful purpose. This "consistency" is the false ideal of those who oppose governmental expediency as contrary to the self-righteous opinion they have of themselves—a pharisaic attitude which deserves no respect whatsoever.

In some instances, a division of labor of the type just illustrated is clearly precluded by the nature of the situation. In 1954, the Indochinese crisis was described as a tragic dilemma for America: either we had to resign ourselves to the loss of Southeast Asia, or a full-scale American intervention in the war was necessary.

Public opinion pressed the administration to state its true objectives so that—Senator Flanders said on April 19, 1954—"a confidence in our purposes may be enkindled where it does not now exist."[15] On the same day, Senator Humphrey called for "clarity, candor, forthrightness and honesty" in regard to French colonialism.[16] Senator Morse went all out in their support and announced that he would "smoke out the administration and make them take a position which the American people can understand."[17] Senator Humphrey added that if the administration did not have the courage to announce to the world that it was standing for freedom, the United States would, in fact, be "taking up the decadent colonialism of the French and replacing it with the virile strength of young Americans." This truth, he concluded, should be told to the French "clearly, and unequivocally and forcefully."

On November 2, 1956, Mr. Nixon declared that in the past, the nations of Asia and Africa had felt that America would, "when the pressure was on, side with the policies of the British and French governments in relation to the once colonial areas." Speaking of the Suez invasion, the Vice-President added that "for the first time in history," the United States had shown independence of Anglo-French policies that seemed to reflect the colonial tradition. This was, he said, a "declaration of independence" which had "an electrifying effect throughout the world."

As Mr. Nixon was speaking, Mr. Stevenson was declaring that the administration's policy had let the Soviet Union achieve "a major victory by splitting the coalition of the free nations, and we find ourselves in bed with Communist Russia and the dictator of Egypt." On April 21, 1956, Mr. Stevenson criticized the administration on the question of colonialism. "The administration has done nothing," he claimed, "to evolve a reasoned and sound American position, linked to our traditions as well as to respect for our friends and a due concern for world stability." Rather, our government "floundered around, trying to be all things to all people and thereby antagonizing everyone." On February 16, 1957, he again referred to that "melancholy spectacle when the American delegate to the United Nations lined up with Russia against our allies to save a dictator's neck, or Mr. Nixon's shocking exultation over what he called our declaration of independence from Britain and France."

In the name of candor and intellectual honesty, pressure is thus applied to obtain from our government a declaration of purpose that is consistent with our tradition, the national interest, and public opinion everywhere. If such a declaration could ever be made, there would be no problem at all; since the situation precludes candor, any declaration actually made by the United States is found shocking. On March 20, 1956, Ambassador C. D. Dillon expressed sympathy and support for the French effort to work out what he called "a liberal solution" of the Algerian problem. This was, of course, an unwanted declaration. Support for the French, though half-hearted, was sufficient to dishearten the Algerian nationalists. In March, 1956, Mr. Dulles extolled before his Indonesian hosts our anti-colonialist tradition and professed American neutrality in the New Guinea dispute. Since the Indonesians had just severed the last of their ties with the Netherlands, the Dutch were angered. On December 2, 1956, Portuguese Foreign Minister Cunha and Secretary of State Dulles issued a joint communiqué which contained the following paragraph:

Various statements attributed to Soviet rulers visiting in Asia, which included references to the policies of Western Powers in the Far East and allegations concerning the Portuguese provinces in the Far East, were discussed by the two Foreign Ministers. They considered that such statements do not represent a contribution to the cause of peace.

This declaration does not sound like the slogan that was immediately attributed to Mr. Dulles by American public opinion. It does not say that "Goa is a Portuguese province." Yet it came after the Soviet Comrades had been treated like Hindu divinities by the mobs of Calcutta. Mr. Dulles explained on December 6 that the communiqué had not been "lightly issued." It was an attempt to express the United States' attitude toward the emotionalism which the Soviet rulers had attempted to create in India, and since Goa had been under Portuguese rule for more than four hundred years, it was not particularly outrageous either.

A similar fate will befall any declaration the United States makes on the issue of colonialism. If we align ourselves with a colonial power, we are not faithful to our tradition. If arms are supplied to Tunisia against the wishes of the French government, we ruin Western solidarity. American public opinion cries out against colonialism as loudly as it shouts against moralizing anti-colonialism. It refuses to follow in the matter the surer guide of the national interest. Again, this attitude cannot be excused. It is not in the interest of the United States to have a power vacuum result from the abrupt end of colonial dominions. The orderly disintegration of Western imperialist influence is an objective as important to all concerned as immediate self-rule. The conduct of public opinion is the more irrational when the United States has been diverted, by circumstances as well as by our own past statesmanship, from the difficult task of liquidating a colonial empire. In the name of anti-colonialism, the American people do their utmost to implicate the United States in this unrewarding process, and they simultaneously accuse the administration of not supporting its colonialist allies.

Neutralism is another striking example of the process that forces public opinion to adopt the approach that is likely to hurt our national interest the most. "It was only a few months ago," Adlai Stevenson declared on September 11, 1956, "that the President was saying that neutralism was fine, the Vice-President was saying that it was terrible and the Secretary of State was saying with his characteristic flair that, while neutralism was indefensible, most of the neutrals were all right." The President had said that neutralism was fine when President Sukarno of Indonesia was visiting the United States. Mr. Eisenhower said on June 6, 1956, that neutralism did not "necessarily" mean what it was so often interpreted to mean—"neutral as between right or wrong or decency and indecency." Many countries were using the term "neutral" with respect to "attachment to military alliance," the President added. So understood, neutralism was not necessarily a disadvantage to the

United States. If a country announced "its military association with another great power," Mr. Eisenhower concluded, "things could happen to it, difficulties along its borders and people would say, 'Good enough for it.' They asked for it."

The President's statement could have received a constructive interpretation. For good reasons, however, it was generally considered to be a blunder. On June 7, the White House issued a clarifying statement explaining that the President believed that there could exist "special conditions which justify political neutrality but that no nation has the right to be indifferent to the fate of another, or, as he put it, to be neutral as between right and wrong." While an association with the Soviet Union could lead to difficulties, the President did not believe that "association for mutual security with the United States will involve any country in added danger, but on the contrary, will provide added security." On June 9, Mr. Dulles declared that the notion of mutual security had abolished, as between parties, the principle of neutrality, "which pretends that a nation can best gain safety by being indifferent to the fact of others. This has increasingly become an obsolete conception and, except under very exceptional circumstances, it is an immoral and shortsighted conception." Finally, Mr. Nixon recalled on July 4, 1956, how many countries had already been enslaved by Communism. "You know the proverb," he said, "he who sups with the devil must have a long spoon." It is not easy to outmaneuver the Soviets, and those who feel that they can do it "are taking a fearful risk," the Vice-President added.

There is nothing in all of this which is not self-evident. The United States cannot coerce neutral nations into some form of association. We must therefore accept neutralism to the extent that it is in the national interest to strengthen these countries and to preserve their independence from Communist dictation. Mutual security should not become a prerequisite for American friendship. The United States must also uphold the usefulness of mutual security, reward its friends, and rebuff the excesses occasionally displayed by neutralist statesmen.[18]

Public opinion considers this flexibility to be an intolerable con-tradiction. "If these various contradictory views were expressed by a single individual," Senator Humphrey said on July 13, 1956, "a psychiatrist would say that this individual did not know what he wanted or where he wanted to go. . . . His basic convictions would seem to be so out of focus that he would be considered un-predictable and unreliable by his friends."[19] Here again, opinion refuses to identify itself with the dialectics of the problem. It plays neutralism against mutual security. The neutrals must be officially branded or the validity of neutralism must be acknowledged. The situation is characterized by irreconcilable elements, yet public opinion demands an immediate, clear-cut answer. It does not want holding operations and delaying tactics. Let the United States stand fair and square on every issue. Let us stop this wobbling from one side to the other. Let us negotiate our path in daylight. Partisanship thus asserts that with creativeness and leadership, any problem can be solved—*a solution that it is careful enough never to formulate.*

At this point, our partisan debates cease to be useful. Taking delight in bright new ideas that cannot be stated, partisan criti-cism ceases to grapple with realities. Like a spoiled child who takes his dreams for virtue and his whims for realities, the dissenter places his little person on the throne of pride. He has the answers, but he will announce them only if the people will cease giving allegiance to their government. Otherwise, he is content to live in the splendid isolation of his own heart. He is not of this world. At this point, partisanship substitutes the governed for the govern-ment. The people are entitled to the truth. "We've got to be trusted," said Mr. Stevenson on October 29, 1956. "We've got to be ready to meet our problems, to face them squarely, to make the great, the wise decisions." During all these years of what he called "unrushing history, we've been patted on the back, we've been patted on the head, we've been told that everything's all right— just relax and enjoy it." The administration has lied. It is guilty. Its crime is that it demanded the faith of the people; it governed. The critic has no claim to the people's trust, other than having sapped their confidence in the United States.

This, then, is the fundamental irrationality of opinion. The natural objective of partisanship is confusion—a state of opinion that is defined as a breakdown in public confidence and political certitude. Apparently, the United States has no policy on neutralism. It has no policy on East-West trade. It has failed in Europe. It was not able to maintain its technological lead. We jump from one crisis to another, improvising answers to Russian moves but having no plans of our own. In the *Washington Post* of April 15, 1956, C. M. Roberts compared America with a "great sleeping volcano, which usually sits quiet, important because of its sheer bulk, but which now and then rumbles and looses an eruption which affects the world around it." Eruptions, but no policy. Dulles finds himself caught between India and Pakistan, France and the Arabs, Israel and Jordan, Britain and Greece. He constantly entangles himself in hopeless contradictions. With each new dilemma, we lose a friend, and possibly more.

As long as public opinion remains in such frame of mind as that described above, every piece of evidence it considers will automatically turn into an accusation. Every demand that is made upon national policy is made to contradict some other demand. Every explanation attempted by the administration is immediately denounced as a new contradiction. Public opinion forces itself to believe that the United States finds itself without friends at a critical moment or that it starts some reckless action at the wrong place and at the wrong time. American blunders invite the enemy to act. No one on earth believes that the great United States means what it says. Partial—and often completely imaginary—reverses are described as the worst in American diplomatic history. The conduct of our foreign policy is so foolish that the administration cannot even find a way out of its own faults. In this manner, public opinion is submerged by a flow of contradictory data and is overwhelmed by pressures coming from every direction. Confusion is therefore characterized by the fact that everything said or done is immediately transformed into a portent force leading to further disorder. The breakdown of public opinion is the objective of our partisan debates. The massive retaliation debate has proved that criticism does not halt its attack until the debate has been led *into the dead end that results from the willful annihilation of the policy it criticizes.*

Several times in the recent past—especially in 1955—public opinion was, indeed, brought to the verge of a breakdown. It was saved from a collapse by forces independent from the people's own will. First of all, it owes to executive leadership its salvation from the consequences of its own deeds. The government must make policy whatever the public says it should be. Decisions, once made, must be carried out. Even if it wanted to yield to public pressure, the government cannot always do so. If it can, it must still save face. The policy-maker is thus bound by the nature of his responsibility to maintain a degree of consistency, without which the process of government could not continue. Let us be frank enough, however, to recognize that the necessary resistance which the government is forced to give public opinion is the reverse of what is naïvely described as democratic government.

Another important safeguard of democratic government is the inconsistency generally displayed by public opinion. The practice of our "Great Debates" has been to raise the most serious of charges, only to forget them in the next instant. A policy is described as mortal danger and utter folly. Then all at once, it ceases to be discussed at all. This happens because the announced tragedy fails to materialize. In most cases, however, new events simply divert public opinion to some fresh object of attack. If a debate continues relentlessly, the greater is the confusion, the greater is its viciousness. This would show that opposition has been organized. The movement for a cessation of atomic testing, sane nuclear policy, and the anti-Chiang lobby certainly fall into this category. On the whole, however, public opinion is aimless; so much the better. The grave faults of American democracy lead us to believe that the more erratic our debates are, the safer our free institutions become.

These reasons suffice to explain why it is not likely that public opinion will ever reach the stage of extreme disintegration that we described as a breakdown of national trust. It might perhaps be good for public opinion not to be always protected against the consequences of its own faults. Opinion might then understand that partisan criticism really intends to make such a breakdown a reality. The fact remains, however, that in emergencies not characterized by actual shooting, the whole force of partisanship is destructive. Not a single instance can be found in our recent past in which partisan criticism succeeded in clarifying an issue or even displaying the most elementary wisdom.

When the United States is not subjected to the stresses of an impending crisis but is, instead, caressed by favorable circumstances, the fundamental irrationality of public opinion takes the form of smugness. Much has been said, of course, by the liberals about national complacency, the rosy picture of the world situation which the administration allegedly tries to make the public accept, and a "characteristic" American boastfulness. They have spoken abundantly about the "cardboard weapons of self-delusion, self-adulation and smug self-satisfaction."[20] They complained again and again about the "national mood" and the people's resentment against the interruption of the soothing dream of prosperity, peace, and power. No accusation could be less founded. The massive retaliation debate has proved conclusively that diplomatic success is a concept that is abhorrent to American society. The deeper motivation for this strange attitude is that *success is often just as much a test of mental certitudes as it is of real failures.*

The liberal opposition has refused to consider real failures. Adlai Stevenson said on October 16, 1954, that the Republicans "have to bear the responsibility for nourishing our thinking since the war on myths." These "myths" are that China has been lost, that Roosevelt was weak at Yalta and Teheran—the myth, in other words, that past American policies have ever had anything to do with Communist advances. In contradistinction, one takes a legitimate pride of things past and remote. The Truman Doctrine saved Greece and Turkey. Berlin was not strangled into submission. The Marshall Plan saved Europe. Yet in the present, when our foreign policy is in the making, public opinion must feed on failures that are hypothetical, on dead ends that do not exist, on risks which are taken to be realities.

Arguing on June 10, 1955, that the American economy could well withstand the expenditures of foreign aid without adverse effects on our prosperity, Mr. Dulles recalled that the Soviets had been "constantly hoping and expecting our economy was going to collapse." Quite to the contrary, he said, "it has been their system that is on the point to collapse." The Secretary claimed that the U.S.S.R. sought new policies in order to give them some respite, and he pointed out that Soviet foreign aid was given "at the expense of the livelihood of their people." The opposition expressed a feeling of outrage at this claim that "the Soviet system was on the point of collapsing." Mr. Dulles again appeared as the accused before the Senate Foreign Affairs Committee on February 24, 1956, and restated his scandalous doctrine. He said that Western strength had forced the Communists to adopt more moderate policies. The Soviets were in the process of revising a bankrupt policy. If the United States ever had to go through such a revision, he added, it would be advertised the world over that American policy has failed. "One thing that is absolutely certain," said Mr. Dulles, "is that the unity and firmness and resolution of the free nations during the past few years have caused the Soviet policy to fail, and today they are trying to figure out how they are going to get a better one." U.S. policy had largely nullified the possibility of the Soviets' relying on force and the threat of force. They turned to peaceful competition—for which the United States appeared admirably equipped.[21]

These statements are true, even in the face of the evidence now available. The new Soviet policy has scored great successes but no final achievement as yet. Economic penetration by the U.S.S.R. confronts the United States with a new challenge, but then economic penetration is a delicate process and requires much time. The dangers involved appear more real than military aggression, but this is so only because the dangers of Soviet aggression have receded. Public opinion could not tolerate optimism about the future and still less an assertion that U.S. policy had succeeded. On February 25, 1956, Mr. Stevenson referred to President Eisenhower as an inept coach. On February 27, Senator Morse claimed that the administration had been "keeping secret from the American people a great many things" which they were entitled to know. It is the people who will die, "and will die by the millions, if Dulles stumbles off the brink," he said. Senator Fulbright, the spokesman of malefic sadness, attributed the Secretary's assertions to an apparent craving for approval. The people long for a diet of half-truths. The Secretary of State treats the American people, Fulbright said on February 27, "as children ready to clap in delight at every fairy story, however fanciful." He also said that Dulles "misleads public opinion, confuses it, feeds it pap, tells it that if it will suppress the proof of its own senses, it will see that Soviet triumphs are really defeats, and Western defeats are really triumphs."[22] And Adlai Stevenson concluded on April 22, 1956, that the administration had been unwilling "to take us into its confidence" because it would not admit its failure. "Reverses have been painted as victories," he said, "and if the administration has not succeeded in misleading the enemy, it has succeeded wonderfully well in misleading us."

These examples show that there is no smugness in America other than the *inflexible, narrow-minded, self-satisfied arrogance of partisan criticism,* which consistently refuses to accept the test of success. When our foreign policy succeeds in one of its objectives, it is high time that its validity is understood. The opposite is done, however. The country cannot stumble from crisis to crisis, it is said, without ever coming to grips with the "real" problems of the age. Between crises, warned Senator Fulbright on June 20, 1958, we succumb to dangerous apathy. We cling "desperately to the ancient pillars of policy," he said, "even as they rot away under the pressure of irresistible international developments." Cold war as usual, defense policies as usual, the same policies in Asia, in the Middle East, everywhere. "Are we destined," he asked, "to see the gradual sinking of the prestige of this nation, the steady dimming of its message to mankind, because we go round and round in the same policies?" Can we not have the imagination or the will to move out of the orbit of inertia?[23] Suez, Algeria, sputnik, Quemoy —all are milestones on the road to disaster. Indeed, we have no reason to boast when we look at the world we ought to lead: a world of seething change, frail alliances, rising unrest and sweeping distrust of the United States. The future belongs to a leadership bold enough to face "stern" realities. It does not belong to those who try to shore up the crumbling remnants of the past.

These great phrases, which appear so appropriate, so sound, so well reasoned, are, in fact, the most convincing proof of the irrationality of public opinion yet offered. Criticism is understandable, if not justified, at the moment when the assumptions of our foreign policy undergo the trial of crisis. When a policy succeeds, we should make use of a favorable wind, but public opinion hauls down our sails. When our ship meets with heavy seas, public opinion cries out in desperation; when the waters are calm, it worries about future storms. Instead of fortifying certitudes and giving encouragement, public opinion refuses to acknowledge success; instead, it demands changes, applies additional pressure, and continues to criticize.

Never in history has the policy of a great power been so fundamentally decent, so necessary, so close to success, and yet *so frustrated by blind obstinacy* as the policy of the United States. The aversion which the American people have for American achievement is perhaps the gravest liability of the free world at present. The Soviet leaders are gamblers, the most successful gamblers the world has ever known. The American people have long had the power to transform Communism into the huffing and puffing dragon which they like to consider Mr. Dulles to be. How will they conduct themselves now that the Soviets are both gamblers and equals? Much better, perhaps. If they do, they, not Mr. Dulles, will have changed.

CHAPTER X

The Deterioration of National Policy

THE TRUE SUBJECT of this case study is ourselves. In spite of its intrinsic importance, massive retaliation has served only as a medium of self-analysis. The massive retaliation debate has thrown more light on the processes of partisanship in the United States than any other debate of past years. But political processes are as old as politics. They are laws, in other words, and they determine our political behavior—when we let ourselves be so determined.

Now that we are about to conclude we shall focus our attention on two important principles. We must first recognize that the follies of partisanship are *ours*; in a deep sense, they correspond to what we want to be. They constitute the evil self of America, and if this evil self did not appeal to our pride in one way or another, our political judgments would be rational, our debates sober and consistent, and our inner attitudes upright and fruitful. As we now know, partisanship is neither honest nor constructive. And if it seems incredible that we can identify ourselves with what tends to destroy us, let us remember that politics is only a part of human behavior. We behave in politics as we behave generally. If our conduct is so often irrational and destructive of our genuine happiness, it is because we let ourselves be lured by a false ideal which we prefer to the vision of the true self. The second principle is that this true self is also known to us, that it is endowed with features which fill the heart with self-love and courage, that we shall truly be ourselves only if we are faithful to its image. The evil self demands of us only sloth and irresponsibility while it enslaves us; the true ideal demands a fully conscious commitment, and it makes us free.

We shall now concern ourselves with this self-duality, which is at the root of the confusion we experience in politics. It explains the constant deterioration of our foreign policy. We do not deny, of course, that foreign policy *naturally* tends to disintegrate in democratic countries. The simple efflux of time blunts its ability to command attention and respect. It becomes subject to the vicissitudes of electoral campaigns. Circumstances change. If the policy is a military alliance, our allies soon choose to act as sovereign and independent nations again; they rebel against the rigidity of collective security. If the policy is to threaten and to warn, threats and warnings, after a while, do not sound as formidable as they did before. The very fact that they have been effective tends to prove that they were empty, blustering words. Even when the policy consists in giving aid, the recipient nation soon becomes anxious to avoid what it calls "strings and conditions."

This process of natural erosion is more marked in the United States than it might be in other countries. We shall limit our exploration to the damage inflicted on American policy by our refusal to yield to the demands it makes upon us. The reasons for our refusal to identify ourselves with a consistent, realistic policy must be the reasons for our feeling so much at ease with an ideal self which we know to be false.

In testimony by Admiral Arthur W. Radford to the House Foreign Affairs Committee in April, 1956, two reasons were given for the difficulties encountered by American diplomacy in its intercourse with the world. One was that "the Russian handling of the situation has been very clever." The other was the "picture of confusion that is presented to the rest of the world by the free press of the United States." This statement was unusually frank. The free press, however, is only one of the instruments employed to spread a confusion that already exists in the minds of newspapermen and those who give them inspiration and support. The root of the problem lies deeper.

The relativity of American political thought generally induces public opinion to listen to foreign criticism of the disturbing yet sacrosanct dicta of impartial observers of American affairs. Stalin said that a Russian tractor was better than ten foreign Communists, and there are good reasons to believe that the American people do not value the opinion of others much more than the British or the French value their own. The real reason why American public opinion so readily identifies itself with foreign criticism has absolutely nothing to do with tolerance. The real reason is *an unconscious fear of the impending revelation of some fundamental weakness yet unknown in American policy.*

This paralyzing fear is a characteristic feature of the national self. In the two debates on the offshore islands, during the Suez crisis, and last, but not least, with the launching of the Soviet sputnik, this strange attitude revealed itself decisively: now it can at last be seen that American policy was all wrong. How naïve and complacent we have been! Every reverse is greeted as a long-expected disclosure of some fundamental blunder. Behind every aspect of the international situation lurks some mysterious evil which will soon be seen and which will completely shatter the simple assertions of Dulles. Can the reality be as clear as the administration makes it? Can the Russians be so vicious? Is American power so great? Hence the constant references in our debates to "oversimplifications" and "complications" and "overconfidence." Hence the success in America of anti-Americanism.

It is true that public opinion listens to foreign criticism with complacent passivity. "We should see ourselves as others see us," said Mr. Stevenson on September 15, 1953. This slogan epitomizes our philosophy on the problem. It is assumed that foreign criticism of American policy is always formulated in good faith, for the sake of peace and truth. The American people are quite familiar with the rabid nationalism of the French, yet if the newspaper *Le Monde* or François Mauriac attack Mr. Dulles, they find a captive audience in this country. When the American liberal reads that some foreigner compares the United States to the antediluvian dinosaur, with its huge body and small head, he searches his own soul.[1] No difference is made between Aneurin Bevan, Herbert Morrison or Marshal Juin. It matters little whether the anti-American pronouncement comes from a critic who belongs to the government or to the opposition in his own country. As long as it sounds critical of American policy, foreign opinion seems to be entitled to respectful consideration in America.

Public opinion thus fails to interpret anti-Americanism in the light of foreign attitudes. It is unwilling to recognize that anti-Americanism often has a vicious origin that has nothing to do with alleged blunders of American policy. It prefers to espouse the lies of anti-Americanism, themselves the product of a treacherous acceptance of the lies of Communist propaganda. Public opinion does not understand, either, that many anti-American issues are often fabricated by American partisan debates, explained, exhibited in every detail, and proclaimed the world over by Americans. The echo of domestic disorder returns to America. When it has returned, what was before fantastic exaggeration or sheer fantasy is taken as reality.

It is the American people who have first pretended that federal security programs created in this country the eerie silence that haunts graveyards. It is the American people who have created the myth of an American pathological fear of Communism, who have spoken of American book-burners and pyromaniacs in a manner reminiscent of the Spanish Inquisition. No one can really believe that American liberties are about to be subverted. How mistaken the people are! The threat is most serious and more certain, said Adlai Stevenson on June 14, 1954, to man's "immortal soul than the blandishment of the flesh and the devil." The threat is serious and certain because no one seems to be aware of the inroads already made upon freedom in America.

"Those were the days," Mr. Stevenson pronounced on April 25, 1956, "when an emotional pressure toward a spurious conformity silenced tongues and shuttered minds throughout the land of the free and the home of the brave." A citizen had to think twice before buying a book, making an appointment, writing a letter. Everyone in America had to stop and consider how his activities would be

made to sound in the mouth of McCarthy and before Congressional committees. Scott McLeod purged the Foreign Service. P. H.
Nitze and G. F. Kennan—the latter being the greatest political
genius of our generation—were forced out. Many resigned. Only
the less able, the less imaginative, the less industrious, the time-
servers remained on the job. They were beaten down spiritually.
They proved it by remaining at the mercy of a ruthless secret political power. And in a copyrighted article which appeared in the
Daily Princetonian of February 22, 1954, Mr. Kennan himself told
undergraduates that he could not, "in good conscience," advise
them to make a career in the Foreign Service.

Who will count the public servants who were irresistibly swept
into a world of guilt and nightmarish fears under the strain of
security problems? Mental health specialists in convention assem-
bled were told of a tangle of neurosis creeping through the entire
government. There was fear on every campus. Senator Fulbright
inserted in the *Congressional Record* of March 29, 1954, the story
of a very learned, very well-read young lady who would not sign
a petition sponsored by a liberal group and who later discovered
that the petition was the Declaration of Independence. R. M.
Hutchins related to a graduating class on June 13, 1957, the remark made by "a great industrialist in Detroit" to a friend of his.
The profound and original remark was this: "You are either a
Communist or a thinker." Senator Mansfield said on July 11, 1955,
that after the Oppenheimer case and the Fort Monmouth investigation, a poll of Ph.D.'s revealed that not more than 8 per cent
would want to work for the government.[2] The administration
boasted that it had rid itself of security risks—men who read
books, join movements, make contributions to humanity. It would
not even employ Oppenheimer as a janitor. This policy exacted a
price: sputnik, our own fizzling rockets, our intellectual decadence.

Who will explain how intelligent people could ever have re-
paired to such extravagant absurdities? Who will account for the
fact that all of these fantastic assertions were put into circulation
by the American intelligentsia and that they received credence
from no one except the educated man? What should be said of a

Ph.D. who refuses to work for the government because he "fears" the procedures of security clearance? If a federal employee sinks into neurosis because he apprehends an investigation, is it not better for all concerned to let him depart? And what should we think of the great Foreign Service officers—we mean the bold, the imaginative, those who read books and join movements—it if were true that they were afraid of Roy Cohn or of a U.S. Senator whom they themselves described as a penny-show effigy? If the morale of the Foreign Service is so important, can we, "in good conscience," refer to those who did not quit as time-servers and morally ground-down individuals?

The flood of McCarthyism receded—and so quickly that it proved to be highly embarrassing for those who described the late Senator as a national threat. Is it surprising, then, that they desperately try to prove that "McCarthyism is not dead"? Passports for travel are still denied to freethinkers. Censorship in federal agencies has not been abolished. The State Department still refuses to underwrite traveling orchestras because of the political tenets of the artists. Tax-exempt foundations have been investigated. Much "useful" information is still classified.[3]

The importance of the McCarthy episode for a comprehension of our mentality cannot be exaggerated. In its passionate defense of its own emptiness, the American intelligentsia drove itself into utter ridicule. After having made itself the laughingstock of humanity, it accused the people of anti-intellectualism. The dogma of nonconformity was enforced in a manner truly suggestive of Soviet society. No intellectual worthy of his name could have departed from the anti-McCarthy line. There was, indeed, a pyromania, an anti-McCarthy fear on the campus, a fear of simple humor and common sense.

There can be no doubt that we strike here at the root of an important problem. McCarthyism, Little Rock, the vagrant talk of Krishna Menon, massive retaliation, the Rosenberg affair, the brink of war—all were godsends to the liberal intelligentsia, which would have had little to talk about otherwise. It was, of course, much easier to exhort the administration to a vigorous, unrelenting search for alternatives than to produce these ideas, which allegedly had to be tapped and distilled. It was easier to blame fizzling rockets on McCarthy than to ask oneself what the universities had done to promote basic research. It was easier to let Dr. Clapp go around the world lecturing on the dangers of fallout than to study the problem first hand or to work in a laboratory.[4] It was easier to describe Mr. Dulles as an elderly governess trying to cope with naughty children than to speak up and rebuke the vicious accusations of anti-Americanism. It was easier because the philosophy of liberalism is in accordance with and nurtures the false ideas that public opinion has about the role which the United States is called to play in world affairs.

It is assumed that America's mission must be noble and rewarding. It is apparently the United States' responsibility to be the standard-bearer of freedom and justice throughout the world. Divine Providence has so disposed the course of human affairs once and for all. We are given to understand, however, that this claim to ideological leadership is not taken in any active sense. To enter into a conflict where people are struggling for independence is *no* part of our business. To be militaristic is *no* part of our tradition. The State Department should *not* interfere with the right to travel. Academic freedom and political expression are areas in which the government should *not* tread.

In contradistinction, American ideology is satisfied to assert that there exists a fundamental harmony in the opinions and interests of righteous people all over the world. "Our allies are," former President Truman declared in his inaugural address, "the millions who hunger and thirst after righteousness." They are, in other words, natural allies. They are anxious to follow American guidance and do not need to be bound by military pacts. To attach them, American policy need only be faithful to American tradition. In due time, Mr. Truman continued, as American virtue and stability become increasingly manifest, "as more and more nations come to know the benefits of democracy and to participate in growing abundance," even the enemies of freedom will "abandon their delusions and join with the free nations of the world in a just settle-ment of international differences."

American democracy has been designed to love and to be loved. It cannot be proper, therefore, for the United States to pursue its national interest. Its mission is infinitely higher. Military expen-ditures, overseas bases, diplomatic pressure, military pacts—every self-assertion, in other words—is found to be inconsistent with the Sermon on the Mount and, consequently, with American de-mocracy. We stand for freedom, self-government, self-develop-ment of people everywhere. "The Republican way," Mr. Stevenson declared on September 26, 1956, "has been the narrow, national-istic one of the low, limited horizon, while the Democratic way has been that of the wide horizon, dotted with the ships and sails of beckoning hope."

Throughout its five eventful years, the massive retaliation de-bate has shown that each time the administration had to take some forceful action, threaten, bargain, insist that the Communist threat remained unchanged, the people responded with a demand for moral justification. How could the United States morally justify its nuclear strategy? By what moral consideration does the ad-ministration pretend to tell a foreign government—Communist though it be—what should be done about territories which it knows belong to China? It takes no imagination to appropriate money for arms; it takes only complaisant taxpayers, and it suf-fices to frighten them periodically. "There is no political risk," said Senator Fulbright on June 20, 1958, "to the proponents of ever bigger defense budgets." If their judgment is wrong, it would never be proved in any case. "The war which is likely to follow a policy of armaments to the exclusion of all else," he said, "disposes of all false judgments in its fiery furnace."[5]

No, the Christian thing to do is to disarm and to discontinue atomic testing. The Christian thing to do is to obtain the sanction of the United Nations before acting, especially when that sanction cannot be obtained. It is to secure the active support of our allies for American policy at the moment when our allies do not desire to give such support. It is to make sure that American actions receive the generous applause of world opinion when world opinion is in a state of confusion. The American liberals moralize, in other words, by appealing to moral principles in a manner that destroys national confidence. They repeatedly claim to be ready to defend causes that are morally justified. *The trouble is, however, that when there is a cause to defend, it never seems to have a moral justification.*[6]

It is therefore quite clear that public opinion never really attempts to give effect to moral principle but, rather, withdraws the moral sanction from national policies. It moralizes but refuses to commit itself to action. So conceived, morality in foreign policy is not only an empty dream but the reverse of moral action. And yet it is typical of the liberal creed to use the very failure of its own moralism to do away with all principles, to denounce as rigid conformism and boisterous self-righteousness the valid picture which the American people have of their own historical role. We do have an intuition of the judgment that will be made by history on the basic validity of American policy. We repeat that this intuition is valid. It is the intuition of America's true self. We do know that foreign criticism is often unjust. We do understand the Communist challenge. We all recognize the necessity of resisting Communist pressure at Quemoy. But the intuition that we have of American leadership—valid though it be—will become a reality only to the extent that we commit ourselves to act. *The great drama of human endeavors—and also its great challenge—is that this broad horizon disappears from our sight when the time has come to move to accomplishment.* It is at Quemoy that we have to stand firm—a few square miles of territory which seem to have no relation at all with our vital interest. We must act alone; we wanted to lead. We know that we are right, and yet we associate ourselves with an old man who has no chance at all. At this moment, partisanship takes over. While sanctioning our intuition as existing reality, it diverts us from accomplishment.[7]

This is *impatience,* the most pronounced characteristic of the American partisan self. It is impatience because it forces us to live in a future that does not exist and in a past that the American intellectuals extol in lyric language. Never are we allowed to live in the present. The Founding Fathers, Abraham Lincoln, Woodrow Wilson, all the leaders of America, as long as they are cold and dead, spoke so eloquently of freedom that the United States won the allegiance of men and women everywhere. The words they used, Mr. Stevenson said on April 21, 1956, were "so inspiring, so sublime, and so inexorably appealing to men's consciences that the old world was shaken to its foundations. Tyrannies dissolved; hope sprang up like a fresh breeze; movements of liberation mushroomed." This was a spontaneous leadership, a leadership based upon ideas, not power. It needed no enforcement. Hope sprang up. Tyranny dissolved. Freedom mushroomed. A leadership of this sort was as worthy of us as it was worthy of the world.

What historical evidence exists for all this, we do not know. It is true that the English speak in the same way—although with more restraint—about the Magna Charta and the French about the French Revolution. What is important is that this past American leadership is asserted as *lost*. We may continue to exhort the world about the virtues of our democracy, but it is claimed that our words have lost their past attractiveness. It is the Soviet Union which is now believed to provide for many countries the type of ideological guidance which the United States used to exercise in the past. Much of the world now thinks of America as a threat to the peace. How could it be otherwise? The administration has displayed arrogance, boasted about brinks, acted with impulsivity. It has imposed loyalty tests for economic aid. It has bribed feeble governments. It has supported reaction everywhere.

Still more important than these profound findings is the assertion that *present* policies must be jettisoned. "We must show," said Mr. Stevenson, "that we care about others in the world, not as bodies we would hurl into the military breach, but as men and women and children who we hope will live lives of dignity and fulfillment." He said on September 11, 1956, that "America's sharpest sword is the power of our ideals." We must recapture the soul of humanity. We should *revive*, he added, "the conception of our nation as the bearer of hope and freedom to oppressed peoples everywhere in the world"—the peoples of the Communist world excepted, of course, because liberation is a gimmick. He said on October 5, 1956, that we will restore our position in the world and become *once more* the trusted and inspiring leaders by making the promise of the American Revolution "a light for all mankind." He said on November 2, 1956, that "we must restore to our foreign policy a sense of human concern; we must persuade the peoples of the world that our concern is not just for military bases, or oil, or alliances, but for men and women and children and their right everywhere to equality and dignity."

If these words were not taken as an excuse not to rise to the requirements of our foreign policy, they would receive no attention. We would dismiss them as old women's talk. Of great consequence, however, is the fact that such things can be said with such insistence. It is a form of *ideological imperialism* which is universally resented. The British, the Italians, the secular culture of India have little to gain from American inspiration. To praise the American way of life in a doctrinaire manner as our liberals are doing is to invite everyone to look for and denounce the shortcomings of American democracy. Is it no wonder, then, that the world is so interested in segregation, the closed shop, and the late Senator McCarthy? The great misfortune is that the pedantic preaching inherent in Stevenson's dogmas is transmuted by anti-Americanism into Dulles' alleged absolutism, while Stevenson himself appears to be the friend of mankind because he is anti-Dulles.[8]

Since the liberal creed is rebellious, this result was inevitable. When the liberal intelligentsia speak of freedom, they mean to say that all forms of "orthodoxy" are cruel and futile. Now this is to claim that the American tradition is "anti-authoritarian." It is to define intellectual freedom as "emancipation." It is to repeat once more that textbooks—and how good—have been "burned at the stake." Leeches have been applied, they say, to the "bloodstream of freedom," i.e., dissent. As Senator Lehman said, it is "in the test tube of ideas" that truth emerges "from confusion and error."[9] The Holmes aphorism that the "highest courage is to stake everything on a premise that you know tomorrow's evidence may disprove" is not only proclaimed as the formula of American wisdom, but it is made to mean that the highest courage is to know that tomorrow's evidence *will* disprove the premises of today's deeds and to stake everything on the premise of nothingness. All dissidence is healthy. Every evidence should be questioned as a matter of intellectual integrity. Every approach is experimental, every solution tentative. This is the foundation of American pluralism. This is Americanism. It lacks the "finality" of any definite creed—except its own—and the mind ought to be "bold."[10]

If this would, indeed, be Americanism, if freedom were truly conceived as dissent and truth as boldness, the Christian people of Europe and South America, the world of Islam and the Buddhists of Asia, would turn away from America with legitimate horror. If this doctrine were true, only one question would remain to be asked: What genuine difference is there between the nihilistic slogans upon which the liberal intelligentsia feed and the assumptions with which Marx and Lenin started?

This self-portrayal of a generous, altruistic, and tolerant America is very much like the defense of thrift made by the avaricious man. *We praise what comes to us naturally and without effort. We condemn what we refuse to do.* America needs no great virtue to wait for the arrival of the cryptic friends announced in Mr. Truman's inaugural address. It is not difficult for us to be patient with criticism. The picture of America we hold in such respect sanctions as moral and necessary our own true weaknesses. It brands as guilty any effort—most of the time, quite half-hearted—that we may put forth in order to overcome our own faults.

Speaking about the past with enthusiasm, looking at the future with suspicion and fear, we feel excused to let the present go by. We dream of the opportunities that are offered to us *if* we would only see that they exist, but we do not seize the opportunities that simply exist. "Just think of Quemoy and the Matsus, as compared to India," said Senator Humphrey on April 28, 1955. "Just think of Quemoy and the Matsus, as compared to Burma."[11] Our allies in Asia are Pakistan, a monster of a state, and Thailand, a corrupt

253

and undemocratic country. Every task at hand is found to be unpleasant and risky. The sword that we should brandish is the power of our ideals. We need in the State Department people who know how to make friends. The United States will never capture the souls of human beings by boasting that the American stomach is full and its arm strong. We must foster a love and the understanding of people.

This process is denounced as culpable *evasion*. Nothing that has to be done is appealing. None of the noble and rewarding tasks that we propose to ourselves is directly feasible. Never is the diplomatic situation suited to our wishes. The very things that the United States is bound to accomplish appear to us to be the opposite of the lofty objectives of Americanism. Public opinion wants peace, and Mr. Dulles threatens. It demands friendly relations with all nations, and the administration signs one military pact after another. In our frantic effort to escape from the labors of waging peace, we let ourselves be deceived by fallacious short cuts and gross oversimplifications. The United States should negotiate with the Soviet Union as if there were no obstacle to peace except our own obstinacy. If Mr. Dulles were more open minded, more imaginative, it would be easy to transform the North Atlantic Treaty Organization into the association of free and co-operating partners which it was supposed to become. If atomic testing were stopped, the danger of atomic war would soon disappear. Let us feed hungry people and they will not be attracted by Communism any more. Let us come to terms with Arab nationalism and Soviet infiltration in the Middle East will instantly fail. Let us surrender Quemoy and we will have peace in the Far East.

The process of evasion is intimately related to the irrationality of our behavior. Public opinion refuses to accept its own ignorance of most of the objects of foreign policy. On the other hand, it rebels against the government's direction and justifies noncompliance with its own ability to dream about noble ideas. This is a form of *double talk*, and double talk is the second most important characteristic of American partisanship.

A curtain of silence suddenly falls on a policy which has previously been described as most controversial and most dangerous, and yet everyone knows that the same policy is continued without substantial changes. Accusations of the most serious nature, just dying on the accuser's lips, are forgotten as if they meant nothing at all. If we were to confront him with his own words, he would laugh contemptuously, as if he never intended to speak in earnest. In the mood of the moment, no words are strong enough, but when the fit has passed, the most reckless abuses are exculpated as "just politics." Massive retaliation was generally considered to be an unfortunate formula which had no meaning, but everyone knows that the whole structure of American policy has no other foundation. War over Quemoy and Matsu was declared to be imminent unless they were promptly surrendered. They have not been surrendered; there has been no war; none of the administration's critics has reflected upon the charges he made. Israel should be supported, of course, and it is equally evident that we should gain the Arabs' friendship. The nations of eastern Europe should be free, but there should be no liberation policy. Our universities hire great men who teach opposing doctrines. Our newspapers alternate—or even publish on the same page—a constructive editorial and a destructive editorial, and C. L. Sulzberger can do both in one column. On every issue everywhere, the ability of partisanship to reconcile opposites by sheer double talk has been noted.[12]

One of the specific features of political double talk is that it presupposes—and even asserts—a full comprehension of the issues. Senator Mansfield said on May 22, 1958, for instance, that trouble in the Middle East did not arise from Arab nationalism but from militarism, mobbism, and terrorism. He claimed that in the past, American policy was "bordering closely on appeasement of arrogance and submission to blackmail, until the Secretary of State put a stop to this nonsense by withdrawing the Aswan Dam proposal." He could only approve what he called Mr. Dulles' "determination to be made a pawn in someone's balancing game." He strongly opposed any "servile tendency to flirt with a rampant nationalism." It was time for the policies of this country "to come to age," to cease playing "the role of indulgent father to errant son." It was time, he said, to direct our policies "strictly in support of those nations which work sincerely for peace, which make an unremitting effort to put the energies of nationalism into the building of peaceful, progressive, and responsible states." Both Iraq and Lebanon were dear to his heart. There was no reason whatever to yield to the aggressive manifestations of Nasserism or to abandon our commitments.[13] But on July 14, 1958, he declared that he would be less than honest if he did not say that he had serious doubts about the wisdom of landing Marines in Lebanon. There were unexplored "alternatives." Military intervention could not be the answer to the multiple difficulties there. Neither was the administration justified in invoking the Eisenhower Doctrine.[14] "The decision having been made," he said the next day, he would do his "very best as a Senator to support the action taken."[15]

The implication was, of course, that support demanded great patriotism, infinite restraint, a superhuman effort of good will. This is the manner in which we "support" our own government. Since we regret the necessity of action and appreciate its tragic implications, we support it, if only because it has been done. It goes without saying that if the administration's policy were to lead us to involvement in war, the American people would close ranks behind the government. This "native trait of our character" cannot be impressed too often on would-be aggressors. Were they to press us "too far," they would discover that they had committed the "fatal error" of mistaking "criticism" for disunity. There is no reason, either, why debating should be cut off. How can the country be "unified in its opinion" if there is no "full" and "free" debate?[16] Thus the paradox of double talk is that it justifies itself in the name of patriotism. *The sound understanding which the critic displays of the policy he criticizes serves to protect him against any allegation of bad faith.*

A particular form of political double talk deserves special attention because of its paramount importance. In times of crisis, the situation is pictured, as we have repeatedly stressed, in terms of war and appeasement, of some actual commitment of force or diplomatic defeat. It seems impossible to have a commitment of force without war or diplomacy without appeasement. We call this familiar process *militarism in reverse*.

The assumption seems to be that the problem of aggression can have no other solution than meeting the aggressor on the battlefield. While we describe every crisis as a choice between abject surrender and outright hostilities, the enemies of America experience no difficulty in pretending that America is obsessed with war. It is the fear of war that makes us warlike, but the obsession is a fact. The war in Indochina should have been "continued and brought to a successful conclusion," said Senator Kennedy on March 9, 1954.[17] Yet on April 6 he said that if the United States were to send troops into the most difficult terrain in the world, it would create "a hopeless situation."[18] At the time, we had 250 technicians in the area. Their presence was, Senator Stennis said on March 9, "an open invitation for Red China to come in."[19]

To compound the problem, the critics asserted that the Communists were convinced that we were afraid of *war* and were begging for peace. There should have been no conference at Geneva; the cards were stacked against us. We were, in other words, in a political hot box, and the only alternative was another *war*. When the President asked Congress for authorization to use U.S. forces in the Formosa Strait, he must have thought that we faced all-out *war* with Red China. Why should he have asked for *war* powers if he did not think that *war* was imminent? The Truman Doctrine did not prevent the rape of Czechoslovakia. How could the Eisenhower Doctrine save Jordan or Lebanon without *war*?

Militarism in reverse is an exceedingly simple form of double talk. It is first strongly asserted that "the only way to negotiate successfully with the Communists is to negotiate from strength." But there should be no war either, no commitment of power. The administration is then accused of walking to the brink of war and also of drifting toward appeasement. On March 22, 1954, Senator Mansfield declared:

The only way to negotiate successfully with the Communists is to negotiate from strength. . . . I want to make certain that the free nations do not abandon the vital perimeter of Southeast Asia for a false peace of appeasement at Geneva. . . . Unless there is unity of purpose and a willingness on the part of all concerned to make sacrifices and to rise to the realities of the situation the only settlement which will be reached will be a settlement of appeasement. . . . While the United States should make a contribution to the defense of Indo-China, we should not commit American forces to the fighting there. . . . American forces must not become involved in the conflict. . . . Is the administration just drifting toward appeasement at Geneva?[20]

Senator Gillette spoke in the same way on April 5, 1954: "A narrow set of ugly choices has been presented to us. In simplest terms, the alternatives in Indochina have been reduced to three: Appease, fight or quit—purchase peace from the Communists, or make war against the Communists, or abandon Southeast Asia to the Communists."[21] In other words, there should be no commitment and yet no appeasement. We should "negotiate from strength" and "rise to the realities of the situation," but it should be made clear that the United States is not going to be involved in a war.

The antinomy between war and appeasement is just as forceful as it is unnecessary. As Senator Wiley remarked in 1954, "it is one thing to avoid American boys shedding their blood in Indochina, and it is another thing to assume that we can avoid any risk whatsoever there, by simply burying our heads in the sand."[22] There is always the alternative of a strong and yet restrained use of American power, the alternative of a resolute attitude that all concerned could well understand if they were not faced with confused and irresponsible pressures within these United States. At the moment when a problem can be taken care of without war and without appeasement by a simple assertion of our determination, American opinion scares itself with the idea of war. Frightening its friends with a belligerency born of fear, it leaves American alliances desperately divided at a time when they should be most united.[23]

Like all forms of double talk, militarism in reverse is self-contradictory. If surrender is an alternative that all want to avoid, what reasons do we have to exaggerate the risks that must be taken, no matter what we say? Why do we make it a point to undermine the efficacy of our warnings? If war is truly such a frightening eventuality, why not unite now and impress the aggressor with the determination we promise to display in war? If it is true that the world is wary of Dulles' petulance, why not denounce Khrushchev's arrogance?

We do just the opposite. We work ourselves into a panic. We fiercely denounce our own government. We take delight in foreign criticism. We still act as if war were no threat at all. As Soviet power continues to grow, Soviet leaders become more daring. We have entered the critical years of human history. For many years to come, the Communist dictators will deliberately engineer one crisis after another. They will also negotiate more earnestly. American opinion is dramatically unprepared for this always renewed, always different, always deadly offensive. Unless our own double talk ceases, we ourselves will expose the whole world to Communist blackmail. Unless we learn, at long last, to be satisfied with letting the administration declare the policy of the United States and then standing by such declarations, we will destroy ourselves. The days when the democracies could still afford the decadent practices of Athenian society are gone forever.

It is astonishing for the foreigner to see this great country of ours constantly worried about the picture it projects to the world, apparently ready to succumb to pressures that are by no means decisive, and upholding a philosophy of collective security that ties the hands of American policy-makers. This *aversion for true leadership* is the third important feature of our national character.

In 1954, lack of British support during the Indochinese crisis proved to be a great stumbling block for American public opinion. During the Formosa crisis of 1955, the grand alliance of free nations was allegedly weakened by our lonely stand in "a sullen and hostile world." The Eisenhower Doctrine forced us to stand alone in the Middle East. The policy of the administration in that area was, as Senator Mansfield claimed on January 29, 1957, "not a policy of isolation, not a policy of internationalism, but a policy of isolated internationalism."[24] It was sheer insanity, of course, to land troops in Lebanon unilaterally. We were alone in 1958 during the second Quemoy crisis and were again placed on the defensive before the bar of enlightened mankind. And while the slightest differences with our allies are exaggerated beyond measure, official silence of controversial problems like Algeria or Cyprus is not tolerated by public opinion either. We make it a point to smoke out the administration. We demand some forceful display of leadership when the diplomatic situation demands patience, vagueness, and silence. And, again, if the administration were to speak up, it will be warned about intimidating our allies, going it alone, resurgent isolationism, ultra-interventionism, and shaking the keystones of collective security.

True leadership demands a willingness to maintain independence of judgment, if not always of action, but this requirement is contrary to the false image we have of our historical role. Public opinion has not been able to keep the ideological distance demanded by political realism. It has been equally unable to accept any assertion of American power. The vague idealism that it mistakes for Americanism claims a right to universal tutelage, but it resents the exercise of true leadership.[25]

Since militarism in reverse is a form of double talk, this professed aversion for unilateral action is a way to evade both reality and duty. With the careless innocence of a child, the dissenter takes refuge in "new ideas." He sets forth the steps that *he* would take to preserve international peace and the security of his country. He says that the administration's unilateral and arbitrary intervention in Lebanon would have been something to laugh about if the results of its action had not been so serious, but *he* has a program in five points. The United States should announce unequivocally that it regards Nasser's policies as a direct threat to its own security. It should announce that it is opposed to the violent and illegal abrogation of contractual agreements. It should openly acknowledge that the West needs the resources of the Middle East. It should immediately negotiate a mutual security treaty with Lebanon. It should also proclaim that the security of

Israel is indispensable to its own security. It matters little if none of these five points is practicable. Still less important is the extravagance of the program. Such an authority as Senator Clark can advocate the repeal of the Eisenhower Doctrine, the establishment of a pro-Western Arab radio station to counter the propaganda of the Voice of the Arabs, and more help to the Palestinian refugees and can brand Secretary of State Dulles as "a man whose only answer to any new thought is always 'No.'"

The most natural outlet of evasion, however, is a recourse to the United Nations. In everything we do, we should first go before the UN and state our case before Krishna Menon. As long as the United States is a loyal member of the organization, it should serve a threatening notice on no one without first obtaining the moral sanction of the General Assembly. We cannot pretend to substitute our own judgment for the general consensus of the world. We cannot disregard the law handed down by the court and resort to the law of the jungle. We cannot confront the United Nations with a *fait accompli* and tell this body to pick up the pieces of a situation that our unilateral doings have worsened. The United States should have made it its business to place the entire question of the safety of Lebanon on the UN agenda. The status of Formosa should be determined by the UN. It is the responsibility of the UN to negotiate and to enforce a cease-fire in the Formosa Strait. Whatever the danger of Communist advances, there is a line of conduct in which every human being is even more vitally concerned, namely, that each step we take, each precedent we set by our actions, contributes to the establishment of the rule of law in the world.[26]

The world organization has good reasons, indeed, to be grateful to American public opinion for its devotion. Unfortunately, this doctrinaire attachment is based on the notion of international legality, and, according to international law, the United Nations is practically undone. The agency established by the Charter for the maintenance of peace is the Security Council. To put it mildly, the Security Council has not functioned as was expected. Like any other legal document, the Charter of the United Nations is indivisible. The organization has proved itself powerless to police the Soviet Union, Nasser, and. India. Repeated challenges to its authority have not left unchanged the obligations subscribed by its members. Furthermore, the UN was never supposed to become a world government; it was to be an association of sovereign nations. The recommendations of the General Assembly are not binding in law. In practice, the United Nations has sanctioned lawlessness and has served to embarrass the free nations in every way.

Now this is not to say that the world organization has no diplomatic usefulness. The services of the United Nations have sometimes been used with profit, and there is no place that is more ideal for dumping untreatable issues. When, for valid reasons, the United States does not want to act alone, when a problem offers no hope for a solution, it is wise, of course, to refer the matter to the UN. At that moment—as could have been expected—the administration will be reminded by its critics that the words of the Charter should not be taken seriously. For the United States to put all its faith in the world organization would be a negation of policy. We should not use the beneficent disguise of a recourse to the UN when leadership is expected from Washington. Our policy should be an American policy, not the tail of the UN kite. This means, in other words, that the administration should go before the United Nations when the United States is likely to suffer a loss of prestige by doing so and that we should not refer a problem to the organization when something could be gained from a UN debate. No words less than partisan hypocrisy can aptly describe such inconsistency.[27]

We know that many loyal Democrats will retort that it is hypocritical for the administration to turn to the United Nations when a problem has become hopeless and to go it alone otherwise. This is, indeed, the great drama of partisanship in America. We intuitively sense our own faults, but we misdirect the criticism.[28] We know that we are entitled to respect, but we dare not rebuke and at the same time claim the birthright of ideological leadership. The administration's alleged inability to solve the complexities of the disarmament issue has caused much furor, and we say that disarmament is not the great issue but only a by-product of more important problems which the administration is accused of neglecting. When the President is ill, all say that he should resign because we need a leader. When he recovers, he should not resign because of Richard Nixon. When the President asserts his leadership, we speak of the "personality cult." When he negotiates with the Russians, he is naïve; if he does not negotiate, he is inflexible. In every emergency, we declaim against the warmongers and the fire-eaters, yet when the Soviets launch satellites and missiles, the United States should go "all out." We oppose unilateral action when the United States has to act alone; we return to unilateralism when collective action is in order. We refer to prudence, compromise, and generosity when the situation demands strength; we propose to settle an issue through negotiations when it cannot be done. When the national interest is a sure guide of action, we speak the language of idealism; when a question of principle is involved, we appeal to political realism. When America is unjustly attacked, we exhort ourselves to see America as others see it, but when our policy succeeds, we accuse the administration of tottering from crisis to crisis. The dialectics of partisanship make us give to each problem the response that we should have given in circumstances diametrically opposed to the issues we now face. Since we consistently give the right response at the wrong moment, there must be some logic in so much madness; this logic is nothing more than appeasement.

Supposedly a by-product of the McCarthyist hysteria, the word *appeasement* is anathema to most Americans. When used, it hits us like a curse. Our reaction is always one of deep resentment, anger, and disgust. No political concept has ever caused greater activity in self-defense or greater mental fixation. The extreme sensitivity displayed by public opinion about the notion of appeasement is so pronounced that we consider it to be the fourth most important feature of America's malicious self.

The violent emotionalism caused by the use of this single word, appeasement, betrays, of course, that on this particular point, we are not willing to subject ourselves to rational self-analysis, for in the light of cold reason, appeasement appears to be one of the great dangers of our time. No conduct is more irrational than to refuse to face the reality of danger. Even if we were not inclined at all toward appeasement, the sheer possibility of any appeasement is by itself a problem serious enough to require constant and sober examination of our foreign policy in that respect. Even if our national attitudes were not what they unfortunately are, appeasement would be a natural and almost inevitable process. We face a dynamic ideology which tends to expand its dominion constantly and in every direction at once. Communist imperialism creates tensions that never truly relax. It is bound to succeed in further encroachments unless it is successfully checked by an equally determined force. The type of determined firmness required by a situation of this sort is not in the nature of the democratic way of life and least of all of American democracy. The moods of opinion change with every new event. Every new crisis releases divisive forces; every peaceful move made by the Communists creates doubts about their basic wickedness. The growing power of their weapons is taken as proof that a relaxation is necessary, i.e., that we have to relax.[29]

It is not denied that the difference between appeasement and legitimate concessions to realities is often difficult to draw, which is an additional reason why the problem should receive utmost attention. This admittedly perplexing question could perhaps be clarified if certain conditions necessary to appeasement were stated. It seems certain that appeasement first presupposes the existence of a dynamic situation. This means that the aggressor has the initiative because he actively pursues the achievement of his imperialist aims. As far as Communism is concerned, it will always have the initiative in that sense, but there are differences in degree. In the spring of 1954, the Communists launched their offensive against Dien Bien Phu. The year after, they announced that they would liberate Taiwan. In 1956, the Hungarian uprising was violently suppressed. In the fall of 1957, the area of tension had moved to the Middle East. The U.S.S.R. violently opposed our intervention in Lebanon in 1958, and this second crisis in the Middle East was followed by the second Quemoy crisis and by the Berlin ultimatum. When pressure is so manifest, any peaceful move that we can make runs the risk of amounting to appeasement. Soviet economic infiltration in Egypt and Syria belonged to a different order of things, and although the stakes were higher than at Dien Bien Phu or Quemoy, the situation did not justify such an ironclad attitude. But it would be appeasement, of course, to assert as a matter of principle that we cannot and should not prevent the Arabs from benefiting from Soviet assistance. Other problems, such as our own trade with Communist countries, also represent another order of things where appeasement seems to be only a remote possibility.

It is of paramount importance, of course, to define the categories of appeasement, but it would be an error to assume that a situation is diplomatically active only when the aggressor threatens forceful action. When General Eisenhower, as a candidate for the Presidency, announced in 1952 that the United States would not acquiesce in the enslavement of any people in order to purchase fancied gains for itself, the issue of liberation made the situation dynamic. It was necessary to take sides for or against the proposed policy, and it was hardly possible to oppose the principle of liberation without succumbing to appeasement. A situation can, therefore, become politically active through our own initiative, and this new principle holds true at all levels of political action. On January 10, 1956, George Meany attacked the late Ernest Weir for what he had written in the *St. Louis Post Dispatch* of May 25, 1955. Mr. Weir claimed that there had come "an auspicious moment" to improve our relations with the Soviet Union, a moment that had to be "fully exploited," he said, to "proceed from the principle that Russia now wants peace and more stable international relations." Whether the American people like it or not, a debate of this kind raises the issue of appeasement. In contradistinction, tough talk about liberation and other subjects is not necessarily anti-appeasement. On June 20, 1955, Senator McCarthy introduced a resolution in the Senate demanding that the satellite situation be a subject for discussion at the UN meeting in San Francisco and at Geneva. The Senator failed to win support for his resolution. Since his move was stillborn, the issue never became politically active.

Appeasement also requires the making of certain concessions to the aggressor. Now concessions can be made in many different ways. We can appease even when we refuse to grant to the aggressor some immediate and tangible benefit, such as a piece of territory which he covets. When the Formosa Resolution was still under discussion, Senator Humphrey wanted to amend it and to have the whole problem referred to the United Nations. This move was rightly considered as appeasement, but on February 8, 1955, the Senator tried to justify himself as follows:

My answer to those particular Senators was that if appeasement was to be done at the United Nations, it would have to be done by this administration because the foreign policy of the United States government is in the hands of the President. . . . If there was to have been appeasement . . . appeasement could only have come as the result of an order of the administration forwarded to those who represent us in the United Nations.[30]

This naïve rationalization stems from the belief that appeasement can start only when final agreement is about to be reached and "concessions" made on the settlement of some problem. *Anything that we say or do can be appeasement.* During the Quemoy crisis of 1958, many critics of the administration proposed that the future of Formosa be determined by a plebiscite, and they formulated several other schemes of "extrication with honor." Just to talk at such a moment of extricating U.S. policy from the bog of its own mistakes is as clear a case of appeasement as could ever be found, even if the administration refused to yield to public pressure.

Obviously, there are two levels of appeasement. One is the outright making of a concession, the surrender to a demand clearly stated by the aggressor, although it is evident that if granted, the demand would only serve to increase his power and lead to still more serious difficulties. The other is hidden appeasement. Since "courage" is a part of the picture we have of ourselves, hidden appeasement is both more likely and more deadly. On January 28, 1955, for instance, Senator Morse said that the Formosa Resolution woud "greatly" increase "the probability of war" in the Far East.[31] Four days later, Senator Humphrey introduced a resolution requesting the administration to take prompt action to bring a "cease-fire" in the Formosa area. Senator Morse spelled out the true intent of this new resolution by referring once more to the "powerful forces in America who at this hour want to go to war." On April 1, 1955, another resolution sponsored by Senators Morse, Lehman, Humphrey, and Long was proposed in order to bar the President from holding the offshore islands. "When we go into Quemoy and Matsu," Senator Humphrey said, "we put an end to all hope for a four-power conference; we put an end to any possibility of working out the German question."[32] Such concerted action is appeasement, and Senator Humphrey's statement is particularly typical of hidden appeasement. For the sake of a still hypothetical meeting which could not have been expected to produce any dramatic results, he saw fit to deliver a deliberate slap in the face to the American government and to undermine the efficacy of a national policy that was most solemnly affirmed. How contemptible must these great acts of statesmanship appear, even to the Communist directory!

It is true that real concessions can be made without any appeasement. The Indochinese armistice was followed by the signing of the Manila Pact. The evacuation of the Tachens, which started on February 7, 1955, was accompanied by such an overwhelming show of strength that it was certainly not appeasement. On August 13, 1958, President Eisenhower announced that the administration was ready to grant economic aid to the Arab nations on a regional basis and to renounce its past practice of bilateral arrangements.[33] The difference between appeasement and no appeasement depends most of the time on the climate in which the problem is approached. In Stalin's funeral oration, Georgi Malenkov made his well-known plea for co-existence and thus raised the question of the advisability of a high-level meeting between East and West. In his speech of April 16, 1953, President Eisenhower listed a few conditions which he thought could be met by the Soviets if they wanted to prove the seriousness of their intentions. Delicate negotiations between the powers led to the Berlin Conference and to the first Geneva meeting. The Indochinese armistice was signed on July 21, 1954. In an all-out effort to stop German rearmament, the Soviet Union repeatedly proposed a new conference. The Geneva settlement had proved, it said, the fruitfulness of peaceful negotiations. Germany acceded to NATO on May 9, 1955. The same day, President Eisenhower expressed his willingness to join in a Big Four conference. Meanwhile, the Chinese Communists had reverted to a more reasonable attitude in the Far East. The Geneva Conference could thus take place without appeasement because of its proper timing.[34]

The difficulties encountered in trying not to appease have been illustrated, and we must now explain why the drift into appeasement is such a natural process. *The typical mark of appeasement is that it always seems so rational.* It seems so evident that Red China has a legitimate claim to Quemoy. We must yield. As between a loss of prestige and the cataclysm of war in a cause which most of the world does not consider just, the choice is clear. "The truth is," Thomas K. Finletter wrote in 1958, "that the defense of these islands is necessary only for the defense of an untenable United States diplomatic position brought about by concessions to a small, vociferous minority in this country."[35] It is pleasant but unrealistic to demand that the U.S.S.R. give up revolution as an instrument of policy, and it should not be demanded. There exists no eternal law that states that the West, and nobody else, should have interests in the Middle East. We must face the fact that henceforth Russia has a right to a voice in Middle Eastern affairs. Could Mr. Dulles deny to Moscow the right to give guns to its friends while insisting on Washington's right to give guns to the friends of the West? Could we remain indifferent to Russia's determination not to have U.S. military power stationed on its southern flank? What would we say if the Soviet Union would station troops in Mexico?[36]

The same false realism makes us assert that there is no connection between a suspension of atomic testing and controlled disarmament. The "fact" is that we can stop atomic testing without waiting for the Soviet Union to agree. It is "unrealistic" for the President to deny the need for a study of a U.S. surrender in any future nuclear war. The possibility that we may lose the war or that it may be "strategically necessary" at some future time to surrender in order to save the remnants of a mutilated population is not a moot question but a problem of grave concern. Political pressures warp any "realistic" thinking by the administration on this point as on others. We say likewise that Dulles has frozen the cold war so irrevocably that a future disengagement is no longer possible, yet in the name of realism, the present situation in Europe is described as irrevocable. It is a lack of "realism" for the administration to accuse the Soviet Union of supporting indirect aggression in the Middle East. Every reasonable person knows these things. To speak of indirect aggression is to devise a formula that is most likely to set off an explosion of vituperative language which will poison the air for many months and render negotiations impossible. "This is not diplomacy," Senator Humphrey said on August 8, 1958, "it is adolescent debate."[37]

Many of these irrecusable realities are not always as irrecusable as is pretended, of course, and some of them are the creation of our fantasy. Moreover, political realism consists less in recognizing facts as such than in the response we give to realities. It is true, indeed, that the United States could not wage war with the Soviet Union without risking its continued existence, but to accept this fact simply as a "fact" is the reverse of political realism. The debate on peaceful co-existence revealed the true nature of this kind of realism. It was said that we may not like our adversaries, that we may not even trust them, yet we must live with them. Frustrating though it be, cold war is preferable to hot war. Senator Fulbright so endorsed the idea of co-existence on July 4, 1954, because, he said, "the only alternative is war," and he added that he was "not ready to attack Russia yet." Adlai Stevenson declared on December 4, 1954, that he was "weary of the long semantic argument about coexistence." It is true that atomic war and surrender are excluded. All we have left, he said, is peaceful co-existence or anything else you like to call it.

In order to avoid what is called a "semantic argument," the realist produces a fraudulent set of alternatives. It is war, surrender, or co-existence. So started, the argument will soon lead to the conclusion that peaceful co-existence with Communism is not only possible but is a fact. We do co-exist now, and we have co-existed ever since Communism was born. The realist will not ask himself in what manner we have co-existed; rather, he will say, as Dean Acheson said on March 16, 1950, that East and West can exist together in the world just as "good and evil can and do exist concurrently in the whole great realm of human life . . . within every individual, within every nation." Is there any reason, after all, why some healthy relationship could not be established between the American people and "Russia," even though their respective "philosophies" remain "theoretically" in conflict?

Public opinion is bored with endless propaganda. There is universal anxiety to explore every possibility of easing tensions through negotiations. Since past experiences in negotiating with the Communists have been disillusioning, the purpose of negotiations should not be to reach agreement but to maintain contact with one another.[38] No stone should remain unturned. Every Soviet proposal should be given an "affirmative" response, and this means that the administration's response has been "negative" and unconstructive, that Dulles is unwilling to examine Soviet proposals in earnest, that American diplomacy is bankrupt.

Step by step, and with the precision of clockwork, this "semantic" debate has drifted into an indictment of American policy. The end result is that we might as well face the facts and try to come to terms with the Soviet Union. If war is not an alternative, then issues have to be compromised. "If we the people are uncompromising," Mr. Stevenson said on June 13, 1955, "if we equate a

270

negotiation with appeasement, if we think war is inevitable, if we regard every Russian proposal as a trick and a trap, if we think that what is advantageous for one is automatically disadvantageous for the other, then we the people will have ruled out bargaining." Let us "take some chances," he added, let us "risk something to win more." Diplomacy prescribes no rigid formula for accomplishing its objectives. "How can we get along with the Russians," he asked on October 18, 1958. "How do we know until we try?"

The real difficulty is, of course, that we the people are only too willing to compromise and to take chances and also that we regard every Dulles action as a trick and a trap. We the people have ruled out appeasement. Mr. Dulles pointed out on May 15, 1954, that "coexistence is not part of a Soviet creed or practice, except in the sense non-Communists are allowed, in a physical sense, to exist." On February 2, 1955, Mr. Eisenhower defined co-existence as "a state of our being as long as we are not attempting to destroy the other side" by the force of arms. Since the United States has never had any intention of doing such a thing, the concept of co-existence means that the other side cannot destroy the United States. So understood, the notion of co-existence can be realistically used as a means of peaceful pressure on world Communism. In contradistinction, the "realists" see in atomic stalemate nothing but the restraint we must place upon ourselves.[39]

Diplomatic recognition of Red China by the United States was similarly demanded because it is a fact that the Chinese Nationalist government will never regain control of the Chinese mainland. Both Mr. Dulles and President Eisenhower insisted that recognition was a privilege and not a right, but this abstract, nebulous "emotionalism" made no sense to the realists. The historic policy of the United States has been to grant recognition to any regime firmly in power, they said, and while we tried to isolate the Chinese Communists, all that our policy actually did was to isolate us. Non-recognition was considered, in other words, to be a short-sighted, hopeless policy. The American eagle came to look like an ostrich. This refusal to face an "immutable fact" will keep us indefinitely at the brink of war in the Pacific. Unless we recog-

nize Red China, there will be no settlement in Korea, no settlement in Indochina, no settlement of the Formosa issue.[40] Let us
enter into the only course that can lead to durable peace in Asia,
i.e., recognition of Red China. What a simple solution to so many
pressing problems! But the Republican administration is inflamed
to *intransigeance* by Robertson and Radford. It forcibly keeps
alive a hatred for Communism, and the "real" meaning of recognition is thus beclouded. Since recognition would bring the Chinese
Communists closer to the West—and thus educate them in freedom—a reappraisal of our Chinese policy is necessary in the name
of reason and realism. For the time being, U.S. policy is committed
to a fiction.

If the fiction is useful, however, who can say that non-recognition lacks realism? Legal fictions are part of our daily life; they
are both legitimate and helpful. Of all the arguments that can be
formulated in favor of recognition, none has less validity than the
one based on "realism." If the question is a question of realism, it
must be proved that the national interest would be better served
by recognition than it is by maintaining vis-à-vis Communist
China a state of quasi-war.[41] As Mr. Dulles said on January 16,
1958, as long as the Communist regime opposes, "by all possible
means, the things which we believe to be in our interest," there can
be no valid reason or advantage to be obtained "by increasing its
authority, its influence and prestige to be used against us." Non-
recognition is an instrument of realist diplomacy, which is consistent with principle. Furthermore, recognition can be granted,
just as it can be refused. "None of us are talking here in terms of
eternity," the Secretary said on February 19, 1957. He added on
January 16, 1958, that "any time it will serve the interest of the
United States" and the interest of our allies, we will grant recognition. "We are not controlled by dogma or anything of that sort,"
he said. "It's a very simple question."[42]

Now this is not true for the pseudo-realists because the pseudo-
realists are idealists at heart. When realism fails them, they automatically turn to pseudo-idealism. National policy is indicated in
terms of values higher than the national interest. Constant appeals

are made, as we know, to the Golden Rule. Mr. Dulles' art of going to the verge of war, Senator Humphrey said on January 17, 1956, "comes precariously close to rejecting the traditional American conviction that we must not strike the first blow; that we must never bear the awful responsibility for beginning atomic warfare."[43] Adlai Stevenson said on March 6, 1954, that "it is only in the humility of all men under God that we can create a future not scratched from the wreck and the rubble of war." This future must rise, he said, "from the love and the faith and the devotion of unconquerable humanity." In an editorial published in November, 1956, in the *Bulletin of Atomic Scientists*, Mr. Rabinowitch called the Stevenson proposal for discontinuing H-bomb testing a possible first step in the formulation of a new foreign policy for this country. He wrote that a test renunciation by the United States could become "the first demonstration in history of the recognition by a powerful national state of the existence of requirements of humanity as a whole, overriding the immediate needs of the segment of humanity which this state represents." This country has always professed to be motivated by the Christian ideal. It should make a venture of faith, and if there is any risk in stopping atomic testing, let us recall the adventuresome spirit that Western culture has always displayed, an adventure that can be traced to the Christian faith in Christ's resurrection.

The same idealism tends to give more weight to the atom-for-peace idea than to the atom-for-war notion—as if they were mutually exclusive alternatives. On April 25, 1956, President Eisenhower proposed that an atom-powered merchant vessel be constructed at public expense to demonstrate to people everywhere the peaceful possibilities of nuclear energy. Atomic Energy Commissioner T. E. Murray proposed a thermonuclear demonstration to educate all the leaders of the world. Paul Hoffman called for the establishment of a Supreme Council for Peace. Adlai Stevenson wanted the Secretary General of the United Nations to appoint a commission of cultural leaders of humanity to examine all the various proposals to end the arms race made to date. Senator Humphrey thought that peace in our time would be achieved if his proposal for an international, interracial, interspatial sputnik were taken seriously. Any such dramatic move is presented as a creative idea. It is said to electrify free men all over the world. It counteracts—or so it is believed—the picture of America as a bomb-happy country. It seems certain, however, that its only usefulness is to give an outlet to a guilt complex and to make it possible to escape from the hard realities of power policy. For the rest of the world, it proves that America, the country of psychology and social science, still has to learn the art of public relations.[44]

It is in the name of idealism that we have always asked ourselves the question of why American policy has gone so wrong that we have to use force. The use of force signifies the absence of policy or the breakdown of policy. "So long as we stand on principle," Senator Humphrey said on August 5, 1958, "we can be firm and unequivocal. So long as we protect the rights of others, we will have the strength of legion."[45] We are part of the human family, and we must learn to live not only with our friends but also our adversaries. Distrust is at the root of evil in the world. Nobody trusts anybody. A way to create confidence, Mr. Stevenson said on June 9, 1958, "might be for us, the West, to accept the principle of Soviet equality in power." He well knew that this principle conflicted with our present policy, but since our policy had accomplished nothing, what was the difference? If we would accept Soviet equality, we would not be "rivals for military superiority," he said, and "our other rivalries are safe, and civilization is safe."[46] Therefore, the time has "now" come to concentrate on the possibilities of agreement rather than on missiles, failures, and the evils of the "past."

Nothing is easier for governments than to incite the people to war by appealing to fear. Now fear is the greatest enemy of peace because it is fear of an enemy. There can be no greater folly than to sit back and do nothing. Let us try again and again. Talk, talk, talk, unhurried talk. The alternative to decreased tension is increased tension. The Pilgrims invited the Indians to dinner. And Lincoln has said that "the only way we can get rid of our enemies is by getting rid of our enmity." But the Republicans stick to the *status quo.* The situation demands patience, a slow and painful process toward carefully thought-out objectives and also, of course, bold, dramatic new concepts to instill vigor and hope. "The way to get started" on the difficult road to peace, Stevenson said on September 29, 1956, is not "to scorn new ideas." Is it because this administration has so utterly failed to make any progress toward peace that progress is forever impossible? "No matter which party wins in November," he added, "another supreme effort must be undertaken, and if it fails, then another, and another, for leaders must lead." Hence a constant worry about the people's apathy and preoccupation for material enjoyment, both material and mental. Hence constant pleas for a new debate which would "air" the issues and produce "something" in the way of "positive" alternatives. Hence the constant references to the "bankruptcy" of our diplomacy.

Let us conclude that this pseudo-idealism has two complementary aspects. First, it refuses to accept the reality of determinant evil in the world, both in others and in ourselves. Second, this refusal is rationalized by the mysticism of the unknown. *American partisanship feels at ease in the limbo of an inexistent future, in the mystery of new ideas that cannot be stated, with new diplomatic moves that cannot be made.*[47] It speaks of leadership, of unconquerable humanity, of the ships and sails of beckoning hope, of the broad horizon, of the Founding Fathers, of the north wind. Surely, it is believed, the present crisis demands a more imaginative answer than massive retaliation and greater statesmen than Secretary Dulles. But, as Senator Bridges remarked on February 6, 1958, those who cry "for imagination and flexibility on our part make no such demands on the Russians." It does not trouble them that the Russian leaders continue "writing the same tedious letters, proposing the same stale plans, and restating the same terms and conditions—all of which, if we agreed to them, would spell the surrender of the free world."[48]

Let us conclude that this idealism is as appeasing as anything can ever be. In order to understand Communism and to understand ourselves, we need faith in a system of values. The whole intellectual creed of this country identifies moral evidence with absolutism, the Inquisition, Beria, McCarthy, and, finally, with Communism itself. As far as Communism is concerned, the process is reversed. Barbarism is nothing new in Russia. The Soviets have not changed. So what? Why should the administration be so panicky about a relaxation of tension? We deprecate an alleged habit of thinking in terms of political absolutes. The Soviet leaders act like they do because of Dulles' moralistic stubbornness.[49]

This is the picture of America, the self-portrait that has been drawn by those who pretend to speak for American public opinion. Do we recognize our own likeness? We certainly ought to recognize the thoughts that have occupied our attention during the past four years. These are not the thoughts of "we the people" but those of a handful of agitators, uprooted intellectuals, all comedians by profession, all to move away from the limelight soon, only to be replaced by others.

This is a time for dissent. The false prophets of public opinion have acquired a monopoly on our political thought, a monopoly they ruthlessly enforce. This monopoly they now enjoy, but for how long? They would not repeat so often that their ideas are unpopular if they were not frightened by our faculty to dissent. They despise public opinion, but only because they fail to control it.[50] They themselves do not believe in what they say. They are better individuals than they lead us to believe, but they are cruel masters. They confuse us and then laugh at us—and at themselves.[51] But there is little to laugh about in such a phony conspiracy.

For their sake, as well as for our own, we must set ourselves *free*. Since we are voluntary captives, nothing could be easier. But we must rise to the seriousness of our age and *use words strong enough to break away*. We must break away from the spell cast upon us. We can be free if we so choose, but not without effort. It is easy to understand *now* the sincerity of our past policy, yet every new crisis will instantly obliterate all valid previous experiences. In one instant, all the slogans whose recklessness has been denounced will be restored to our consciousness, as vivid and disturbing as before. Fallacies repeatedly disproved by reason will recover their fascinating charm all the more. We will be surrounded once more by a choking atmosphere of bland lies, accusations that are not intended as accusations, exaggerations that we do not pretend are true and yet feel ready to accept. It is *not* in our power to prevent the rebirth of the destructive patterns of partisanship, for partisanship resembles the mythological Hydra. It presents a new face as soon as a head has been cut off. Because of its iniquitous omnipresence and infinite versatility, the monster seems real. However, the only reality it has is its very existence, which is, indeed, ominously real. But the only power it has upon the will and the actions of free men is the power that they themselves have freely surrendered to the beast.

It is not within our power not to succumb again, yet if properly directed by a sincere will, our reason can break the spell and transcend it to the light of reality. We therefore issue a challenge. We assert that the weird atmosphere in which political debates are presently conducted is the price that the United States must pay for the political nihilism of an increasingly large fraction of its intelligentsia. We well know how easy it is for the liberal intellectual to condemn every possible aspect of our foreign policy and then shower his noble phrases upon the world. But we also know that the policy-maker must act and that action means commitment. We know that as soon as our foreign policy has committed the people, it becomes the object of the liberals' systematic question, if for no other reason than that they are committed to nothing but their own pride.

This finding goes, we earnestly believe, to the very root of partisanship in America. The type of attack of which the Eisenhower administration has been the object during the past five years is directly related to the slow erosion of moral certitudes, which is particularly noticeable in the ranks of the liberal intelligentsia. It is not by chance that the individuals who are the most confused about our foreign policy have been the philosophers, the political scientists, the newspapermen, the scholars. It is not by chance, either, that the great statesmen of this country and those who have the clearest insight into the issues of the present day are men of simple and deep intuition and, very often, men of faith. Nothing is more appropriate for the scholar than to be deeply conscious of the limitations of his own knowledge, but when this relativism is turned into a doctrinaire denial of all certitudes, it spells disaster in politics, just as it does in every other field of human conduct.

Our challenge is this: Will the liberals be willing to speak a language that all can understand? Will they part from their lofty jargon? Will they cease to call the real public opinion of the United States reactionary when *they themselves are the reaction?* Will they have a soul high enough to rise above themselves, or, rather, will they themselves be real citizens of these United States and not citizens of a dream world? Will they speak the truth?

For our part, as *free* men answerable to no one or nothing but our own conscience, we must now decide to break away from divisive partisanship while there is still time. It is the continued existence of the free commonwealth that is at stake. Plato wrote his *Republic* to show, in the body politic, the enlarged picture of the human soul. Now the massive retaliation debate has revealed, in magnified features, the working of evil in the human spirit.[52] It is within our power—let us repeat it once more—to run away from the mirage of despair, but in order to be free, we must ponder the Bible's warning that man is a liar to himself. With this observation, we rest our case.

Notes

NOTES

For the most part, the material we have used has been identified in the text by a date. When such information is identified only by a date, the reader is referred to the daily press, the *New York Times*, the *Washing Post and Times Herald*, and the *New York Herald Tribune* in particular. Many magazine articles and many editorials published in the press are to be found in the Appendix of the *Congressional Record*. Many of the quotations included in the text are identified in the footnotes; they are generally short and the reader might want to place them in their context.

We have tried to choose our samples carefully, and we believe that they are truly representative of "public opinion." The amount of material we processed was overwhelming in its bulk, yet as our work progressed, we realized that everything said or done by the administration and its critics was falling into well-defined categories and that further research would cease to be fruitful. We therefore invite the reader to read some of the past Senate debates in full, not only to check on the validity of our conclusions, but also to free himself from the slavery of political conformism. As a matter of fact, this work is unnecessary. Any *critical* analysis of an article or speech by Adlai Stevenson, Walter Lippmann, James Reston, Hubert Humphrey, William Fulbright, or others would suffice. It is a fact that the minds of the intellectual leaders of public opinion are so transparent that any competent writer should be able to write their speeches for them in advance.

Preface

1. *Congressional Record* (hereafter designated as *CR*), March 30, 1954, p. 4072.
2. *CR*, June 20, 1955, p. 8686.

Chapter I

1. *CR*, January 21, 1954, p. 577.
2. *CR*, January 17, 1955, p. 393.
3. "We cannot afford to revert to the 'feast and famine' pattern of our past history, not just because of the effect upon our economy, but primarily because we cannot take the military risks involved in such a policy." (C. E. Wilson, Testimony to the House Armed Services Committee, January 26, 1955)

4. *CR*, January 5, 1956, p. 136.
5. *CR*, January 6, 1955, p. 122.
6. V. M. Molotov, February 8, 1955.
7. *Foreign Affairs*, October, 1957, pp. 27-28.
8. *CR*, January 5, 1956, p. 138.
9. See the State of the Union Message of January 6, 1955: Our military planning must be "flexible enough to utilize new weapons and techniques which flow in ever more speedily from our research and development programs." See also President Eisenhower's press conference of November 5, 1958: "If we are going to defend ourselves by what we called the 'new look' in 1953, we have got to do some good, hard-work thinking on the thing, and not just pile one weapon and one system of weapons on another and so in the long run break ourselves."
10. *CR*, January 16, 1957, p. 606.
11. *CR*, January 5, 1956, p. 138.
12. *CR*, January 6, 1955, p. 123.

Chapter II

1. On massive retaliation and Congress' war powers, see Secretary Dulles' press conference of March 16, 1954, and President Eisenhower's press conferences of March 10, 1954; March 17, 1954; March 24, 1954; and April 4, 1956.
2. "God keep us out of war but if war must come let us not draw a line and say that beyond that line is a sanctuary which the enemy may occupy and behind which he may retreat. . . . Let us say that wherever the enemy is we will strike." (Senator George, January 27, 1955) This repudiation of the "sanctuary" doctrine was dynamic when it was first stated, and it remains valid, of course, as an essential ingredient of massive retaliation. Yet it is a law of diplomacy that valid notions tend to lose their impact precisely because they are generally accepted. The new notion that now imposes itself is a more explicit doctrine on war's limitation. See Chapter V.
3. *CR*, January 24, 1955, p. 601.
4. "We must, if occasion offers, make it clear that we are prepared to stand firm and, if necessary, meet hostile forces with the greater forces that we possess." (J. F. Dulles, March 8, 1955)
5. See *CR*, January 26, 1955, pp. 736-68.
6. See *CR*, January 5, 1957, pp. 224-27.
7. A declaration is correct, in other words, when it serves the national interest and when the proposed policy is not contrary to principle. When public opinion requests declarations that are *factually* correct, it reveals a certain absolutism in thought or simply attempts to evade the labors of waging peace. See Chapter X.
8. *CR*, January 22, 1954, p. 651.
9. Daily issue of the *Congressional Record* (hereafter designated as *DCR*), February 27, 1957, p. A 1569.

10. On SAC's personnel problems, see *DCR*, February 28, 1958, pp. 2752-68.

11. *CR*, January 17, 1955, p. 395.

12. General LeMay testified in 1956 that he could sink any carrier at sea in two hours, and it has been pointed out that German submarine attacks during World War II almost succeeded in their mission. But it has also been said that in war, "almost" is a synonym for "defeat." It is hoped that the Navy will succeed in achieving its objective of six atom-powered aircraft carriers by 1966.

13. This reasoning presupposes, of course, the successful completion of the Polaris submarine. Let us repeat once more that weapons on the drawing boards do not have deterrent power.

14. *CR*, January 17, 1955, p. 394.

15. *DCR*, August 21, 1958, p. 17407, and the State of the Union Message of January 9, 1958, *DCR*, January 9, 1958, pp. 171-75. See Chapter VI for a fuller discussion of relative American power.

CHAPTER III

1. Local defense means either defense *by* one locality or defense *at* one locality. Both forms of local defense are as unfeasible without massive retaliation as they are conceivable with it.

2. *CR*, January 7, 1954, p. 79.

3. *CR*, January 17, 1955, p. 393.

4. *Foreign Affairs*, October, 1957, pp. 31-33.

5. *Foreign Affairs*, April, 1954, pp. 352-64.

6. Although it is true that the Communists would never take great risks for marginal areas like Formosa and Laos, the theory that the Soviet Union might feel that it is a "good gamble" to seize western Europe is unsatisfactory. It was at the root of some of the difficulties encountered by the administration when the continued importance of NATO had to be emphasized. If NATO did not exist, the Soviets might be tempted to seize western Europe. Now that NATO does exist, they cannot seize other areas without first taking over western Europe, and this they cannot accomplish without risking their very existence.

7. See Chapter VII.

8. Even if it were fully accepted by the various NATO countries, the atomic-stockpile concept should not interfere with the United States' right to use—independently and in the best interests of the Alliance—atomic weapons in case of Russian aggression in Europe.

9. *DCR*, June 23, 1958, p. 10789.

10. See *DCR*, June 23, 1958, pp. 10787-10802, pp. 10649-57, and pp. 12031-35. The United States should always be able to rely on either the United Kingdom or the Continental nations, and we can never become entirely committed to any one of our NATO partners. It is to NATO that we are committed, not to England or France.

11. In the event of aggression in Southeast Asia, the United States

would cease "to exercise restraint on the Republics of China and South Korea." (J. F. Dulles, March 15, 1955)

12. *DCR*, February 9, 1955, p. 1167.

13. Many will claim that properly speaking, the Formosa Resolution is not a declaration of war, but all must agree that it is a broad grant of authority that would make a declaration of war unnecessary in case of Communist aggression.

14. Despite these repeated applications of the doctrine, it is generally asserted that the Middle East Resolution has not been used thus far. See Senator Mansfield, *DCR*, June 17, 1958, p. 10347.

15. Progress on the alliance's programs was obviously hindered by the dislocation of its secretariat. The Baghdad Pact suffered its severest test in the Iraqi revolution and survived. It thus proved both its weakness and its resilience. Were it to have no use except to permit Iran to accede to formal American protection, the Pact would still be important. New economic and defense agreements with Iran, Turkey, and Pakistan, long desired by the United States, were concluded on March 5, 1959. As Mr. Dulles said on January 27, 1959, "there are two ways in which the United States can assume international engagements. One is by treaty process, the other is acting pursuant to legislative authority which has been granted by the Congress." The Secretary indicated that the United States was not willing to go beyond what he called "the maximum consistent with the legislative authority which has been granted by the Congress." The Eisenhower Doctrine is unilateral; the Baghdad Pact is a multilateral treaty; the forthcoming agreements will be bilateral; all are overlapping, complementary, and necessary. The whole arrangement is a classic example of diplomatic refinement. As far as Turkey is concerned, the new agreement will spell out arrangements for installing American missiles on Turkish bases. The Baghdad Pact is especially important for Iran, which does not belong to NATO (as does Turkey) or to SEATO (as does Pakistan). A new treaty between the United States and Iran would irritate the Soviet Union and some Arab countries even more than the continuation of the Baghdad Pact—or rather give them an excuse for showing their irritating displeasure.

16. *CR*, January 6, 1955, p. 122.

17. It is regrettable, of course, that the President did not attempt to develop a more dynamic doctrine on this notion of "stalemate."

18. See also the President's press conferences of June 30, 1954, August 11, 1954, and January 19, 1956.

Chapter IV

1. Professor A. V. Baez, Letter to the Editor, *New York Times*, September 9, 1957.

2. *CR*, April 29, 1954, p. 5742.

3. *DCR*, January 30, 1956, p. A 879.

4. *DCR*, January 23, 1956, p. A 627.

5. *DCR*, April 14, 1954, p. A 2832.

6. W. W. Kaufmann *et al.*, eds., *Military Policy and National Security* (Princeton, Princeton University Press, 1956), p. 24.

7. *DCR*, January 24, 1956, p. A 716.

8. *Military Policy and National Security*, p. 21.

9. *Ibid.*, p. 20.

10. *Ibid.*, p. 38.

11. *Ibid.*, p. 27.

12. *Ibid.*, p. 34. See exactly same reasoning process in G. F. Kennan's *Russia, the Atom and the West* (New York, Harper & Brothers, 1958), pp. 50-56.

13. The critics of massive retaliation have inverted this self-evident notion. Senator Fulbright claimed on June 20, 1958, that massive retaliation was "irrational because of the degree of rationality it requires." It was "irresponsible because of the very degree of responsibility" it places upon so many people. (*DCR*, June 20, 1958, p. 10703) This glib formula has been repeated hundreds of times in various forms by liberal intellectuals. Although it is both vain and fallacious, it shows that the very people who claim that foreign policy is the people's business seem to believe that a policy is irrational when it necessitates rationality on the people's part.

14. Letter to the Editor, *New York Times*, March 9, 1955.

15. American opinion further considers any use of force—or threat of using force in international relations—as conclusive proof of the failure of U.S. policy. "Why did foreign policy go so wrong," it asks, "that we have to dispatch troops?" Using the same reasoning process, we can put the blame for broken families on social workers and claim that the very existence of physicians proves the failure of medicine.

16. *DCR*, July 11, 1955, pp. A 4989-90.

17. On the clean bomb, see the President's press conference of March 26, 1958, and Secretary Dulles' press conference of April 1, 1958. Senator C. P. Anderson said in a televised program on April 27, 1958, that the military forces were "not only supporting" the dirty atomic bomb but that "they have pulled bombs out of the stockpile and inserted something that makes it dirtier." He added that "we talk clean on one side and we stockpile dirty on the other side." See the text of the interview and debate on this scandalous incident in *DCR*, May 1, 1958, pp. 7013-15, and *DCR*, May 5, 1958, pp. 7154-61.

18. See *Hearings* before the Special Subcommittee on Radiation of the Joint Committee on Atomic Energy (hereafter designated as *Hearings*), Eighty-first Congress, First Session, pp. 73-76.

19. On the various forms of fallout, see Dr. W. F. Libby, *DCR*, May 3, 1956, p. A 3562, and *Hearings*, pp. 54-60, 141-62, *et passim*.

20. Furthermore, cesium is not retained by the body; strontium 90 is. See *Hearings*, pp. 742-45. On carbon 14, see the AEC's *Biological*

hazard to man of Carbon 14 from nuclear weapons. Calculations made on carbon 14 and conclusions reached about it do not seem to differ from those obtained on strontium 90.

21. *Hearings,* p. 65. "As long as fission occurs, the probability is 1 in 20 that roughly 5 per cent of the fragments which are produced will be strontium." (Dr. Graves, *ibid.*)

22. *Hearings,* pp. 508-23, 710-14, and 719. On strontium concentration, see Mr. Eisenbud, *ibid.*, pp. 588-89. Dr. W. F. Libby reported on November 7, 1958, that the use of certain fertilizers might reduce plants' intake of strontium 90.

23. Dr. Crow, *Hearings,* p. 1013.

24. It is often said that fallout creates a hazard over which an individual has no *free* control. Unlike driving or smoking, fallout radiation is not a risk that we are willing to take as payment for our pleasures. It would be interesting to formulate the notion of liberty that is used as the basis for this argument.

25. *Hearings,* pp. 1433-34.

26. *CR,* March 29, 1954, p. 4024.

27. When the AEC does release information about the effects of atomic weapons or fallout public opinion expresses a feeling of outrage at such a "factual," "matter-of-fact" description of horror.

28. In other words, the essential points concerning the physical aspects of fallout have been largely agreed upon, and the issue is therefore mainly political.

29. Dr. Libby, *Hearings,* p. 1223.

30. *DCR,* June 17, 1957, pp. 8350-51.

31. *DCR,* August 1, 1958, p. A 6913. Further testing seems particularly important for the development of low-yield hydrogen weapons and missiles warheads.

32. It cannot be denied that most of the difficulties encountered here by the administration were caused by its failure to stand firm against public pressure. Anything that a government official says— even in answer to honest queries from the people—automatically becomes a part of national policy. This means that no government has the right to take a purely passive view of domestic opinion. Concessions to public opinion should never be made candidly or by chance, nor should the primary objective of speeches and press conferences be to "explain" the foreign policy to the "people." The objective should be to state it.

33. *DCR,* June 17, 1957, pp. 8350-51. Senator Gore proposed on November 17, 1958, that the United States end all atomic tests that pollute the air in order for the United States "to seize the initiative." In another "statesmanlike" effort to prevent the complete failure of the Geneva talks, Senator Church proposed, on March 2, 1959, a suspension of nuclear testing in the earth's atmosphere "within the framework of a trustworthy and sufficient international control system, adequate to reliably detect and report any violation." (*DCR,* March 2, 1959, p.

2810) This proposal would make it possible to establish a threshold below which underground explosions would be permitted. Mr. Dulles declared on January 13, 1959, that these ideas had been considered by the United States as "a possible fall-back position." The threshold principle was reportedly discussed by British Prime Minister Harold Macmillan and Soviet Premier Nikita S. Khrushchev. President Eisenhower declared on March 4, 1959, that the study which the United States has given to these ideas "so far does not reassure us that they are completely practical." Explosions in differing rock and soil formations obviously produce varying seismic signals, and for this reason, endless disputes can arise over allowable yields. Any intelligent person can come forward with a proposal of some sort. When a proposal is divorced from the "intricate" technicalities of actual negotiations, it is worse than useless. Even intelligent proposals can hide the kind of naïve idealism revealed by Senator Fulbright in the statement we have quoted.

34. See the sad collection of editorials inserted in the *Congressional Record* by Senator Humphrey on April 1, 1958. (*DCR*, April 1, 1958, pp. 5268-73) "I don't think we are being negative when you are firm but are standing on what you believe to be the truth, the facts, and the welfare of the free world, including specifically the welfare of the United States." (President Eisenhower at his press conference of April 2, 1958)

35. On January 5, 1959, the United States announced that American seismologists had discovered that underground nuclear explosions were more difficult to distinguish from earthquakes than had been previously estimated by the Geneva conference of experts. Is it necessary to insist upon the difficulty of detecting explosions in outer space?

36. *DCR*, August 22, 1958, p. 17698. Senator Humphrey said on February 4, 1958, that "we have appeared before the world as if we favored radioactive fallout, as if we positively enjoyed bomb testing." (*DCR*, February 4, 1958, p. 1401)

37. Public opinion seems to assume that a movement of opinion is Soviet-inspired only if and when it is actually led by card-carrying Communists or "spies." The Communist challenge is so fundamental that any form of moral evil is, in fact, an accomplice of the Communist conspiracy. When the psyche of individuals is sufficiently well known to us to permit legitimate inferences, we can often trace mental confusion back to envy or avarice, for instance. Any search for the root of moral evil in a human soul is not admissible except within a relationship of love and authority. If we cannot accuse others of evil because of the confused state of their minds, we must denounce the confusion (and, if necessary, accuse others of being confused) and assert that moral evil always creates mental confusion.

38. Senator Humphrey declared on January 20, 1959, that he wanted "the Senate record to note that while our government was proposing to the Soviet Union a total disarmament program, one of the points of which was the prohibition of further nuclear tests with inspec-

tion," the United States had "no inspection system based on scientific fact that could have policed such an agreement had the Soviet Union accepted it." Fortunately, he said, the Russians "accommodated us" and refused. If they had accepted our proposals, "we would have found ourselves in a situation where the Soviet Union could have gone ahead with a series of underground explosions." (*DCR*, January 20, 1959, p. 895)

Chapter V

1. *DCR*, February 1, 1954, pp. A 727-28.
2. *CR*, January 22, 1954, p. 653.
3. *New York Times Magazine*, March 28, 1954, p. 77. Lieutenant General J. M. Gavin wrote in *Life* magazine on August 4, 1958, that he once heard Secretary Wilson say that we cannot afford to fight limited wars. He claimed that Mr. Wilson had said that "we can only afford to fight a big war, and if there is one, that is the kind it will be." Gavin added his own conclusion, namely, that "if we cannot afford to fight limited wars then we cannot afford to survive, for that is the only kind of war we can afford to fight."
4. *CR*, January 22, 1954, p. 648.
5. *DCR*, April 16, 1956, p. A 2993.
6. *Ibid.*, pp. A 2993-94. Mr. Murray has consistently opposed an absolute atomic test ban. See, for example, his speech of November 15, 1958.
7. See *DCR*, May 6, 1957, pp. A 3379-82, and *ibid.*, July 2, 1957, pp. A 5276-77.
8. *DCR*, June 27, 1955, p. A 4638.
9. *CR*, February 16, 1954, p. 1783.
10. *DCR*, August 3, 1955, pp. A 5712-13.
11. *CR*, January 22, 1954, p. 648.
12. *CR*, April 19, 1954, p. 5297.
13. *CR*, April 6, 1954, pp. 4672-74.
14. *CR*, February 9, 1954, pp. 2904 *et sqq.*
15. *CR*, February 16, 1954, p. 1782.
16. Admiral Radford, as quoted by Representative Wigglesworth, *DCR*, May 11, 1955, p. 5205. It seems quite certain that actual nuclear warfare might require more manpower than conventional warfare, as was shown in the study released by the Army on October 26, 1958, but that is not the question at all.
17. *CR*, June 20, 1955, p. 8689.
18. *CR*, April 25, 1956, p. 6927.
19. *CR*, January 22, 1954, p. 652.
20. No author is more frequently quoted by the critics of massive retaliation than Henry Kissinger, and none has bothered less about understanding what he criticizes. We invite the reader to count the num-

ber of times Kissinger quotes Mr. Eisenhower or Mr. Dulles. It seems to us that his thesis is directed against the United States' pre-Korea strategy and has been hastily recast in an effort to apply it to massive retaliation. Valid criticisms of pre-Korea defense thinking applied to massive retaliation (itself misunderstood by Mr. Kissinger) make an awkward ensemble.

21. *CR*, April 28, 1954, p. 5685.

22. *DCR*, May 27, 1957, p. 6897.

23. *DCR*, February 2, 1954, p. A 749.

24. *CR*, January 22, 1954, p. 652.

25. In this particular instance, pure defense was not only feasible but dynamic and offensive. This was not the case in Korea or Indochina, where defense was not real defense, but it was the case in the Battle of England in 1940. Perhaps this "offensive defense" is linked to island and naval operations.

26. As we have seen, NATO's strategy calls for a nuclear counter-attack on the Communist heartland and the forward defense of the NATO area in case of Soviet aggression. The administration's critics do not seem to understand that these two tasks are complementary but distinct. Many contingencies which do not call for nuclear retaliation can arise on the ground. The forces that compose NATO's shield might be unable to deny territory to advancing Russian armies, but how far will the Russian armies advance? It makes little sense to assume that they would ever overrun western Europe while Russia itself is destroyed, especially when one considers that this destruction will occur in the first hours of the war. As General Maxwell Taylor testified on March 11, 1959, before the Senate Preparedness Subcommittee, the Soviets are "tremendously vulnerable in the satellite area, and the consequences of starting any kind of a shooting operation there must look very dangerous to them, indeed."

27. The fact that the Korean War was kept localized is "a tribute to long-range American airpower." (General Twining, April 25, 1956; see *DCR*, April 27, 1956, p. A 3457)

28. *DCR*, May 14, 1958, p. A 4432.

29. See D. Acheson, *New York Times Magazine*, March 28, 1954, p. 78.

30. Massive retaliation provides for the build-up of the conventional forces of allied countries all over the world. It would have suited us much better if the Lebanese army had been able to cope with the rebellion without American intervention. We must therefore beware that the principle of collective security does not become a way of escaping from the tasks of leadership. To some extent, our allies' forces must remain inadequate and in need of our backing. American interventions are vociferously denounced, but they produce long-range results that are often intangible and difficult to prove at the moment the intervention takes place.

Chapter VI

1. *CR*, March 29, 1954, p. 3987.
2. *New York Times Magazine*, April 15, 1956, p. 69.
3. *DCR*, February 18, 1959, p. 2359.
4. *Washington Post and Times Herald*, February 5, 1959.
5. It would be a miracle if Lenin had never said that the United States would spend itself into bankruptcy; if it were true, he might not have been a Marxist. According to Marx, the economic value of a piece of goods is determined by the quantity of human labor normally necessary for its production. Values thus decrease constantly because of technological advances, which, in turn, require larger and larger investments that fewer and fewer capitalists can afford. The process is inevitable and self-destructive. It leads to increasing production and shrinking consumer markets. The capitalist world literally spends itself into bankruptcy.
6. *CR*, May 9, 1956, p. 7802. Representative Mahon said on May 24, 1957, that new weapons are "fabulously expensive. The country cannot afford to provide these new weapons and also support an outmoded military structure." He added that "the taxpayer's head is on the block" and his security is also at stake. (*DCR*, May 24, 1957, pp. 6788-89; see also his speech of June 3, 1958, in *DCR*, June 3, 1958, pp. 8981-83)
7. *DCR*, July 1, 1957, p. 9611.
8. The cry for more imaginative answers merely serves to disclaim responsibility. See Chapter X.
9. "I have pointed out a number of times that I am not going to deliberately and try continuously to, as you say, thwart the will of Congress. I think Congress is sometimes mistaken, and I think in the past they have made some very bad mistakes in dealing with defense." (President Eisenhower, March 11, 1959; see also Representative Mahon's remarks in *DCR*, May 28, 1957, p. 6964)
10. *CR*, May 10, 1956, p. 7962.
11. *CR*, January 7, 1954, p. 80.
12. See *DCR*, January 22, 1956, p. A 618.
13. *DCR*, January 23, 1958, p. 650. Senator Symington said on March 12, 1959, that people become "mystified" when military chiefs make speeches "which read against each other." Why, then, does Congress force them to speak and to state their differences publicly?
14. "And that is the end of that, constitutionally and every other way." (*DCR*, May 9, 1956, p. 7013)
15. *CR*, June 22, 1956, p. 10814.
16. *DCR*, May 29, 1957, p. 7082.
17. *CR*, February 10, 1956, p. 2499.
18. *CR*, June 29, 1956, p. 11445.
19. *DCR*, August 14, 1958, pp. 16207-12. This speech is literally full of paralogisms, and it illustrates quite well the dangers of ghostwriting and shallow brilliancy.

20. *CR*, May 9, 1956, p. 7815.

21. See General Twining, *DCR*, May 9, 1956, p. 7009.

22. *CR*, June 29, 1956, p. 11448.

23. *DCR*, January 9, 1958, p. 172.

24. The same arguments will be used again and again with every new Soviet advance, one of which could be the atom-powered aircraft. They should therefore be refuted, if necessary, in the same way. On the atom-powered aircraft, see the Budget Message of January 19, 1959. Until the nuclear power plant is successfully developed, the Message said, "and the technical problems involved in operating a nuclear-powered aircraft safely are solved, there is no practical military value in attempting to build the airplane itself." (*DCR*, January 19, 1959, p. 759)

25. *DCR*, January 9, 1958, p. 172.

26. Hanson W. Baldwin wrote in the *New York Times* of March 15, 1959, that according to the administration, our radar surveillance in Turkey showed that the Soviets had fired only seven missiles at ranges of more than 3,000 miles. Although the United States has no plan to match the Soviet Union numerically in the production of ICBM's, no one knows, of course, how many missiles we may order once our missiles are ready for mass production. Is it necessary to say that no one knows how many missiles Russia can manufacture now and in the future? See the President's press conference of January 14, 1959.

27. "The bugs in our missile production are not in our assembly lines," Senator Symington said on January 23, 1959, "but in our policies." It must also be kept in mind that only a certain amount of power is required to deliver a thermonuclear warhead. Since our missiles are powerful enough for that purpose, rocket horsepower has become of secondary significance.

28. "I believe that we are making," said President Eisenhower on January 28, 1959, "within the relatively short space of time we have had, remarkable progress." However, this rapid progress makes the neglect of missile programs until 1953 all the more inexcusable.

29. These alleged fears about dictatorship in America are no more reasonable than fears of an Iroquois attack on Chicago. Since they are unreasonable, they deserve no praise at all. Our Revolutionary creed would not do us much harm if it would limit itself to inspirational Fourth of July oratory. Unfortunately, it has become an important expression of national indiscipline, a vice as serious as French nationalism or German militarism. It is no virtue to have a vice different from somebody else's.

30. *DCR*, February 10, 1958, p. A 1189.

31. The *Washington Star* of February 3, 1958, reported that Adlai Stevenson had referred to Explorer I, our first earth satellite, as "long, thin, and not much to it." This remark is not very important, of course, yet it is revealing. It is neither mockery nor humor. It is not serious enough to be dispiriting. It is not derisive enough to bring discredit to

its author. But the touch of irony it contains suffices to push the debate into the undeviating groove of self-accusation.

32. *DCR*, August 14, 1958, p. 16242.

33. *CR*, February 10, 1956, p. 2499.

34. *Ibid.*, p. 2494.

35. Admiral Arleigh A. Burke remarked in January, 1958, that there was "nothing secret about basic national strategy or national policy." (*DCR*, January 8, 1958, p. A 68) These two things are secret and mysterious only to the extent that they are not properly understood.

36. We do not mean to say that the British and the French experience no pleasure at our reverses but that any such pleasure cannot be condoned.

37. See Senator Fulbright's "great" speech of June 20, 1958, in *DCR*, June 20, 1958, pp. 10702-10707. Referring to the "gap" in a speech on August 21, 1958, the Senator claimed that we have "covered over" it "with the smug complacency of the ever-easier life, with a desperate pursuit of material success, and with a moratorium on creative thinking." (*DCR*, August 21, 1958, p. 17414) See also Hans J. Morgenthau's article in the *New Republic* of December 9, 1957. Morgenthau wrote that the prestige which the United States enjoyed throughout the world, "especially," he said, "in Asia and Africa," derived "primarily not from the qualities" of American democracy but from its "standard of living, and its technological achievements which, in contrast to these other qualities, are visible, tangible, demonstrable, and seemingly attainable by all through imitation." Adlai Stevenson said on September 27, 1956, that compassion and generosity have failed in America. These are the emotions, he added, "that can save us from brash materialism"; these are the feelings that "redeem wealth and power by getting them to serve the humblest human needs."

38. *DCR*, August 23, 1958, p. 17763.

39. *CR*, February 1, 1956, p. 1765.

40. *CR*, May 9, 1956, p. 7802. "All the talk about massive retaliation," Senator Jackson said on October 10, 1957, "is so much massive nonsense." (See *DCR*, January 9, 1958, p. A 97)

41. *DCR*, August 14, 1958, p. 16209.

42. *Ibid.*, pp. 16213-14.

43. By and large, the critics of the administration have appealed to the fear of Soviet strength. Since it could be said that they have lost faith in America, they have protected themselves against any such charge by saying that it was "neither pleasant nor popular" to contest the idea of American supremacy. (Senator Fulbright, January 23, 1958) They also complained, of course, that the greatness of America had been sacrificed "on the altar of fear." On July 13, 1957, Senator Mansfield warned against a "laden inflation of the Soviet threat." He said that "fear as the predominant base of foreign policy must yield to faith." (*DCR*, July 13, 1957, pp. 10433-41) The emotionalism of faith

is no better than the emotionalism of fear. It is one more example of the split personality of America's partisan self.

44. This remark does not refer as much to missile development as it does to the global military and economic effort that the United States will have to support in the years ahead. We do not deny that "for sacrifice to be effective it must be intelligent." (State of the Union Message of January 9, 1958) Yet there is no doubt that great sacrifices must be accepted. It is a tragedy that the Republican party, which has consistently upheld a realistic foreign policy for many years, has become the standard-bearer of economic Malthusianism.

45. It has become necessary to emphasize again the futility of any strategy based upon a date of maximum danger. See the words of the Budget Message of January 16, 1956: "In the words of Washington's Farewell Address, we must meet our defense needs by maintaining a respectable posture of defense. There is no magic number of dollars or of military units and weapons that would solve all our defense problems and guarantee our national security. Neither can total mobilization in peacetime be the answer to our defense needs. It is essential to have a stable, long-range defense program suited to our needs which avoids fluctuations in response to transitory pressures." (CR, January 16, 1956, p. 562)

46. We should not forget, however, as the President warned in his press conference of November 5, 1958, that new weapons "displace"—and not merely "supplement"—the old.

47. If the Soviets ever come to think that they can do so with impunity, the American scholars who have deliberately attempted to tear massive retaliation to pieces will have to bear a heavy responsibility indeed.

48. Dr. A. R. J. Grosch, manager of space programs for the International Business Machines Corporation, New York Times, March 21, 1959.

49. DCR, January 27, 1959, p. A 527.

50. DCR, February 9, 1959, p. 1941.

CHAPTER VII

1. CR, May 10, 1956, pp. 7939-40.

2. DCR, February 10, 1958, p. 1682. See also DCR, February 16, 1956, pp. 2295-99, on the "Goa blunder." Jordan, of course, is no nation at all and is hardly worth the effort to save her. "A mapmaker's dream," Jordan was created "by Churchill and T. E. Lawrence over brandy and cigars to pay a feudal debt." (C. L. Sulzberger, New York Times, July 19, 1958) This kind of talk would not be out of place in a back-country general store or in a classroom. Publicized at a moment when Jordan was struggling for her independence, it reveals a certain coarseness of feeling and serious impropriety.

3. *DCR*, May 21, 1956, p. 7659.

4. *DCR*, July 13, 1957, p. 10440.

5. *CR*, March 2, 1957, p. 2942.

6. "Nowhere in Asia, with the exception of Japan, is the conflict between Communism and democracy relevant or even intelligible as a philosophic contest between tyranny and freedom," wrote H. J. Morgenthau in 1956. But he immediately added that in "the battle of the minds," Marxist philosophy triumphs because it contains certain "hard-core" elements "which are politically relevant and without which the persistent intellectual attraction of Marxism could not be explained." (*DCR*, July 13, 1956, pp. 11484-85)

7. *DCR*, February 10, 1958, pp. A 1189-90.

8. This desire for more independence from American influence is entirely legitimate. NATO can be "de-Americanized" only by limiting the American commitment to guns and dollars. This is as hard for American public opinion to accept as it is for the European countries to accept American power supremacy vis-à-vis their own inability to cope with Soviet power.

9. On the whole, the British White Paper suffers from a plainness that is sometimes close to a lack of depth. This weakness does not affect the American version of massive retaliation.

10. The same principle applies to any resurgence of dynamic nationalism in any European country to the extent that nationalism is anti-American, anti-German, or anti-British.

11. The "respectable military posture" principle thus applies to NATO. As Mr. Dulles said on September 27, 1958, "we do not devote our energies and our resources so wholly to the prolification of such weapons that we undermine the economies which the weapons are designed to defend."

12. The alleged "realism" of our allies is opposed to our "moralism" in much the same way that the principle of collective security is opposed (by American opinion) to the United States' national interest.

13. *CR*, February 1, 1956, p. 1763.

14. *CR*, March 28, 1957, p. 4628.

15. *CR*, February 29, 1956, p. 3597.

16. *DCR*, March 4, 1954, p. A 1721.

17. "We think of allies as people who should agree with us. We expect them to do what we want. We protest when they do not," said Senator Jackson on June 18, 1956. (*DCR*, June 18, 1956, p. 9438) In reality, we do just the opposite of what the Senator said. Instead of a "drive for conformity," criticism of American policy is accepted as normal in view of our "blunders."

18. Mr. Dulles said before the NATO Council in Paris on December 14, 1953, that if the European Defense Community should not become effective, "if France and Germany remain apart, so that they would again be potential enemies, then indeed there would be grave doubt whether Continental Europe could be made a place of safety. That

would compel an agonizing reappraisal of basic United States policy."

19. In contradistinction, British statesmen are constantly cast in the beautiful role of rescuing the free world from Mr. Dulles.

20. Senator Kennedy said that "the war in Algeria confronts the United States with its most critical diplomatic impasse since the crisis in Indochina—and yet we have not only failed to meet the problem forthrightly and effectively, we have refused to even recognize that it is our problem at all." (*DCR*, July 2, 1957, p. 9719) He then introduced a resolution demanding that the United States actively pursue the solution of the Algerian problem through NATO and the United Nations. (See the text of his resolution in *ibid.*, p. 9726) "Nothing could be more injudicious than this proposal," wrote Dean Acheson, "except making it." (Dean Acheson, *Power and Diplomacy* [Cambridge, Harvard University Press, 1958], p. 123) The former Secretary of State added: "Keep well thy tongue and keep thy friend." (*Ibid.*, p. 135)

21. See *Russia, the Atom and the West*, pp. 59-60. Writing in the February, 1958, issue of *Harper's*, Mr. Kennan said that he could not overemphasize "the fatefulness" of arming NATO with atomic weapons. If the "Western continental countries are to be armed with them, any Russian withdrawal from Central and Eastern Europe may become unthinkable for once and for all." (*DCR*, June 19, 1958, p. 10659)

22. *DCR*, February 12, 1959, pp. 2037-41.

23. See *DCR*, February 16, 1959, p. 2098.

24. *DCR*, February 12, 1959, p. 2035.

25. The *New York Times*, March 15, 1959.

26. *DCR*, February 18, 1959, p. 2360.

27. *DCR*, February 19, 1959, p. 2473.

28. *DCR*, February 26, 1959, pp. 2720-25.

29. *DCR*, February 26, 1959, pp. 2724-25.

30. *DCR*, March 16, 1959, p. 3786.

31. G. F. Kennan, *Realities of American Foreign Policy* (Princeton, Princeton University Press, 1954), pp. 89-90.

CHAPTER VIII

1. *CR*, April 28, 1955, pp. 5207-5208.

2. *DCR*, February 17, 1954, p. A 1317.

3. If the election is favorable to the opposition, it is said that if our foreign policy is not radically changed, there is no point in voting. If the administration then appeals to bipartisanship, it is claimed that the people are no longer free to determine their own destiny and that their vote means little more than it would under a dictatorship. In reality, the people are neither ignorant nor infallible.

4. Quoted by Representative Price, *CR*, June 8, 1955, p. 6710.

5. *CR*, February 10, 1956, p. 2166.

6. *Realities of American Foreign Policy*, p. 70.

7. This type of accusation is a slogan. It is bound to be repeated, not only in this country, but the world over. See Chapter X.

8. *DCR*, February 9, 1955, p. 1184.

9. *CR*, January 26, 1955, p. 764. See also Senator Morse, *ibid.*, pp. 736-68.

10. *CR*, March 30, 1955, p. 4041.

11. See L. J. Halle's revealing article in the *New Republic* of August 18, 1958, and Howard K. Smith in *DCR*, July 24, 1958, p. 13644, who claimed that our Middle East policy was based upon "such wrong premises that it was bound to lead into dead-ends in which, no matter which way you move, you are blocked; no matter what you do, it is wrong."

12. *CR*, April 28, 1955, pp. 5237-42; italics added.

13. *CR*, February 12, 1954, p. 1699.

14. See *DCR*, February 27, 1957. On March 31, 1958, the U.S.S.R. announced a unilateral suspension of atomic testing. "The world should realize that the Soviet Union is not making a single concession in terms of its own security in this announcement," said Senator Humphrey. He added that the Soviet Union would "resume testing when its research indicates that another test series is ready." But he also said that the United States had been "delivered a terrible propaganda blow. For months we have had the opportunity to negotiate a satisfactory test suspension. . . . I hope we shall not again see the specter of the Soviet Union literally keeping our Nation punch drunk from one propaganda blow after another, leaving us standing before the world in ugly nakedness, because of the sterility of our international policies on this great issue." (*DCR*, March 31, 1958, p. 5112)

15. *CR*, March 1, 1957, p. 2881. It was also said that the approved text had "the virtue of remaining silent on the question of the relationship between the Congress and the President with respect to the use of force." (*DCR*, March 4, 1957, p. 2685)

16. *DCR*, May 22, 1958, pp. 8329-35.

17. *CR*, March 1, 1957, p. 2881.

18. *DCR*, August 5, 1958, p. 14862.

19. See also *DCR*, July 14, 1958, pp. 12343-45, and *DCR*, August 8, 1958, pp. 15263-65.

20. See also Senator Morse, *DCR*, August 5, 1958, p. 14862. On August 25, 1958, Senator Morse said that we should "guard against further erosion of the congressional power in the field of foreign policy. In the Lebanon crisis, the President acted without congressional sanction. He acted arbitrarily and without showing a desired sensitivity to democratic checks." (*DCR*, August 25, 1958, pp. 18089-90)

21. *CR*, January 22, 1954, p. 654.

22. Senator Jackson, Letter to Secretary Wilson, *DCR*, June 28, 1955.

23. Great Britain acted unilaterally in Kenya and Cyprus, as did France in Indochina and Algeria. Although public opinion accused the

administration of not considering these various problems as its own, it never accused our allies of acting alone.

24. The various crises created on purpose by the Communists are often described as "probings" of Western determination. Personally, we do not think that Soviet moves are always carefully planned and skillfully executed. If unsuccessful, a good deed can be repeated. A crime that fails is a blunder. Since Soviet maneuvers can be nothing more than manifestations of disorder, let us beware of rationalizing them more than is necessary in order to oppose them vigorously.

25. This letter was published in the press on April 3, 1955.

26. D. M. Figart, Letter to the Editor of the *New York Times*, October 21, 1958. "If there is one single factor which more than any other has undermined the prestige of the United States before the world," said Senator Mansfield on August 8, 1958, it is "the negative attitude" that the administration has manifested "toward efforts to get at basic international tensions. It has acted at times almost as though it has a vested interest in the perpetuation of these tensions." (*DCR*, August 8, 1958, p. 15265)

CHAPTER IX

1. See also Senator Mansfield's speech of July 13, 1957.

2. To be bored by truth is a fundamental attitude of the evil or superficial man.

3. This statement is remarkable in that it shows that there is a manner of relying on fission bombs and massive retaliation which is appeasement. The policy of containment was a policy of "massive retaliation"—understood as passive reliance on atomic power. As we noted earlier, much of the criticism of massive retaliation is relevant to containment. The critics, in other words, criticize themselves.

4. Four months before the Hungarian revolution, G. F. Kennan wrote that "evil, like good, produces its own vested interests" and that there is "a finality, for better or for worse," in what happened in eastern Europe. (*U.S. News & World Report*, June 29, 1956, p. 74) This fake realism is a sharp contrast to the deep realism of Secretary of State Dulles, who said on April 22, 1957, that peace will remain in jeopardy "until the divided nations are reunited and the captive nations set free."

5. This assertion is policy.

6. *CR*, January 12, 1956, p. 394.

7. *DCR*, June 2, 1955, p. A 3890.

8. As Professor D. N. Rowe noted in his letter to the editor of the *New York Times* on September 23, 1958, the Quemoy crisis forced us to recognize "what we should have learned long ago in Korea—that we cannot deprive allies of offensive weapons (supposedly to prevent their taking the offensive on their own) without risking serious danger to their own minimal defense against aggression."

9. Until this hysteria sets in, agitators complain that the crisis is "debate-less."

10. Nor was Lebanon like Korea. See Senator Morse, *DCR*, July 17, 1958, pp. 12915-16. But when the Soviets decided to press the Berlin issue somewhat, the German capital soon appeared to be another "untenable" position like Quemoy.

11. *New York Herald Tribune*, September 21, 1958.

12. This will be defended as "political realism." See Chapter X.

13. Mr. Finletter took this stand in his recent book, that is, *before* the last Quemoy crisis. *During* the crisis, everyone agreed that Formosa had to be defended in keeping with our treaty commitment and in the interest of the free world. As soon as the crisis was *over*, it was said, with equal unanimity, that the administration was right in scotching the idea that an abandonment of Quemoy would bring peace to the Far East. The real problem, of course, is Formosa and the administration's entire Chinese policy.

14. Neither was it lost to the common man of America. After having published a report about the State Department's flood of mail opposing the administration's policy on Quemoy, the *New York Times* made its own survey of public opinion. It found that the man in the street was calm and unworried. A well-indoctrinated Columbia University student declared, of course, that he did not want to die "redeeming Dulles' pledges." But, except for a clergyman, all seemed to agree that there was no question but that the United States had to draw the line and fight if necessary and that the Reds were bluffing. The most "distressing" sign of public "apathy" was the people's anxiety to attend to their own business and leave U.S. policy in the hands of the administration.

15. *CR*, April 19, 1954, p. 5281.

16. *Ibid.*, p. 5292.

17. "Have we gone down the middle of the road," asked Senator Douglas on April 18, 1956, "or have we wobbled from one side to the other like a drunken sailor trying to negotiate a path in the darkness of the night?" (*CR*, April 18, 1956, p. 5293)

18. The fact remains, however, that it is better not to make a formal statement of policy on such subjects.

19. *CR*, July 13, 1956, p. 12654.

20. Senator Lehman, *DCR*, June 14, 1956, p. A 4756.

21. See Senator Fulbright, *DCR*, July 14, 1958, p. 12345. As Mr. Dulles said on June 22, 1956, "we need not fear the results of the peaceful competition which the Soviet rulers profess to offer." This new challenge must be met. It must be met with economic aid and *also* with means of military pressure, as in Lebanon. Since the Soviet Union uses military pressure against countries that it cannot penetrate by means of subversion, it is unavoidable that the use of American power may become necessary, on occasion, to curb Soviet infiltration. But partisan criticism will then demand that the United States react to Soviet eco-

nomic aid with more attractive offers, and it will call this dancing to the Soviet tune "initiative."

22. *DCR*, February 27, 1956, pp. 2940-47.

23. A comparison of the Senator's speeches is interesting. Except for Adlai Stevenson, no American statesman has called so much for "imagination" and displayed so little intellectual creativeness as Senator Fulbright. See *DCR*, August 6, 1958, pp. 14958-60.

CHAPTER X

1. We found this phrase in the first French newspaper we read upon arriving in Europe in the summer of 1953. It is one of G. F. Kennan's favorites. Mr. Kennan often expresses the thought that we should refute, with utmost care, every individual lie of Soviet propaganda. He cannot hide his annoyance when he hears somebody say: "It's just Communist propaganda." The most effective way of refuting a lie is to denounce it as a lie. On the other hand, any refutation that takes a lie as something to be refuted in earnest cannot be effective.

2. *CR*, July 11, 1955, p. 10151. Fear of social reprisals allegedly deterred many intellectuals from espousing "unpopular" causes, even though they deeply believed in them. But why were they unpopular? And if faith was so deep, why so little courage?

3. The anti-Communist affidavit that must be filed by students who obtain federal funds under the National Defense Education Act is considered to be the latest slap at the intellectual community.

4. And who will explain why the subversion of intellectual integrity seems to have become the specific responsibility of so many scholars in America?

5. *DCR*, June 20, 1958, p. 10706. See also a typical editorial, "Middle East Disaster," in the July 30, 1958, issue of *Christian Century*.

6. Even when the question of principle overrules all other considerations, as in Berlin, public opinion succeeds in withdrawing the moral sanction from national policy. The administration said that we will not be driven from Berlin. "It is a sound position," Senator Mansfield said on February 12, 1959, but it is not enough. "That is a slogan, not a policy." Or it is asserted more crudely that the situation is so grave that we have no right to be inflexible.

7. Senator Clark said on July 28, 1958, that Mr. Dulles' position with respect to the Baghdad Pact was like the old nursery rhyme:

Mother, may I go in to swim?
Yes, my darling daughter,
Hang your clothes on a hickory limb,
But don't go near the water.

The rhyme is a perfect description of the Senator's own attitude and the attitude of many of his colleagues.

8. The fact that great American statesmen like Secretary Dulles can

be unpopular in Europe—while so many others enjoy a reputation of greatness that is utterly undeserved—is the most convincing proof of the shocking ignorance of American foreign policy to be found in Europe.

9. *DCR*, July 3, 1958, p. A 6051.

10. President Eisenhower said on April 22, 1956, that "our fore-fathers did not claim to have discovered novel principles. They looked on their findings as universal values, the common property of all mankind." In the fear of arousing accusations of moralism and absolutism, American statesmen—from George Washington to John Foster Dulles —often limit themselves to praising the expediency of principle.

11. *CR*, April 28, 1955, pp. 5237-42.

12. Double talk presupposes evasion or the absence of any commitment and so leaves the mind free to go in every direction at once.

13. *DCR*, May 22, 1958, pp. 8333-36.

14. *DCR*, July 14, 1958, p. 12343.

15. *DCR*, July 15, 1958, p. 12531. Senator Mansfield, who chose to become the standard-bearer of appeasement during the Berlin debate, declared on February 19, 1959, that he would "support the President of the United States and his Secretary of State to the hilt, and we will, of course, when the decision has been made, put our shoulders to the wheel and get right behind them." (*DCR*, February 19, 1959, p. 2471) "The purpose of my speech today," he said on February 12, 1959, "is to suggest, respectfully and constructively, some possible alternative which may be of value to the Department of State." Evidently taken aback by the violence of the reaction to his talk, the Senator declared on February 16:

> What matters most is that there be a full discussion of this situation, which, obviously, contains within it the seeds of world-shattering war. We have needed this discussion which is now beginning to gather momentum. We have needed the outspoken thought—the deepest thought—of American citizens on this vital issue. We have needed it for a long time. The hour is already late. If my remarks have helped to pull the plug which has kept this thought bottled for too long, then they will have served their purpose.

(*DCR*, February 16, 1959, p. 2089) He then inserted in the *Congressional Record* a collection of editorials which proved that none of the thoughts he had expressed on February 12 was new. All were plagiarisms. Another of the tricks used to justify double talk consists in pretending either that national policy is not supported by the people or that the people are not well informed. "There is a strong presumption that in each country the opposition approach more nearly reflects current public opinion than does the official policy of the conservative government leaders," wrote the *St. Louis Post Dispatch* of February 15, 1959. "I personally think," declared President Eisenhower on March 11, 1959, "that the American public is more soberly aware of the true situation than a lot of people around this town. We are so close to ourselves around here that we have a great possibility of stirring ourselves up. It's like one staff officer making work for another, so you get still another one to do it."

16. When the situation is dialectical, partisanship practices double talk in reverse by translating U.S. policy into terms of double talk. "We have never made the fundamental policy decision as to whether Arab nationalism—epitomized in Nasser—was a force which we should try to work with, or a force which we should oppose," said Senator Fulbright on July 16, 1958. "As a consequence our day-to-day actions have vacillated" as if U.S. policy practiced double talk. (*DCR*, July 16, 1958, p. 12666) See also the Democrats' policy statement of October 11, 1958.

17. *CR*, March 9, 1954, p. 2904.

18. *CR*, April 6, 1954, p. 4676.

19. *CR*, March 9, 1954, p. 2904.

20. *CR*, March 22, 1954, pp. 3611-13.

21. *CR*, April 5, 1954, p. 4577.

22. *DCR*, March 22, 1954, p. A 2153.

23. We do not mean to excuse Allied opinion for the blind opposition it often takes to U.S. policy.

24. *CR*, January 29, 1957, p. 1114.

25. "Instead of trying to mold other peoples in our image," Senator Jackson said on June 18, 1956, "we think of allies as people who should agree with us. We expect them to do what we want." This formula shows that an abdication of leadership can be combined with the unbearable pretense of molding others in the American image.

26. International law, like the UN, is a means and not an end in itself. No act can be more contradictory than to use law to destroy the rule of law.

27. It is hypocrisy because it is entirely within our power to understand when the United Nations is the proper venue for the solution of a problem and when it is not.

28. We intuitively sense our greatness, but we praise our weaknesses. Since we know our own faults, self-criticism seems justified. We know our own virtues, and we feel that praise is deserved. Partisanship thus seems to be rational. This situation is no Humpty Dumpty, as G. F. Kennan has so often said. Let us praise what deserves praise and blame what should be blamed, and we will be ourselves again.

29. We repeat here that this type of relaxation can go hand in hand with a hysterical fear of Communist power.

30. See also *DCR*, July 24, 1958, p. 13634.

31. Speaking about the Formosa Resolution, Senator Morse said on January 26, 1955, that he could reconcile with his religious principles "some issues and questions of morality" involved in the Public Law. (*CR*, January 26, 1955, p. 739) See the entire debate in *CR*, January 26, 1955, pp. 736-65, and *CR*, January 28, 1955, pp. 920-95.

32. Senator Humphrey starts from a hypothetical fact and discusses a hypothetical situation and yet arrives at a conclusion that can be strongly asserted!

33. The President's proposal came after the situation had been stabilized by our landing in Lebanon. We have said that almost anything can be appeasement. We must add that most concessions can be made without appeasement.

34. The Berlin crisis has shown that demands for a summit meeting can be more annoying and come closer to actual appeasement than the meeting itself if it were to be held.

35. Letter to the Editor of the *New York Times*, September 6, 1958.

36. "Could Mr. Dulles or President Eisenhower demonstrate before the United Nations Security Council that Moscow or Cairo was responsible for the revolution in Iraq? . . . Would Mr. Dulles deny to Moscow the right to give money and guns to the friends of Communism in the Middle East while insisting on Washington's right to give money and guns to the friends of the West?" (J. Reston, *DCR*, August 5, 1958, p. 14776) See also the unusually inconsistent editorial of C. L. Sulzberger in the *New York Times* of July 30, 1958.

37. "Are we merely going to have a display of vituperative debate to prove to the world that the Soviets are tyrants, to again prove to the world that the Soviets are conducting a conspiratorial activity, and that the Soviets enjoy the confusion and disorder which prevail in many parts of the world, and profit therefrom? We do not need to prove those things. Every reasonable person knows them. . . . This is not diplomacy, it is adolescent debate." (Senator Humphrey, *DCR*, August 8, 1958, p. 15259)

38. In his scandalous Nobel Prize Lecture of December 11, 1957, Lester B. Pearson said that "it is essential that we avoid this kind of dangerous stalemate in international policy today. The main responsibility for this purpose rests with the two great world powers, the United States and the U.S.S.R. No progress will be made if one side merely shouts 'co-existence'—a sterile and negative concept—and 'parleys at the summit,' while the other replies 'no appeasement; no negotiation without proper proof of good faith.'"

39. This purely negative conclusion precludes realism. Even if the United States did not have the power it still has in its possession, a realist could not accept this notion of atomic stalemate.

40. In a letter to Senator Humphrey, James P. Warburg wrote that "our refusal to recognize change keeps us perpetually at the brink of war, alienates the uncommitted peoples, divides us from our allies, and cements the Moscow-Peiping axis." (*DCR*, July 14, 1958, p. A 6255)

41. There is nothing that can be done to pierce the mystery of China's future, but contrary to what is generally said, the policy of keeping the Red Chinese regime in exclusive trust of the U.S.S.R. seems to have immense potentialities. Soviet power might now give reasons for Red China to be bold, but the day might come when this boldness will

have to be restrained by Soviet power. Chou En-lai himself showed a map of Eurasia to a friend of ours and pointed out that most of Russia was, at one time, a Chinese province.

42. See the State Department release of August 9, 1958, in *DCR*, August 13, 1958, pp. A 7245-48. As Eugene Lyons wrote in the *New York Times* of November 26, 1958, "revolutions always appeared 'impossible' before they occurred and 'inevitable' after they occurred." Before they do occur, any intelligent person can misuse his intelligence to find reasons why no parallel should have been made between Hungary and China.

43. We have already noted that President Eisenhower rejected this notion formally—at long last—in his press conference of August 27, 1958.

44. This emphasis on "public relations" and social science in itself is revealing with respect to national attitudes. If international relations were a science, they could be achieved without a commitment. There is the same difference between foreign policy proper and international relations as a science as there is between "good" manners and friendship or love.

45. *DCR*, August 5, 1958, p. 14843.

46. *DCR*, June 9, 1958, p. A 5201. When he says that rivalries other than military rivalries are safe, Mr. Stevenson implicitly recognizes the validity of massive retaliation. But he wants us to accept the principle of power equality between the U.S.S.R. and the United States as if the United States had aggressive intentions and is responsible for civilization not being safe.

47. The limbo of "new ideas" is the counter-image of the valid intuition we have of America's historical role. The "broad horizon" should inspire all of our undertakings. When we see where we are going, we should tell ourselves that our intuition is not yet reality. When the broad horizon is lost to our sight, we should know that it is still there and go through the crisis with the courage derived from our knowledge of its reality as experienced in better times. Let us add that appeasing idealism also takes refuge in a pessimistic mood that is justified by accusations that cannot be clearly stated. Adlai Stevenson said, for instance, on December 9, 1957, that "when Sparta was frightening the Athenians Pericles said: 'I am more worried about our own faults than about the plans of our enemies.' And so am I." An apparently brilliant quotation is used here as a screen to hide poor, vicious reasoning.

48. The inroads made by Soviet propaganda prove, in other words, that our political judgments are not ruled by sound reason. Our own daily life bears witness that any one of our faults, even the greatest, can be rationalized by reasonings that are often too subtle to be refuted by other reasonings. But we can, and should, always see where these rationalizations carry us and judge the tree by its fruits. Not all reasonings are reason.

49. At this point, idealism returns to realism. This schizophrenic jumping from realism to idealism and then from idealism to realism is typical of appeasement. It is also typical of partisanship in America. See Representative Vorys, *DCR*, January 27, 1958, p. 935.

50. They *do* control public opinion to the extent that public opinion is not free. A master despises those who serve him as slaves, but he fears their capacity to emancipate themselves. The slave fears his master, who controls him only because he fears.

51. After having stirred up trouble and creating confusion in 1957 with his notion of disengagement, G. F. Kennan excused himself by denying that he had found a new formula for the solution of East-West tensions. He merely said "things" about which the Western governments should "think." In concluding his book *Power and Diplomacy*, Dean Acheson expressed "a measure of assurance" on what he called "the rightness of contempt for sanctimonious self-righteousness." He added that if the reader found "a tinge of dogmatism" in what he had said, he would be reminded of Montaigne's words: "I should not speak so boldly if it were my due to be believed." (*Power and Diplomacy*, pp. 136-37)

52. While showing quite clearly the *workings* of evil (not evil itself) in man's mind, politics does not reveal man's goodness as well. Moral values generally belong to a level much higher than politics. We make this point not only because this particular problem has long baffled us but also because we want to defend ourselves against the accusation of pessimism. The real pessimist is one who seeks love and the higher forms of human morality at the political level—the true pessimism of those who want, for instance, atomic testing to be discontinued because they have faith in Christ's resurrection. A person who says a thing of this kind seriously might be a humanist, but he is not a Christian.

CPSIA information can be obtained
at www.ICGtesting.com
Printed in the USA
BVHW091528020119
536873BV00032B/1571/P

9 781258 338831